"Drucker is the great connector," says Leo M. Cherne, Director of the Research Institute of America.

"He is perhaps the most unallied, unaffiliated authority in the whole business world—he belongs, and will belong, to no one else's school," says David M. Ewing, the Executive Editor of the *Harvard Business Review*.

Now John J. Tarrant has written the first book-length study of this towering and original business thinker in action. Tarrant covers Drucker's career with a perceptive eye, outlining the process, the spark of originality that sets Drucker apart. He blends actual interviews with Drucker with his published works and comes up with a remarkable, rounded picture of the man whose ideas on the management-ordered society stimulate debate and improvement in the performance of managers.

Drucker:

The Man Who Invented the Corporate Society

Drucker:

The Man Who Invented the Corporate Society

John J. Tarrant

Foreword by
C. Northcote Parkinson

WARNER BOOKS

A Warner Communications Company

WARNER BOOKS EDITION

Copyright © 1976 by Cahners Books, Inc.
All rights reserved. No part of this book may be reproduced in any
form without permission.

Library of Congress Catalog Card Number: 75-44265

ISBN 0-446-81318-4

This Warner Books Edition is published by
arrangement with Cahners Books, Inc.

Cover design by Gene Light

Cover photograph by Tony Ruta

Book design by Milton Batalion

Warner Books, Inc., 75 Rockefeller Plaza, New York, N.Y. 10019

A Warner Communications Company

Printea in the United States of America

Not associated with Warner Press, Inc. of Anderson, Indiana

First Printing: February, 1977

10   9   8   7   6   5   4   3   2

Contents

Drucker:

*The Man Who
Invented the
Corporate Society*

Foreword

To understand Peter Drucker's career we have to grasp, first of all, the American attitude towards commerce and industry. Modern industry (that is, originally, iron and steel) was born in Britain. But the soil of Britain, ideal for planting the seed, was not quite favourable for the growth of the industrial plant. London was like Vienna, the centre of an empire which would soon cease to exist. But while it remained in being and for years, indeed, after its disintegration, the brains available were directed into public rather than into business administration. For the British chessboard was already occupied by King and Queen, by bishops, knights and castles, and there was only a limited space and opportunity for the pawn who aspired to royal importance. There could be wealthy industrialists but they were outrated in esteem by admirals, generals, ambassadors and judges. There would be men like Hudson, the railway king, or Armstrong, the British answer to Friedrich Krupp. But Armstrong with all his cannon was of small consequence beside a Viceroy of India, and was a poorer man than the Duke of Westminster. The British had a scale of values in which an Earl comes below a

Marquess, in which an actor-manager may become a knight, in which the millionaire (as such) comes practically nowhere. Room was found for the industrialist as time went on but the tradition remained that talent should go into the diplomatic corps or the Indian Civil Service, should go into the Navy or out to the Sudan. Younger sons without obvious ability might go into the City and a banker might have a modest position in society but the businessman was taught to know his place. He might sit near the foot of the table or he might not have been invited at all. He could at any time be brushed aside by even relatively penniless officers in the Household Cavalry. In many a context his millions might be irrelevant, his manners less than acceptable, his origin all too apparent. It was right and proper, no doubt, that businessmen should discuss business in a Chamber of Commerce but all this was of far less importance than anything discussed at Whitehall. And what was true in London was as true, more or less, in Paris, Vienna, Berlin or Rome. Prestige in France centred upon members of the Academy and Graduates of the Ecole Polytechnique. Prestige in Vienna centred upon Archdukes, in Berlin upon the Prussian General Staff, in Rome upon the Vatican and the College of Cardinals. In whichever way he might look, the European pawn could see that the chessboard was largely occupied.

In the United States the aristocracy hardly survived the Civil War, a whole continent was all but blank and for the railway magnates the sky was clearly the limit. Little prestige attached to politics and the senator who seemed too dignified was liable to lose his seat to someone whose image was more democratic. Big business was essentially the invention of Cornelius Vanderbilt and millionaires enjoyed an eminence they could never have achieved in Europe. They were aided at first by the fact that there were, in those days, four dollars to the pound. To be a millionaire in Britain was then four times as difficult. But millions multiplied and people looked upon the great companies as the very pillars of

American society. There were criticisms, too, but it became the accepted fact that all the brightest talent should be drawn into industry or into the ancillary professions of accountancy, banking, insurance and law. American romance centred, above all, on the oil prospector or inventor, the storekeeper who ended as head of a retail chain, the corporation's founder who came to dominate a whole industry. Then the scene changed in another way. Engineers had been men associated with coal and soot, with grease and lampblack. With the coming of electricity there appeared a new breed of engineers, cleaner and more scientific. They were socially on a higher level and the whole world of industry became more worthy of study. Just as scientific agriculture began with the inventions of gumboots—without which the scientist never went beyond the farm gate—so the science of management began with the electrical plant, which was clean enough for the theorist to explore. In America some serious thought was now given, not merely to economics but to the art—and in time, the science—of management.

A pioneer in this field was F. W. Taylor, whose success was such that the American Efficiency Society was founded in 1912. Efficiency was the American word, European practitioners calling themselves Industrial Engineers, as they still do, and British practitioners being Management Consultants. The analysis of industrial method began at rather a humble level with time and motion study but accountants soon invaded the head office with new ideas about paper work. Other theories, bolder still, advocated business education. The oldest business college in the United States is believed to be the Wharton School, founded in 1881 as a part of the University of Pennsylvania; a useful experiment but rather ahead of its time. The foundation of the Harvard School of Business Administration in 1909 is the real landmark as giving Harvard's academic blessing to a new development and to one at which the established academics were looking askance. From that date the business schools have been accorded a grudging recognition, at first in the United States and later, and far more

11

slowly, in Europe. There is still a question mark suspended over each one of them. It is doubtful, for one thing, whether there is an accepted body of theory which a school can safely teach. It is doubtful, on the other hand, whether the teachers (many of them lacking business experience) are well qualified to explain and justify what theory there is. With these limitations, and with many doubts about their curriculum, the business schools have come to stay.

Parallel with business education and essential to it, there has appeared the literature of management books for the academic shelf providing topics for the academic seminar. These begin with F. W. Taylor's *Scientific Management* (1911), *The Modern Corporation and Private Property*, A. A. Berle and G. C. Mezas (1932), and Dale Carnegie's *How to Win Friends and Influence People* (1936). These made a beginning and one thing at once apparent was that few of these books were written by men who had themselves been successful in business. Such books were not unknown—one or two, for example, by Andrew Carnegie—but these contained little but dreary platitudes about thrift, integrity and honest toil. The books which could be actually read with profit came from people whose own success, except perhaps in authorship, had been far from outstanding. Books, however, were multiplying, some about bookkeeping and commercial correspondence and some, more ambitious, about personnel management, and company law. And one thing apparent was that the United States in this field must lead the world, not because Americans are more intelligent but because intelligent Americans go into business. A brilliant Frenchman becomes a civil servant and a brilliant Italian makes himself a cardinal. Only in the United States is the Presidency of General Motors the ultimate goal of the intellectual elite. Only in the United States is the businessman completely dedicated to business.

Then came the computer, a development of the cash register, invented in 1942 and since become widely available. The breakthrough in this development is represented by I.B.M.'s 701 machine which gained its reputation during the Korean War. By 1958 there were 1000 computers in the U.S. and 160 in Europe. Computers have multiplied since then, with various results but with one of greatest significance. With the coming of the computer, management has become less of an art and more of a science. The computerized head office has the cathedral-like solemnity of the research laboratory. The manager begins to think of himself as a scientist. There are instances, even, of the scientist becoming manager; not with invariable success. Management decisions take place above the cloud level in some modern highrise in Sinai. It has all become a matter of higher mathematics and scientific forecast, beyond the mental range of middle management and not really open to discussion. Books written on management in its scientific form included *The Managerial Revolution* by J. Burnham (1945), *The Organization Man* by W. H. Whyte (1950), *The Hidden Persuaders* by Vance Packard (1957), *The Affluent Society* by J. K. Galbraith and *Up the Organization* by Robert Townsend (1970).

From the above list here has been omitted *The Practice of Management* by Peter Drucker (1954), not because it is unimportant but because it deserves more careful comment. Drucker, whose ideas are the subject of this book, is perhaps pre-eminent among management consultants and also among authors of books on management. To what does he owe this pre-eminence? This is for our author to explain at length. Here, however, at the outset, three general comments may serve as preliminary. First of all, Drucker, coming originally from Vienna, is concerned not with the practice but with the philosophy of management. Looking beyond the details of office work, he seeks for general principles which are applicable to every solution. He would not claim to know what all these principles are but he is groping towards them, convinced from the outset that they exist. "Build on strength" may be elementary, and is based, of course, on army tactics, but it leads on to other conclusions, some of them far from obvious, and others perhaps still to be defined. Drucker has no interest in a managerial drill, an application of a text-

13

book solution to a problem defined in text-book terms. He is a philosopher and seeks the solution based on a principle that is intellectually satisfying. It should have a rightness which goes beyond mere success. To have the right answer means to have asked the right question: and the right questions are those which answer themselves.

In the second place, Drucker is a non-specialist, a man who has lived in different countries and learnt from experience in different trades. He has a law degree but would regard that as representing an intellectual approach to life, not as the preliminary to a professional career. He has been a journalist but not as the sequel to any training in journalism. Given a wide reading, a varied career, some powers of observation and a gift for analysis, he seeks to approach any new problem with an open mind and child-like innocence. His is the Socratic method, the art of asking the simple and devastating question: "What exactly are you trying to do?" —to be followed by that other question: "Why?" Drucker is a consultant and with a wide general knowledge of the world and of business. But what he brings to a problem is not so much his knowledge as his ignorance. The man absorbed in the routine of industry has a mind littered and obstructed with prejudices and mental habit, current sayings and tired jokes. His cluttered blackboard has no space for any new calculation. It is often the function of the consultant to wipe the board clean, eliminate all the accepted wisdom, destroy every known and revered truth and start afresh as one who has never seen a factory before. Legend has it that Drucker was called in as a consultant by a company which manufactured glass bottles. At his first meeting with the Board he asked the simple question, "Well, gentlemen, what is your business?" Surprised at his ignorance, the Chairman replied, "Our business is in the manufacture of glass bottles for soft drinks or beer." To this Drucker replied, "No, I don't agree. You are in the *packaging* business." A great light dawned. It was as if he had kicked away the legs of the boardroom table. The directors could begin to think

14

again and they would realise afterwards that they had themselves provided the solution to each of their problems. Drucker had merely asked the right question—perhaps even the one basic question—and left the rest of it to them. It is the non-specialist who can do that, the man who comes to the problem without any prejudice or preconception.

In the third place, Drucker is essentially unworldly. There are problems to be solved and he takes an interest in at least considering them, but not with the primary object of making money for the firm nor with the secondary object of making money for himself. The late Mr. G. K. Chesterton commented once on the fact that the newspapers often call for "a Practical Man," to deal with the current situation, whatever it may be. He went on to point out that the really difficult problems call for an unpractical man. In fact, the greater the difficulty the more vague and absent-minded will the professor be who can find the answer. He went on to illustrate this theory by writing the "Father Brown" stories.

The point of each story is twofold. First of all, the worldly and knowledgeable people, the experts and criminologists, are all baffled by an unusual crime presenting an apparently insoluble problem. Second, the unworldly and innocent priest solves it, not by a brilliant deduction but by the application of a philosophic principle. G. K. Chesterton, himself the most vague and absent-minded of men, was the model for Father Brown and each story, in effect, is a portrait painted from the mirror. And from each story we remember afterwards not the motives and clues—the tale being often highly improbable—but the cosmic truth he has set out to illustrate. In similar fashion Drucker is the very opposite of a go-getting and aggressive American executive. Had he wanted success, American style, he would have formed a corporation, Peter Drucker Inc., with five directors and a hundred consultants. He would have been a rival to McKinsey, a threat to Booz Allen and the death, perhaps, of Cresap McCormick. He would

15

collect $10 million a year in fees and would eventually go public, selling his shares for a fortune. For a real businessman this would have been the right thing to do. But Drucker has never shown that much interest in money, refusing more in fees than he has ever made. And in this he exemplifies for all time the true character of the business consultant, the last man in the world to follow his own advice. When theorists write books on how to make millions, the more cynical of us are apt to ask, "But if you know how to make millions, why don't you do it? If you are so smart, why aren't you rich? And if you are rich why write books or offer advice?" The logic of this objection is answerable. But we know from observation that the chief executive and the consultant have quite different abilities to offer. They do not respectively represent practical success and theoretical failure.

How do they differ? They differ in the way that the real Prince of Denmark must differ from the actor who plays the part of Hamlet. The Prince has to decide on a policy. The actor has to ask himself how he would have behaved if he were Prince of Denmark. The skill of the Company President is in handling the board meeting. The consultant's skill is in putting himself in the President's place—and next week stepping into the shoes of someone else. This calls for a special kind of imagination, a gift the real President can do without. If we consider the relationship, in the abstract, between the Company President and the Consultant, we are bound to ask: "But if the President does not know how to run the Company, who does? And if he doesn't know, why should he have his position and salary?" But it is not as simple as that; nor can we safely propose that our best policy would be to replace the President and put the Consultant in his chair. Why not? Because, for one thing, the work which is to continue for twenty years would bore the consultant in a week. He has a real contribution to make but he does it quickly if he can do it at all. We hope to have from him a flash of brilliance. We cannot live with a series of such flashes and he cannot produce them in the context of a single business. So the consultant, a man like Peter Drucker with a touch of genius, has a place in the world but not, as a rule, in the presidential chair. His function can be compared with that of the signpost at the crossroads; a device which points the way but does not follow it.

Surrey, England　　　　　C. NORTHCOTE PARKINSON
October 1975

Preface

A preface should explain why a book has been written.

In candor, it is easy enough to say how a book about Peter Drucker got started. I am a professional writer, and I often write about business and management and the human dimensions of corporate enterprise. Peter Drucker is a towering and controversial figure in the world of management. Mike Hamilton of Cahners was enthusiastic about a book on Drucker and so we came to quick agreement.

That is the inception of *a* book on Peter Drucker. Why *this* book?

When I started, the job seemed challenging but straightforward. I had worked with Peter Drucker some years ago. I had read most of his books and many of his articles and essays; I set out to read them again, analytically, from the beginning. I knew of Drucker's success as a consultant, starting with the landmark project for General Motors in the 1940s. I began to talk with businessmen who had dealt with Drucker as a consultant. I knew people who had been close to Drucker at various stages of his career. I set out to talk with them also. I got in touch with educators who might comment on his role as a teacher; I started to delve into the copious references to Drucker in books and magazines.

And then there was Peter Drucker himself. While he observed that he was "appalled" at the thought of a book about him, he made unpublished material available to me, arranged for me to sit in on sessions that he conducted, and was extremely generous with his time and energy in permitting me to spend days with him at his home in Claremont, California, for tape-recorded question-and-answer research. At this point it may be useful to emphasize that this book is neither "commissioned" nor "authorized" by Drucker. It is a totally independent project.

So far so good. A tough job, but a clearly laid out one. However, as I proceeded with the project I began to confront a multitude of complexities and paradoxes.

A writer's difficulties in doing a book are his problem, not the reader's. But this is a case in which the subject has turned out to be bigger and far more variegated than the writer first supposed, and this has a considerable effect on the book. There are, in the life and work of Peter Drucker, strands that connect with the central questions of the way we live our lives today, and what those lives mean. I have tried to trace those strands as best I can; the reader is entitled to know this.

In a very real sense Drucker invented the concept of "management." Forty years ago most managers did not think of what they did as "managing." Books and courses concerned with business focused on the efficiency of industrial processes, not on the tasks of planning, decision making, and so on that we now recognize as lying at the heart of the executive discipline. Drucker first described the enterprise as something to be managed. Then he defined the job of the manager. And then he began to devise the tools that would help the manager to do his job better.

The manager of today may never have met Peter Drucker, never heard him speak, never worked with him as a consultant. He may have read some of Drucker's books and articles. But even if he has never come in contact with Drucker's work in any form, the businessman's life, day-in-day-out, year-in-year-out, is profoundly affected by Peter Drucker. What Drucker dreamed of thirty years ago, the manager now takes for granted.

But even close students of management are often unable to see the full spectrum of Drucker's influence. For example, while Drucker's pioneering work on such concepts as management by objectives is generally recognized, there are other ideas in wide use that are ordinarily associated with the names of other men. Two such concepts are "Theory X and Theory Y" and the "Hygiene Theory," both widely influential in shaping our approaches to motivating people on the job. Other thinkers are credited with the development of these theories; but the reader of this book will find evidence that Drucker at least anticipated them.

While Drucker is often not identified with concepts that he did originate, he is at the same time frequently cited in support of positions that he has never taken. For instance, the idea of the interchangeability of the manager—the notion that an executive who has mastered "the art of management" can move from a shoe company to a construction firm and practice his art with undiminished success—had a great vogue a few years ago and is only now being called into serious question. Drucker is assumed by many to have been the moving spirit behind the concept. He is not; not only does he stress the necessity for the manager to know the business he is in—he is scornful of the proposition that management is an "art."

There are other contradictions. Drucker says that the quantum jumps of technological change make it impossible to predict the future; but he is an inveterate predictor. In some auguries he has been wrong; in a great many he has been right. Today he has some fascinating and, perhaps, ominous visions of the years ahead of us. He is noted for the facility with which he adduces details and statistics to support a premise; yet he confesses he has little patience with statistics, preferring to "make it up as he goes along." The details that he makes up are often more revealing of the real truth than objective data would be.

It is said of Drucker that he is cold, lacking in humanity ("no awareness of the victims of the marketplace, no anger, no compassion"). An old acquaintance says that Drucker, before even arriving in the United States, laid out his career with deliberate calculation. "He determined to make a lot of money by writing and consulting, and then do what he pleased. He has accomplished this." (A professional writer might be permitted the observation that the individual who sets out to make a lot of money through writing is, indeed, a visionary.) An eminent professor of management remarks that "many people believe that Drucker will never do anything which is not of benefit to himself; will not do much for others. There may be some truth in this. . . ." The professor, however, then goes on to say, "So far as I am personally concerned, this has not been true. On the contrary, he has done much for me over the years."

For my part, I found Drucker sensitive if not demonstrative; concerned with human beings if not emotional in his manifestations of concern.

Most observers admit that Drucker is a good writer. But there are qualifications and caveats. Some point to what they consider Drucker's trick of stating the obvious with the implication that he has just discovered this truth. Another criticism is expressed by one management writer who declares that Drucker, in his writing, gets away with using "a bagful of tricks."

Drucker, who takes most criticism calmly if not indifferently, responds with considerable heat to such observations. He considers himself, above all, a professional writer. He points out that he has earned his living primarily through his pen since he was twenty. Long before he became known as a management writer —indeed, long before he became interested in management—he had been accepted as a leading magazine author. His work covered foreign affairs and economics, but he also wrote about American and European history, philosophy, education, religion, and the arts. His work appeared in magazines ranging from the old *Saturday Evening Post* to the *Virginia Quarterly*, from *Reader's Digest* to *Harper's* and *The Review of Politics*.

21

Up until the early sixties, when his consulting work began to take more of his time, Drucker wrote and published fifteen to twenty articles a year, and few of them had anything to do with management.

As for his writing "tricks," well, every writer has them; but I believe that an objective reading of Drucker does not bear out the charge that he invariably tries to hoodwink the reader into thinking that the author has freshly minted all of his thoughts. Drucker is generous in his acknowledgments of predecessors. If he is proud of his own original contributions, well, what writer is not?

More than this, Drucker is a philosopher who has made a bold and breathtaking attempt to probe to the real meanings of life in what is often a mechanistic and cruel world. He has given much thought to the confrontation of God and man in today's society—though he does not preach a gospel. In talking with him I have found what I think to be fresh and workable answers to the problems of alienation, depression, and disintegration that appear to infuse the society we live in. I have tried to present them here.

Drucker's most enduring contribution may be the one he makes in the role of a teacher, not just of management but of life. He has always taught. Irving Kristol says (in a review of *Management*, Drucker's most recent book) that Drucker has never received his due recognition from the academic and intellectual communities. Drucker disputes this, pointing to his nine honorary doctorates from leading American, English, Belgian, Japanese, and Swiss universities. But Drucker's influence as teacher rises high above the relatively minor question of enshrinement by academia. He has contributed in awesome quantity and quality to the shaping of the world. He has had his failures, some of which he feels deeply. He takes responsibility for his concepts and is used to being attacked for them; most recently he is under fire as the conceiving spirit behind the concept of the "global shopping center" and the multinational corporation. Drucker responded eloquently when I pressed him on the salient points raised by his adversaries—but he disdains to enter the arena.

Although Drucker's fame rests primarily on his contributions to business management, his influence and perceptions range well beyond those boundaries. Indeed, he has always thought of himself as a student, not primarily of business, but of institutions; today, he is much more caught up in the overhauling of a government (and he has many governmental clients) or of a hospital system, than a corporation. He has ideas about education and politics that have proven to be prescient and that will come into increasing acceptance. (Again, here he has pioneered concepts later seized upon and promulgated by others; the idea of the "new majority" is just one example.)

I have tried to penetrate the image and contradictions to the heart of Peter Drucker's ideas, influence, and meaning. This book is neither endorsement nor attack. It is, I hope, a critical examination and presentation of a man who is important to both businessmen and non-businessmen.

If I am in any way successful, the book is several things. For one thing, it is useful. Drucker is the most sought-after and highly paid individual consultant in the history of that industry. His consulting approach —which I have tried to set forth—is so simple and logical that any manager can apply it himself, if he has the objectivity and the guts to do it.

I would hope the book is entertaining—because Drucker is a stimulating and refreshing person. His observations, often barbed, and his anecdotes, always pertinent, stem from a unique combination of intellect, energy, and immense learning and culture. Apart from making frequent use of his remarks in the contexts where they are appropriate, I have given in to the temptation to include an appendix comprising nothing but Drucker's epigrams—on business, on education, on politics, on himself, and on life in general.

Most of all, I hope this book is in some way enriching to the reader, in the sense of conveying a feel for the meaning of society and the institutions through which it operates. If the book does not do this, it is my failure, because Drucker is enriching and rewarding. He has had an influential hand in shaping our world;

he can tell us how it works and how to live with it and in it.

Peter Drucker may or may not be a man for all seasons, but he is, I think, a man for *our* season.

1.

The Man and the Reputation

Peter Drucker is famous in the management community.
He is well-known to a large segment of the literate
population of the world. Many like him, and agree with
what they think he has said. Others dislike him. There
is general concurrence that he is Important and Influential.

But Important and Influential for what?

Let's begin with the biographical facts.

Peter Drucker was born in Vienna in 1909. The family
was originally Dutch. The literary thread is evident
from the beginning. In the seventeenth century the
family published bibles, sermons, and other religious
books in Holland. The name "Drucker" in Dutch (and
in German) means "printer."

Drucker's father, Adolph, became, at a very early age,
a high official in the government service. He left the
civil service in 1923 in protest against the Austrian
government's trend toward clericalism, and became an
international lawyer. But Adolph Drucker's main interests were literary and cultural. While still in government service he had founded the Salzburg Festival

25

(a major international musical event), which he served for many years as chairman of the board.

Adolph Drucker was a leading and outspoken liberal. When Hitler invaded Austria in 1938 he came to the United States to become Professor of International Economics at the University of North Carolina, later assuming a similar post at American University, Washington, D.C. Upon reaching the age of 70 in 1946, Adolph Drucker retired to Berkeley, teaching European literature at the University of California for a few more years. He died in 1967, aged 91.

Peter Drucker speaks of his father with great pride and respect: "He and I were totally different people. We never saw anything—events or people—the same way, never shared any interest. Yet we were very close and had tremendous respect for each other. From early childhood I admired my father's absolute moral integrity, his genius for friendship (which I totally lack), his courage. And he in turn was totally tolerant even though he could make little sense out of anything I was doing."

Peter Drucker's mother, Caroline, was one of the first women in Austria to study medicine. "And," Drucker says, "I am very much *her* son. Where my father had principles, she had perception. Till the last years of her life, when she was very ill, we always understood each other without having to discuss anything."

Peter Drucker was graduated from the gymnasium in Vienna in 1927. He then worked for a year and a half as a junior clerk in export houses in England and in Hamburg. Drucker recalls fondly a Dickensian milieu in which he sat on a high stool and scratched illegibly with a quill pen in brass-bound ledgers. He moved to Frankfurt in 1929, receiving his LL.D. from the University of Frankfurt in 1931. In 1930 he began to teach international law and constitutional history at the university.

Until then, Drucker had been working at two jobs in Frankfurt. One was with the local office of an American banking firm. The other job was with the *Frankfurt General Anzeiger*, where he was primarily an editor and financial writer. The newspaper did not boast a large staff; Drucker soon found himself writing about everything, including sports.

Drucker was young, talented, and apparently a conservative. So, when the Nazis came to power in 1933 they offered him a job in the Ministry of Information.

The answer to this was the publication—a few weeks after the Nazis had taken over—of Drucker's first book.

Berthold Freyberg, who served as fellow clerk with Drucker in Hamburg, and is his closest and oldest friend, has just retired as head of Europe's largest fishing and fish-preserving company (Nordseefischerei A.G. in Bremerhaven, an affiliate of Unilever). He recounts that he visited Drucker in Frankfurt in the spring of 1932. Both young men decided that they could not accept Nazism. Freyberg decided then to stay in Germany but in opposition; he became one of the leading spirits of the Protestant opposition to Nazism. But Drucker told Freyberg that he saw no way he could stay, since he could not continue as a journalist or as a university teacher, precisely because he was a conservative committed to constitutional government, the rule of law, and the tenets of Christianity. Indeed he felt that he could not even live as a businessman under Nazism without loud and clear protest. He accordingly set to work on his first book, the thirty-two page monograph entitled *Friedrich Julius Stahl, Konservative Staatslehre und Geschichtliche Entwicklung* (Conservative Political Theory and Historical Change).

Drucker was then an unknown author. Apart from feature articles in the newspaper, he had published a few articles, mainly on economics and econometrics, as well as a doctoral thesis in international law which he declares to have been "as trivial, as boring, and as deservedly neglected as Ph.D. theses usually are." Yet the monograph was immediately accepted for publication by Germany's most prestigious publisher, Mohr, in Tuebingen. It was published as the "jubilee number" in Germany's most respected series of legal and political monographs: Mohr's series on "Law & Government." Mohr published the essay two months after the Nazis had come to power, in late March 1933. By sheer coincidence, but to Drucker's delight, the publication date coincided with the first big Nazi rally after they had seized power. The result went far beyond the expectations of both publisher and author.

Stahl's name was in every German history text; but he had been neglected for almost a hundred years. He had been an important thinker of early nineteenth-century Germany, who had succeeded Hegel in 1831 as Professor of Philosophy at Berlin and then dominated German academic life for twenty-five years. He was originally a Munich Jew who became both the leading supporter of the Hohenzollern Crown and the leading philosopher of German Protestantism. However, he opposed Prussia's drive for hegemony over Germany and nationalism altogether. He was a lifelong political conservative but he rejected the concept of absolute monarchy as "no longer legitimate" and created the legal foundations for German constitutionalism. And despite his Jewish birth—he wasn't converted until college days —he strove mightily to develop a political philosophy for German Protestantism.

All this made Stahl an uncomfortable subject for politicians and philosophers alike. He was paradoxical; he could be classified neither within a Marxist frame nor within a Nazi frame. Liberals saw in him the great parliamentarian and espoused many of his doctrines; but they could not swallow his premises. Conservatives felt at home with his premises; but they could not figure out how he applied them to create a strong parliamentary system and were altogether uneasy because he was by no means an extreme right-winger. And in every aspect—as a Jew by birth, as a Protestant by conversion, as a conservative and as a constitutionalist—Stahl was anathema to the Nazis.

The Nazis had already instituted censorship; but the censor was fooled by the book's title—especially probably the word "conservative" in it; and the book slipped through. It became the subject of instant and widespread attention and something of a sensation. Indeed, a few years back when Drucker attended the twentieth anniversary party of his German publisher in Salzburg, he was told by several of the high officials in the present German government that this little book—which they read while still students or just starting on their first job—had prevented them from joining the Nazis and had induced them, despite all pressures and risks, to stay aloof during the entire Nazi period. The Nazis were also completely taken by surprise. But within a few weeks they had banned the book—one of the earliest manifestations of the bookburning that was later extended to embrace all "hostile" books.

Drucker clearly understood that this meant he had to leave, and fast—his Austrian passport wouldn't have protected him long. But he also felt that now he could leave with honor and a clear conscience. In April 1933 he left for England and a job in a merchant bank. Then Drucker was offered the chance to serve as American correspondent for a group of British newspapers; two in London, one in Sheffield, one in Glasgow.

In 1937 he sailed for the United States with the half-finished manuscript of his next book, *The End of Economic Man*, in his bags. It was his first full-length book, and the first to be published in English.

Drucker spent considerable time in Washington during the war working on intelligence about German industry. He began to teach, first at Sarah Lawrence College in Bronxville, New York, and then from 1942 to 1949 at Bennington College in Vermont, where he taught philosophy, government and religion. In 1950 he became professor of management at New York University; he still lectures at NYU. In 1971 he assumed the chair of Clarke Professor of Social Science at Claremont Graduate School in California.

In 1943 Drucker took on his first consulting project, a momentous one. He was retained to conduct a massive study of General Motors. (As we shall discuss, GM was thoroughly discomfited by Drucker's findings, and, so far as the management of the firm was concerned, he was treated as a nonperson for many years.)

By now Drucker had written *The Future of Industrial Man*. The General Motors experience provided the basis for his next work, *Concept of the Corporation*. Since then he has written ten more books and hundreds of articles. As an author he is a phenomenal seller; his books remain in print, and some have gone into dozens of editions. His byline remains potent in magazines. When, for example, *Harvard Business Review* publishes a Drucker piece, the staff braces itself for a flood of reprint requests.

The GM project was the start of an enormously successful consulting practice. Drucker has worked with hundreds of clients. He has never had a staff; he works alone.

Drucker's influence is worldwide. One reason that his thinking is valued by politicians and managers in many countries is that he does not just enunciate principles. He tries to get inside the traditions and culture of a particular place, to understand how things really work, so that he can focus on what is truly important.

For example, Drucker has been a welcome guest in Japan for many years. He first went there during the occupation, to lecture to Japanese businessmen. In the beginning, one observer reports, Drucker's lectures were popular but not necessarily productive. Typically, there is a story of two Japanese executives meeting after one of Drucker's sessions. One says, "My friend, you enjoyed Drucker-san?" "Oh, yes, very much." They talk about the brilliance of what they have heard; how important it will be to them. Then one asks, "What have you done about what you heard last year from Drucker-san?"

"Nothing," is the reply.

"Will you return next year to hear him again?"

"Oh, yes."

For some years Drucker told the Japanese wise and sometimes brilliant things, but he was talking from the outside. He realized this. He dedicated himself to penetrating and understanding the Japanese culture. Now his thinking on management and organization is tempered by his sense of Japanese tradition. His words are welcomed—and acted upon.

In turn Drucker's experience in Japan has enabled him to bring new insights to Western organizational thinking, notably in his analyses of the decision-making process.

Drucker is a conservative and a moral opponent of Communism. This does not keep Soviet management technicians from studying his theories and appropriating what they think is relevant. The Soviets approach Drucker on the basis that, while he cannot be trusted at all in terms of overall political and economic theory, he is nevertheless a valuable thinker when it comes to practical matters of organization policy and procedure. Soviet experts acknowledge that it is Drucker who has formulated the definition of management that has become the standard in "bourgeois" writings. Moreover, Drucker even wins grudging praise from Communist management theorists. For example, one leading professor of organizational science in the USSR concludes a lengthy analysis of Drucker's description of the tasks of the manager by saying, "We consider this approach rational even though it exaggerates the distinctive features of the manager's work, and unnecessarily sets it up against all other forms of administrative activity." The Soviet expert goes even further. He quotes Drucker's remark that "the average businessman, when asked what a business is, is likely to answer: 'An organization to make a profit.' And the average economist is likely to give the same answer. But this answer is not only false; it is irrelevant." The Soviet management expert then adds, "Thus, by emphasizing the perfectly obvious distinction between management and ownership of the means of production, noted by Marx in his day, [capitalist] management theoreticians are trying to draw a picture of the gradual elimination of capitalism's vices."

Drucker would probably be somewhat amused and gratified by these words; he would not be likely to regard them as altogether appropriate. His low opinion of the thinking of Karl Marx is amply recorded; indeed, he has been attacked by some critics who say Drucker goes much too far in that regard.

One can get an idea of the seriousness with which Drucker is taken in the USSR by examining *Organisation and Management: A Sociological Analysis of Western Theories*, by D. Gvishiani. This treatise, translated into English and printed in Moscow by Progress Publishers, is described as the first Soviet study of the main trends and schools of bourgeois theories of organization and management. The book is remarkable in its dual approach. It contains concise and accurate summaries of Western management theory, starting with Frederick W. Taylor and coming down to the present day. The exposition of capitalist theory is interspersed with political commentary that provides the required Communist viewpoint—but the theories themselves are treated with considerable objectivity and the strong implication that there is much to be learned from them.

Peter Drucker is by far the management thinker who is covered most fully in the text. There are twenty-eight separate references to him in the index. This is exceeded only by the number of references devoted to Marx and Lenin. In terms of space, however, Drucker is central to the book. There is much more space devoted to him than to anyone else. Sections many pages long are given over to Drucker on the practice of management and the tasks of the manager. Drucker is presented as being superior to his colleagues: "Drucker shows a certain farsightedness and understanding of the development prospects of modern production when he opposes the view that the worker is no more than an appendage of the machine."

And, again, "As distinct from many other bourgeois sociologists, Drucker realizes that the progress of industrial production demands that the sphere of management be extended and that it should enlist the help of more people at present engaged in the process of production, since isolated individuals are unable to carry out the complex set of operations linked with the management of modern industry."

Having thus been singled out for moderate praise, Drucker is then immediately condemned for failing to see that capitalism is "organically hostile" to the proper execution of his theory. Sometimes the reader gets the feeling that the author thinks, wistfully, that everything would be fine if only Drucker would see the light and enroll under the red banner.

This book is only one of the numerous manifestations of the interest that Communist management theoreticians have shown in Drucker's work and of the influence he has exerted—indirectly—on Communist organizational structure.

Now Peter Drucker lives in Claremont, California with his wife Doris, whom he married in 1937. His four children are grown. He is still fully active, but he restricts his traveling. Clients come to see him, and pay a lot of money for the privilege. He is in great demand as a speaker; he accepts no engagement that will take him away from home overnight. He continues to write, and think.

These are the bare facts of a life. Drucker is well known. He is successful. But these things do not make a man significant. What is Drucker saying when he writes? What does he teach? On what principles is his consultation based? What ideas does he have, to whom does he transmit his ideas, what has happened to his ideas in the marketplace of world affairs?

How does Drucker *reach* people—and whom does he reach? As we approach this question, the image of Drucker begins to fragment into a series of prismatic images. Many different people see him in many different ways.

Arjay Miller, dean of the Stanford Graduate School of Business Administration and former president of the Ford Motor Company: "Throughout the years, Peter Drucker has provided an effective bridge between academe and business, to the benefit of both. His teachings and publications are supported and enriched by 'real world' experiences, and business in general has gained from the application of his ideas and insights."

Chester Burger, consultant: "I have studied Drucker's theories of managerial communications closely. Although they are articulately expressed, there is nothing new in them."

Richard H. Buskirk, Herman W. Lay Professor of Business Management, Southern Methodist University: "He escorted management theory and thinking from its ivory tower and put it to work on the line. He made management aware that it was something separate and distinct from the simple administration of some technical operation . . . He has communicated managerial thinking to the operating executive."

Robert Townsend, writer and executive: "He is completely ill-at-ease with people, in a real in-depth relationship . . . He can't really understand people, empathize with them, figure out what they want out of their jobs, and try to structure the organization so that everyone is working toward the same goals . . . He's very comfortable in the world of ideas, and that's where his role has been."

Harold Koontz, Mead Johnson Professor of Management, University of California, Los Angeles: "He is certainly the greatest management philosopher of any time. He has had extraordinarily perceptive insights . . . 'management by objectives,' 'control by self-control,' 'federal decentralization' and many others. These insights have had great impact on practice and on management thinking."

Ernest Dichter, writer and consultant: "I am convinced that he has stimulated American businessmen in particular to think about their roles in more 'time-binding' fashion, relating past, present and future . . . Where I do disagree with him and where I have had to develop a different approach is based on the fact that I found a wide discrepancy between management accepting a theory and putting it into practice . . . I have become somewhat anti-Drucker, if this is not a sacrilege. Based on my disillusionment with management by objectives and the demand that management roles be clearly defined, I advocate that influencing managers to learn to be flexible, to operate much more by the seat of their pants, to become speculators with courage and verve, is more important than neatly formulated philosophies. In other words, I feel that Drucker may not have gone to the fuller implementation of his statements. He must ask himself what happens when a manager is psychologically incapable or unwilling or afraid (all of them interrelated) of putting a far-reaching theory into practice."

Lawrence J. Peter, author, teacher, creator of the "Peter Principle": "His writing is clear and at times brilliant. I have frequently quoted from his writings. As a writer, Peter Drucker is well established."

Leo Cherne, Executive Director, Research Institute of America: "Drucker is the great connector. His greatest gift is the ability to take disparate threads of society and history and show the connections among them."

David W. Ewing, Senior Associate Editor, *Harvard Business Review:* "Peter Drucker has done more than any other person—or group of people—to shake businessmen and business students out of ruts in their thinking."

Charles Dailey, Management Consultant and former Professor of Psychology, Dartmouth College: "The full value of Drucker's ideas . . . has yet to be fully exploited by industry and government."

Leonard Silk, financial writer, the *New York Times:* "A lot of people who consider themselves sophisticated in management look upon Drucker as a kind of amateur, not 'washed in the blood.'"

Chris Argyris, Harvard University Graduate School of Education: "Peter Drucker has the rare ability of high analytical competence coupled with the capacity to understand the underlying requirements of effective administrative action, especially at the top. . . . Some social scientists may fault Peter for not being more of an empirical researcher. I do not, for if he were, I wonder if he could have made the conceptual path-clearing contributions that he has made. If I were to fault Peter, it would be that he never seemed to realize that embedded in his 'nonscientific' consulting-based methods of inquiry were the seeds for a new methodology for social science—one that it needs desperately if it is to become genuinely applicable."

John L. Cobbs, Editor, *Business Week:* "The world is full of people who have important understandings, but who sit and commune quietly with themselves, maybe sharing a few thoughts with their dogs. The significant thing about Drucker has been that, when he has an idea, he can push it. He comes over as a very exciting man and people listen to him."

Frederick C. Dyer, author, consultant, and lecturer: "Whenever I pick up the writings of Drucker, I feel that I am in the presence of genius."

Howard W. Johnson, Chairman, Massachusetts Institute of Technology: "I am a great admirer of Drucker and think he has made seminal contributions in consistent ways for over forty years."

Lawrence E. Fouraker, Dean, Harvard Business School: "I have read all of Drucker's books and think he is a major contributor to our understanding of general management."

Simon Ramo, Vice-Chairman of the Board and Chairman of the Executive Committee to TRW, Inc.: "[Drucker's] books speak for themselves—that is, they are successful and obviously fill a need . . . He not only says highly intelligent things, but says them well."

These are just a few characteristic examples of variations in the way Drucker is perceived. That he has played an important role in the shaping of management thinking is usually acknowledged. His influence on the course of society—in many of its aspects—is often recognized. But it is impossible to fit Drucker into any neatly defined compartment. He is a European who has, for many years, commented on many facets of American life. He is frequently thought of as an economist, but his degree is not in economics, and he is often caustic about economics and its practitioners. He is a consultant and a highly successful one, but he rarely imparts to his clients any specific advice about operating methods. He is known as "Mr. Management," but he has never met a payroll. He has devoted years to the study of organizations—and has had enormous effect on the structure and functioning of organizations—but he has, himself, no organization, and has never had one.

To point up just one aspect of the difficulty that arises when one tries to categorize Drucker, we may consider for a moment the basic matter of his role in establishing the very concept of management that is now so widely accepted and that infuses the society we live in to such a great degree.

The question is not whether Drucker originated the concept of "scientific management." He did not. There was a "management movement" long before he arrived on the scene. It began with the work of Frederick W. Taylor in the late nineteenth century. Taylor was, in Drucker's words, "the first man in recorded history who deemed work deserving of systematic observation and study."

The three decades that followed Taylor's pioneering

work were fertile. From 1890 to 1920 the "classic" school of scientific management produced a wealth of ideas. Taylor's disciples, among them Henry Gantt and Frank and Lillian Gilbreth, developed the pioneer's theories.

However, after 1920 the "classic" movement seemed to lose impetus. Although there were exceptions, the range of the problems treated by "scientific management" theorists grew narrower. Their volumes grew longer and more abstruse, their subject matter narrowed down to particular technical questions of production and organization of labor.

Over the years there has existed a dedicated body of students of the practice of management. There are some eminent thinkers among them: Gantt; Mary Parker Follett; Henri Fayol. James Burnham's book *The Managerial Revolution*, published in the 1930s, is a masterful exposition of management concepts. The Society for the Advancement of Management and the American Management Association emerged to try to give form and impetus to the new discipline.

But, before Drucker's arrival on the scene, how much had resulted from this thinking and effort? Drucker offers thorough praise and recognition to his predecessors in the field. But he is—understandably—extremely conscious of what had happened before him as compared to what he caused to happen.

Drucker does not feel that the believers in management as a discipline had cut any great swathe, despite all of their dedication and insight. In the span of his working life he has seen the concept take hold with great force, influencing to a revolutionary extent the conduct of business and affecting greatly the whole society, which has become, in his view, a society of institutions, with the business corporation only the forerunner. Here are some unvarnished comments by Drucker:

"When I got the assignment from General Motors, I knew nothing about management. I gave myself a quickie course, finding to my surprise that I could read all of the significant books about management in two days. There were just seven books on general management, in all languages except Japanese, and most of them repeated each other. The other business books were on specific operational areas—accounting and taxation, salesmanship and advertising, and so forth.

"Nowadays, of course, even a huge barn would be inadequate to hold even one-tenth of the books on management. Our awareness has changed. Before World War II managers did not know they were managing.

"There was a cult of practitioners of the discipline of management. When they met in international congress they did not need the Waldorf Astoria. The Tavern on the Green was plenty big enough for them. In fact, there could be three high school graduations there at the same time, and the management cultists would still have enough room.

"The Harvard Business School did not concern itself with management before World War II. Nobody did. It was all production management, factory organization, industrial engineering, etc.

"There's been a very great change. We have had a management boom for twenty-five years; today, the most junior filing clerk in the shoe store is management conscious. The corporations were the first; now the public service institutions are becoming management conscious.

"One of the greatest changes has been the growing consciousness of the importance of structure. When Harold Smiddy began his reorganization of GE most of the managers readily admitted it was an organizational monstrosity. They were not opposed to reorganization. But they did not see why they should waste any time on it. After all, what difference did it make?

"In those days GE was run by two secret societies, the ex-Schenectady works engineers and the ex-traveling auditors. GE was run completely by people elected by the secret societies. Only the lamp division was exempt; it was the only division that had remained profitable during the depression. Otherwise, two men ran the firm; they met once a month at the board meeting, but they never exchanged a word. They couldn't stand each other.

"Just after World War II each of the two proposed lists of men for the top job. Charley Wilson was on neither list; and so he got the job. And the first thing

Wilson said was, 'We have to do something about reorganization.' That's when he brought Ralph Cordiner back from Washington. But nobody took it very seriously; they said, 'Who cares about organization, we've got dynamos to sell.'

"Today the pendulum has swung in the other direction; sometimes too far. Far too much reorganization goes on all the time. Organizitis is like a spastic colon. You get a pinprick and the colon acts up. Two junior people have a fight, and the reaction is that we have to reorganize.

"I have learned to be very conservative. Reorganization is surgery. One doesn't just cut."

Nowhere does Drucker maintain that there was no body of management thought, or no group of practitioners of scientific management, before his entry into the field. His role was to make the concept of management a matter of everyday thought for people who conduct the affairs of organizations. The record bears this out. But, beyond that, it is one of the propositions of this book that Drucker has made a vast number of original contributions to the concept of management; and that he has been uniquely effective in helping to get those concepts accepted and practiced.

Drucker has done this. In doing it he has been a shaper of our world. He has received formal recognition. He holds every management honor that it would be possible for him to receive. He became an officer of the American Political Science Association nearly 35 years ago. He has been president of the Society for the History of Technology, and a vice-president of The Institute of Management Science. None of this has happened because Drucker is an enthusiastic committee-man. On the contrary, he says "I do not like to take part in associations, and I am very poor on committees—and very bored. I work best alone and do not greatly enjoy meetings of any kind."

Nevertheless, there are many purists of the management "establishment" who are still grudging about their acceptance of Drucker.

Why? A veteran participant in the professional management movement speaks of his reactions to Drucker, yesterday and today.

"Originally, I was very much put off by the fact that he was an outsider working in my field. The group I belong to felt then—and to a great extent still feels— that this man had no business representing himself as a management authority.

"Worse, I think, was the fact that he was so much more successful than those of us who did not pretend to be anything but management experts. It used to bother people that he was just too damned good as a writer.

"Much of the criticism has abated. Most of the members of the 'establishment' will admit that Drucker was of great help: that he taught new ways of thinking and of looking at the organization, and that he gave the field new phrases and concepts. He has never attacked the people in the field; we have received nothing but help from his fame and success.

"But he is by no means fully accepted as an important figure in the history of professional management, in spite of his success. He is still, I regret to say, considered an outsider. It may take Drucker's death to establish his reputation in this field to which he has contributed so much."

It would be utterly wrong to infer that there has been no interrelationship at all between Drucker and the advocates of management science. For example, in June 1967, Drucker was the principal guest at the annual awards dinner of the Society for the Advancement of Management, which presented him with its highest award, the Taylor Key. In his speech, Drucker attacked those who belittle Taylor as making no more sense than those who belittle Newton because he did not anticipate quantum mechanics. Drucker affirmed Taylor as being the first to apply quantitative analysis to the study of the labor process, and went on to include "all the vaunted 'Management Sciences' of today—Operations Research, Systems Analysis and, indeed, Human Relations"—as part of the Taylor heritage.

Drucker's sweeping praise of Taylor and the scientific management movement was enthusiastically received.

Nevertheless, it is fair to say that, while the invitation and the reception indicated a cooling of earlier resentments, the occasion did not mean that Drucker was now accepted as a full member of the dedicated band of management scientists.

Though the upholders of the faith still withhold their full acceptance, Drucker goes blithely on, spreading his ideas, in the United States and all over the world. It is, perhaps, one of those unfair manifestations of life that he has become far more influential than any of the small band of idealists who have worked so hard to establish the concept of management as a discipline.

That is just one example of the impossibility of putting a label on Drucker. As we explore what he has done, we will come upon many others.

In the end, what is important is not the categorization of a man but rather the weight of his impact. On this basis, let's look at some of the faces of Peter Drucker.

2.

Drucker's Vision
of the New World

By 1936 Drucker was looking at a world in chaos. Total-itarianism and militarism were in the saddle. The tra-ditions of centuries were being destroyed. Civilization thrashed in a gigantic convulsion.

Drucker permitted no unwarranted optimism to give a roseate cast to his somber view. He saw that the old order was crumbling. That destruction, he concluded, would be complete. Hitler would be beaten in the end; Drucker was sure of that, because he was sure that totalitarianism could not sustain itself. But a thousand years of civilization was likely to fall along with the dictators.

These thoughts Drucker was preparing to put into his first book in English, *The End of Economic Man*—if he could find a publisher for such a depressing docu-ment. Drucker saw little that could be said to give hope to the anguished free world, and he was unwilling to provide spurious messages of good cheer. The rise of fascism was more than a spasm of history; it marked an end to a way of living that had been the under-pinning of freedom and progress in the world. The current situation was not merely an episode of history; it was the death agony of a scheme of economic, political, and social existence that had been constructed and nurtured since the end of the Dark Ages.

Yet, within ten years, Drucker had forged a philosophy by which he felt free men could live and grow again. In three remarkable books—*The End of Economic Man, The Future of Industrial Man,* and *Concept of the Corporation*—he completed the building of an ideological framework for peace, freedom, and human development. Much of what he said has become part of our intellectual paraphernalia—but not all. "Industrial Man" has not behaved or fared altogether as Drucker hoped he would. By examining the strong points and the weak ones in this vision of the industrial society we may find out some things, not just about Peter Drucker, but about ourselves and where we are going.

The End of Economic Man starts as an analysis of the roots and the nature of fascism. But totalitarianism is not really what the book is about. Drucker says that civilization had been based on a concept of the supremacy of economic values. The systems of government by which the world had been run—socialism no less than capitalism—were grounded in the assumption that human beings, on the whole, tend to act in accordance with their economic interests. A rational world view had been based on this proposition. Man, if he was anything, was Economic Man. There would always be aberrations, but man's values were essentially economic values; and thus an ordered and professedly more decent world order could be sought and achieved through the satisfaction of economic needs.

Drucker contemplated Economic Man and saw a corpse. It would be convenient to say that Hitler, Mussolini, and Stalin were the murderers; but it was not that simple. Totalitarianism was the immediate instrument of destruction, but it was also the terminal excrescence of organic decay.

In those days the rise of the dictators was generally attributed to economic phenomena. Totalitarianism was seen as a bill of goods that had been sold to mankind as a solution for economic problems. Drucker agreed

43

that this was a factor—but only one factor: "I believe that the material, far from being the foundation of human society, is but one pole of human existence." Unable to accept the usual explanations for the totalitarian revolution, he undertook to break new ground.

He dismissed the argument that fascism was succeeding because the desperate capitalists had turned to it as a bulwark against communism or because its practitioners were fiendishly clever propagandists. He acknowledged that fascism offered "no positive creed"; but he took issue with those who assumed that this meant the dictatorships would soon fall apart because their subjects would see through them. Drucker pointed out that the abundance of negative concepts in the totalitarian credo gave ample nourishment to the people of the "enslaved" countries. In commenting on the believers in the power of propaganda, Drucker showed an early flash of the biting sarcasm that helps to make him such an entertaining observer (if you are not the target) : "Learned scholars in learned books on mass psychology have come to the conclusion that it is only due to the chance absence of the right kind of demagogic mass-leader that we do not go on all fours or are not all nudists, since the masses 'probably' fall easy prey to any superior salesman, whatever his goods." (Drucker has never had much good to say of advertising!)

Drucker saw fascism as the final product of the collapse of Europe's spiritual and social order. Capitalism was doomed, at least as far as Europe was concerned. Capitalism had not brought freedom and peace to the people; it had led inevitably to class warfare among rigidly defined classes. Socialism had shown that it could not abolish those classes; all it could do was exacerbate the stresses between them. As for Marxism, its promise of the classless society had been shown to be empty.

These creeds had all purported to exalt the situation of man by improving his material status. They were based on "laws" that simply did not hold up, such as, Henry Ford's quest for a monopoly through lower prices and greater production, in defiance of the well-known "law" that monopolies cut production and raise prices.

So the concept of Economic Man was collapsing, and

the individual in society was not only not free; he could see no function for himself at all. As the walls of the old edifice crumbled, fear, superstition and belief in "demons" came flooding through.

People looked around for the "demons" responsible for their disillusionment and confusion. Fascism provided demons. The profit motive was gone; but there was no positive quality to take its place. So the Jews became the personification of the forces that were bringing evil to the world.

But even the handiest scapegoat can serve as a diversion for only so long. The masses could not be satisfied forever by the punishment of others who were said to be responsible for their discomfiture. Economic rewards were equally unsatisfying, because they did not bring *equality*. And equality, not material goods, was what people were demanding from their leaders. The leaders were preaching a new equality—but it consisted of the right of the majority against the individual.

Historically, organized religion had provided a refuge for the individual against the inhuman pressures of the world. Because religious institutions were not built exclusively on the discredited concept of Economic Man, there was some hope for religion in the ordering of a new society. But this could happen only after "the routine of the churches has been destroyed or, in other words, after persecution or social revolution [had] rendered impossible the maintenance of the outward institution."

A dismal prospect. Capitalism was finished. Socialism and Marxism offered no hope. Religion was an empty shell. Only totalitarianism appeared to be flourishing, because it nourished to some extent—even if spuriously —man's need for *noneconomic* fulfillment. The underprivileged were being given some of the noneconomic paraphernalia of economic privilege—high-sounding party titles, entertainment, special consideration in a host of trivial areas, such as the right to wear a resplendent uniform. Rational observers might scoff at this, but totalitarianism was in some measure responding to the individual's need to consider himself a functioning member of a society. The older creeds had offered nothing like this.

However, these attempts at conferring the trappings of status on the citizen were at best a poor substitute for the real thing; and totalitarianism could never offer the real thing. To the economist of the free world, fascist economics were a joke. To believe in what the totalitarians were saying about their system, one had to abandon all rational thought and revert to a belief in miracles. But Drucker pointed out that this was the very strength of fascism.

People were disillusioned with the nonrewarding nature of what they were getting under the "rational" creeds; they had never lost their willingness to believe in miracles, and credence in demons and faith in the nostrums of magicians were preferable to the sterile adapters of Adam Smith.

Fascism was attempting to replace Economic Man with Heroic Man. Each individual in the Nazi sphere was given some reason for thinking that his role had some heroic meaning in accomplishing a grand new world order. Of course this would be, in the end, as futile as all the other creeds. No amount of drumbeating and posturing could conceal forever the fact that the individual, far from being rendered a mythical hero, was now even more a victim of rigid class society and lack of true function. The miracle was a mirage. But the masses were turning to it because they had to have something, and they were being drawn away from the traditions they had supported and that had nurtured them for so long. To go back to bourgeois democracy or to socialism would be to return to a collapsed world, devoid of sense or freedom, ruled by malignant, unpredictable, and implacable demons. The old values were gone; at least fascism gave one some oratory, some color, some music, a chance to march, and the incessant reminder that other people were worse off.

But totalitarianism was not the beginning of a new order. It was only the result of the total collapse of the old. There were no miracles; only mirages The mirage would dissolve—if a new concept of man were to appear.

But—what would that new concept be, and where

would it come from? Drucker was confident that there would be one. He looked back to earlier collapses of European civilization, in the thirteenth and sixteenth centuries. He gave some general guidelines for the new order—but these were more negative than positive. The new society, whatever form it might take, would try to give people freedom and equality, but it would not work through the economic sphere. "We must try to develop," he said, "a new, free and equal noneconomic society on the foundation and from the premises of an existing economic society." Since Drucker had just finished saying that the "foundation and premises" were rubble, this did not seem a very promising proposition. But he was quite clear that economic considerations would have to be subordinate: "If it is recognized that necessary social policies must to some extent be economically harmful, they can be properly weighed as to their social benefits in relation to the economic sacrifices which they involve. And we would cease pretending that any such policy would be 'good for business . . .'"

So there it was. Economic Man was dead. The "free" world would have to find a new concept. What this would be, who could say?

This was indeed a stark document. Many observers at the time found it overly pessimistic and scornful of cherished traditions. But there is something even more interesting about *The End of Economic Man*. It is not only bluntly negative. It is revolutionanry in its treatment of established institutions—the *science of economics, established religion*, the *capitalist system*. It is unlikely that many of those who now celebrate Drucker as "Mr. Management" are aware that he was once proclaiming the doom of capitalism.

When the *End of Economic Man* appeared, Drucker was attacked by the Left. Drucker had just been appointed to the faculty at Bennington. There was a determined effort to persuade the president of Bennington, Lewis Jones, that he should cancel the appointment since Drucker was obviously a "reactionary," if not a "fascist," for predicting the Hitler-Stalin pact.

If *The End of Economic Man* were the sum of Drucker's work, it would have a certain historical importance.

47

Scholars looking backward would point out that he was, by and large, correct in his analysis of totalitarianism and his projection of where it was headed, if a little too sweeping in his nihilistic condemnation of the established society.

The book was negative. Drucker announced that just about everything on which the world order had been based was finished. The messenger who arrives with the bad news is not a popular figure; and there were those who were, at the time, only too ready to behead Drucker, at least figuratively. However, history would have, on the whole, substantiated his dismal pronouncements.

But *The End of Economic Man* was only the beginning. Drucker had said a new world order was needed. Within three years he was to offer his vision of the new society.

The Future of Industrial Man came out in 1942. Drucker was now in the United States to stay. This was his first "American" book. The whole world, now including the United States, was at war. The theme of world conflict runs throughout the work.

But in a way that is peculiarly Drucker's, he looks beyond the cataclysmic but temporary fact of war toward what he sees as the more important truths. He uses the war as a framework within which to present the concept of the new order that he had by now developed.

If one is old enough to remember the kind of thing that was being said about the "war aims" in 1942— the predictable, patriotic reverences being paid to the "traditional" virtues, to "freedom," to "democracy," to "our way of life," and so on—the opening words of Drucker's book are striking in their cool assurance and their acerbic indifference to popular trend: "This war is being fought for the structure of industrial society— its basic principles, its purposes, and its institutions. It has one issue, only one: the social and political order of the entirely new physical reality which Western man has created as his habitat since James Watt invented the steam engine almost two hundred years ago."

This is not the stuff of Fourth of July orations, particularly in wartime. It was not intended as an inspirational tract. It was a blueprint for the future. In many ways—not all of them pleasant ones—the world we live in now resembles this blueprint of more than three decades ago.

Drucker began by emphasizing the preeminent role of industry in the war. The industries of the contending nations were not merely adjuncts to the war effort; the war was being fought primarily between industries. The statement is a little sweeping, a little grandiose, perhaps; to most observers the events that seem like the turning points of World War II are battles on land, sea, and in the air, not contests of productivity. No matter; the statement gave Drucker his theme—that the peace following the war would have to be an *industrial peace.* The new society we were to live in, if we were to have a viable life on earth, would have to be an *industrial* society.

Typically, Drucker proceeds from this broad statement of his grand theme to what might be called a "brush-clearing" operation. He tries to put things in perspective, to dispel the confusions that keep the reader from seeing clearly through the mists of passion and self-interest. War is meaningless, he says. It solves nothing. But it is a fact, and wars are fought to be won. But the larger question is, what happens next?

We must not be misled into repeating the mistakes of Versailles. Germany must not be regarded as a national villain, somehow bearing, alone among countries, the mark of Cain. Every nation has the capacity for good or evil. Nazism does not grow out of "national character" or "national history." Totalitarianism and anti-Semitism are far more inventions of the French than of the Germans. And so forth. Drucker warns urgently against the translation of understandable short-term hatred of the foe into disastrous long-term policy.

The postwar society will, says Drucker, inevitably be an industrial society. It is up to us to keep it free and to make it work.

The functioning industrial society was not a reality at that time. The Western World was a magnificent technical machine, but not a workable civilization. What would it take to make it that?

And now Drucker comes to a point that would underlie much of his work for the next three decades. At the same time, he poses a philosophical problem for himself, which he will return to grapple with again and again—and which in the end he will have to admit he has by no means overcome. For here he sets forth the touchstone for the free industrial society of the future: "No society can function as a society unless it gives the individual member *social status* and *function,* and unless the decisive social power is *legitimate* power." (Emphasis added.) Status, function, legitimacy; the essentials of the new order. As we follow the course of postwar society and Drucker's observation of it, we shall see his attempts to find ways to install these essentials into the industrial society—or to find rational ways to get around their absence. Here we will see Drucker fail in certain important respects and admit that he has failed.

Drucker's starting point is the fundamental conservative concern with the legitimacy of rule. His first book, written as an anti-Nazi manifesto, was about the philosopher Friedrich Julius Stahl. Stahl tried to solve the problem of legitimacy of the rules that followed the French revolution; and did not succeed. Stahl was for twenty years the most influential academician in Germany; yet his failure to solve what he perceived as the central problem of conservative political philosophy meant that within five years after his death he had become irrelevant. Drucker had started on his central concern early; and he has also foreseen the ultimate failure of the attempt.

But that is yet in the future. At this point, in 1942, Drucker is still sketching the blueprint. But again and again he is drawn to his "musts": "For the individual there is no society unless he has social status and function." The individual must know where he stands in the order and be able to feel with good reason that he fills a role in making that society work. The rulers must be legitimate rulers, representative of those whom they rule and responsive to their needs.

The individual who lacks status and function is not only unhappy; he is dangerous. Lacking a fixed (though not immutable) place in the order of things, he is a destructive wanderer through the cosmos. Feeling no responsibility to a society in which he has no place, he sets little value on life. He will destroy and kill because he has no reason not to destroy and kill. Here we see prefigured the current, awful realities of the rootless destroyers—the Symbionese Liberation Army, the Weather Underground, the Palestinian Liberation Organization. "Status-seeking," Drucker was saying, is not an egocentric foible. It is a part of the human condition. When human beings seek status and do not find it, the world is in trouble.

As to legitimacy, legitimate rule is that which derives its claim from the basic beliefs of the society. The legitimate ruler need not be invariably chosen by a great mass of the people. The British landed gentry represented a tiny fraction of England; but for a long time it held the decisive power because its beliefs were accepted as the basis for British social life, and its standards were the standards the British people wished their leaders to uphold.

When the leadership does not meet these critera, it is bad leadership. It is illegitimate—and "No illegitimate ruler can possibly be a good or wise ruler." (Drucker is digging his philosophical hole very deep; when, thirty years later, the question of the legitimacy of the managers of global corporations will be raised by critics of the multinationals, Drucker's response will be articulate and passionate, but not notably consistent with his earlier utterances.)

And now Drucker touches on another cornerstone of his thinking, one that bears out the subtitle of *The Future of Industrial Man:* "A Conservative Approach." He anticipates the debate that was to grow over the question of "relativism versus eternal verities." He scorns both extremes—but he is a lot tougher on the relativists. He dismisses the "masses" and derides the kind of thinking that glorifies the faceless crowd. The masses are not glorious; they are "a product of social decomposition and a rank poison." Cold? Remote? Cynically snobbish? Maybe; but Drucker's aim is to take people out of the mass and make them functioning individuals in a functioning society.

At this point Drucker recognizes that he is beginning

51

to confront a major difficulty. He is proposing an industrial society. The managers of industry will become all-important. They will be, in effect, rulers. But—what makes them legitimate rulers? And how does industry bestow status and function?

Characteristically, Drucker goes to history for his answer. He examines the mercantile societies of Europe, Great Britain, and the United States. And he concludes that the mercantile society did indeed give status and function to its members because the member was integrated in the market. Furthermore, the rule of the managers was "socially decisive" in the market—and thus legitimate.

But the days of the mercantile society are gone. Can the new industrial society build on the positive foundations left behind by the old order? There have been few political thinkers, Drucker says, who had the vision to see ahead to the rise of industrialism. Only one great figure of the late eighteenth century understood the significance of the Industrial Revolution: Alexander Hamilton. Drucker finds the proposals that Hamilton made as Secretary of the Treasury to be prophetic. (It is probably safe to say that few business consultants have read the business correspondence of Alexander Hamilton with nearly as much care.)

What would the industrial society be like? The possibilities of an industrialized world had already been probed by various writers and artists, and they were not pleasant. Fritz Lang's film *Metropolis*, made in 1926, fantasized about the horrors of a mechanized utopia. In the shadow of gigantic machines, human beings are dehumanized and turned into virtual robots. In *Modern Times*, Chaplin did it with humor but no less savage bite. Already the idea of an industrialized world was acquiring an ominous ring, and many thinkers were attacking the coming of the machine as heralding an end to freedom. And here was Peter Drucker, telling the world that, far from destroying freedom, the machine would help to reinforce and ensure it. How?

Drucker now sounded another theme that was to recur again and again. He designated the corporation—along with the assemblyline—as the representative social phenomenon of the era. This was, at the time, a surprising choice. The world had been engulfed in turmoil and war for years. The headline-making institutions were political and military. The idea that the *corporation*, of all things, was the representative institution of life on earth was certainly a novel proposition in the context of the time.

The corporation is not just an economic entity. It is social and political. Its purpose is the creation of *legitimate power*. This was a logical development; the corporation emerged as Rousseau's social contract in its purest form.

Moreover, the corporation worked; very few institutions in history had been as successful. Already, executives of big companies held more sway over people's lives than most political authorities.

But here a knotty problem arose. It was an intellectual problem Drucker had created for himself, and he had the courage to face it. Once the corporation had been truly responsive to its shareholders. The power of the managers of the corporation grew out of the property rights of the individual. Thus, this power was *legitimate* power.

But not any more. Now the vast majorities of shareholders did nothing but sign proxies. They had no say in the management. The stockholder had not been deprived of his rights; he had abdicated them because he could not be bothered to do otherwise. But no matter how the situation had come about, the management of the corporation was no longer responsible to the ownership. It ruled independently, controlled by no one and responsible to no one.

By definition then, corporate power was *illegitimate* power. And "no illegitimate ruler can possibly be a good and wise ruler." How could a free, beneficent industrial society work with illegitimate sovereigns?

Not that the managers were not good people; on the contrary, "there has never been a more efficient, a more honest, a more capable and conscientious group of rulers than the professional management of the great American corporations today." Furthermore, the managers were aware of the abdication of power by the stockholders and uncomfortable about it. Absence of good qualities can undermine legitimacy, but a good man's goodness cannot make him legitimate.

The ruling power in the system would have to be made legitimate, Drucker said. The principle was clear; the "how-to" was to prove elusive.

Nor was this the only problem. The nightmares of *Metropolis* were not merely the creations of fevered minds. Workers were falling victim to the machine. They were being put out of work, or they were being reduced to robot status—and this was not the status that a society should confer on its members. Unemployment was not just an economic deprivation. When a man lost his livelihood he was cut off from society, because his work was what had given him status and function. It was not enough to give an unemployed worker the dole; his predicament stemmed from far more than just lack of money. Somehow the industrial society, in addition to solving its problem of legitimacy of leadership, would have to assure status and function.

Economic security was a beginning, not a cure-all. There would be a basic measure of economic security in the industrial society. The poor would be subsidized; people would not be allowed to starve.

But this was not enough. At this point in the development of his thought (as we examine elsewhere) Drucker clearly prefigured the famous "Hygiene Theory" of human motivation; that economic satisfactions are only negatively effective. When they are absent, the absence creates problems. But their presence by itself accomplishes little. It certainly does not make a functioning society. Economic satisfactions are vitamins, not calories, in the social diet.

At this point the reader has been set up. Peter Drucker has drawn, with broad strokes, the picture of the imminent industrial society. He has implied that there is great hope for this new order—but that, first, a couple of big problems must be solved. The rule of the managers must be made *legitimate*. The individual has to be given *status* and *function*. The reader is ready for the answers—but he is not going to get them. Drucker does not have the answers. And herein lies not just a problem with a book. It is a central intellectual and philosophical problem that has confronted Drucker since he wrote *The Future of Industrial Man*. Even this would not make the difficulty one of major significance for the world if it were not for the fact that these problems have turned out to be real problems of total existence. They underlie much of the anguish, disillusion and despair with which we now try to live. Drucker has not given us the solutions; but he was right about the magnitude of the problems.

Instead of coming forward at this juncture with some positive suggestions (which, as an American political leader of recent vintage was wont to say, would be the "easy thing to do"), Drucker grapples with the monster, and lets us watch him grappling with it. He reviews and dismisses facile and futile solutions that have been advanced by various leaders in various areas. He ridicules the pretensions of "advertising sages" who think that the problems can be solved by slogan. He returns to the cruel follies of totalitarianism to demonstrate how Hitler's regime conferred a spurious facsimile of status, but in reality held status and function in the utmost contempt.

And then Drucker provides a kind of answer: "The only basis of freedom is the Christian concept of man's nature: imperfect, weak, a sinner, and dust destined unto dust; yet made in God's image and responsible for his actions." For many readers this seeming reflection of a Calvinist heritage must have come as a surprise, and not an altogether agreeable one. Drucker is insistent; humanity is not perfectible, and the assumption that it is leads to tyranny. Good government cannot be planned or legislated; it is the product of the "moral character of society, and the genius of the individual statesman." Liberal rationalism has always failed, and will always fail.

No one would call Drucker a mystic; in his pronouncements on management he seems the most hardheaded and practical of men. But there is, and always has been, in Drucker a strong sense of other worlds and other values, exemplified by his fascination with

Kierkegaard's concept of man's simultaneous existence in time and eternity.

So we are not going to get any step-by-step blueprints for building a legitimate industrial society. There are no gimmicks, no devices that will straighten out our problems. (Indeed, when one examines it, he sees the same kind of dynamic at work in the most apparently down-to-earth Druckerian utterances on management. He does not give easy solutions.) The answers, or at least the hopes, lie in a more nebulous but nonetheless potent realm. We are not dealing with tangibles: "Above all, American freedom has been resting on American invisible self-government."

Self-government tends to degenerate, because people abdicate their roles in making responsible decisions. They shift the burden to the shoulders of those who are "paid to do the job"—call them bureaucrats or managers.

We are nearly at the end, and we can see that the problems raised by Drucker will not be dispelled. America is the hope of the future. America must take the lead in building the free industrial society. That society must somehow be given legitimacy and be capable of offering the now-familiar blessings of status and function. Government must be limited, controlled, responsible. The bad trends of the last fifty years must be reversed and we must return to the principles of 1776 and 1787—but with a difference that makes industry socially meaningful.

But how this will come about, no one can now say. "The absence of a basic social purpose for industrial society constitutes the core of our problem." And then, at the very end, Drucker sounds the first faint notes of a theme that he will later try to develop—futilely, as it will turn out—into the way in which the worker will, indeed, find status and function. He says that "the only solution which makes possible both a free and a functioning society is the development of the plant into a self-governing community." Later Drucker will look back on this proposition, and his subsequent development of it, sometimes as a kind of intellectual Edsel. At other

56

times he will speculate, wistfully, that more could have been made of the "plant community" idea.

But here Drucker leaves his readers, ushering them into the age of industrial man with armloads of difficult problems.

I have spent considerable space on *The Future of Industrial Man* for several reasons. In many ways it is the essential Drucker: coming forth with a bold conceptualization, spotting the problems in it, implying that the problems can be solved and then implying that no one has the answers; and then offering, tentatively, an answer. Furthermore, the industrial society that Drucker talked about has come to pass; and its problems are manifold. He was able to see it coming. Perhaps he has not helped us to master it as much as he might have liked, but he did spell it out, and this is a philosophical contribution that was undervalued at the time and has been since.

Drucker had designated the corporation as the "representative social institution." He had spoken with about as much reverence as one has ever seen him muster of the immense virtues of professional managers; of their efficiency, honesty, and dedication. He has been writing about the corporation from the outside. Now he was about to step over the threshold and conduct a monumental study of this vital institution from the inside.

Late in 1943 Drucker was approached by General Motors. Would he undertake a study of the organization? He was not able to find out the identity of the prime mover in GM who had advocated his retention. This individual probably was not boasting of his idea a year or so later. General Motors was emphatically not happy about the book, *Concept of the Corporation*, that resulted from the study. While the concepts it embodied were adopted in the following quarter of a century by many large corporations, including Ford, GM ignored the work. Alfred P. Sloan did not mention the book in his *My Years with General Motors*.

While General Motors ignored the book, other companies did not. Ironically, the competing automobile makers were among those who paid the most attention. Arjay Miller, former president of Ford, recalls, "When

I left the Army Air Force to join Ford Motor Company in January 1946, Drucker's *Concept of the Corporation* had just appeared and I found it extremely useful in forming my own judgments regarding what was needed at Ford. It was, by considerable margin, the most useful and pragmatic publication available, and had a definite impact on the postwar organizational development within the Ford Motor Company."

General Motors was dismayed by the results of the study and the inferences that Drucker drew from them. Although readers and reviewers looked on the book as being probusiness and favorably inclined toward its subject, the GM people felt that Drucker had been hostile and had singled them out for unfair criticism. Ironically, the book has led numerous companies to try to make themselves over into the image of General Motors as they see it in the study.

But the touchiness of GM is of only passing interest. The greater significance of *Concept of the Corporation* was that it completed the trilogy in which Drucker laid out his blueprint for the new order. He had proclaimed the end of Economic Man. He had envisioned the rise of Industrial Man. He had focused on the corporation as the essential institution of the new society. Now—what was the institution like? What should it be like? How could it be run?

Drucker begins with an attempt to give big industry a historical perspective. He asserts that he will study the corporation, not as a purely economic organization, but as a political and social entity, which establishes standards of living; leads, molds and directs the citizenry; determines the perspective with which we view the world; and which gives rise to a host of problems—solutions which we seek from the corporation itself.

The corporation, Drucker emphasizes, is a self-renewing, permanent institution. The stockholder is transitory; the idea that he owns the corporation is a fiction. Today the corporation is based on the concept of mass production, which is not a matter of machinery but of ideas: design, analysis of individual parts, merging parts, merging the production of each part into a plant producing the whole.

The corporation needs leadership, esprit de corps, organization. But it runs into difficulties. There is a tendency toward one-man rule. Initiative is discouraged. Men do not get the opportunity to prove themselves as leaders or decision makers. Fearful for their jobs, older managers keep younger managers down. The whole structure runs the constant risk of falling into ossification and bureaucracy. There is a premium on conformity. All of these difficulties must be surmounted by management while the enterprise is making a profit—because the first rule of the corporation is survival. The answers to survival rest within the problems of oranization.

Drucker discusses decentralization as a working principle for profitable survival. He provides a detailed analysis of the ways in which GM uses decentralization to make the most of its resources, human and otherwise. While he appears a little skeptical about the ways in which it all works out in practice, in general he accepts the validity of the concept.

But the problem of breaking through the isolation of the corporate executive is a tougher one. Relations between managers are difficult. Decentralization, an approach that has much to recommend it, has not been a panacea here.

Even with decentralization, some of the units of the giant corporation remain very large—and tend toward centralization. There are continuing problems with marketing efforts and dealer relationships. However, the principle of decentralization emerges from Drucker's scrutiny with a mark of about "B."

But how does the huge corporation contribute to the workings of the free industrial society? How does it confer status and function on its citizens? Drucker approaches this dilemma using GM as a reference point. (For the time being he seems to have forgotten about the other big problem, that of the lack of legitimacy of the corporation manager, except for reiterating that it is a problem.)

The corporation must give "equal opportunities" to workers and foremen. This is not easy to work out. In the case of the foreman, at this time there was increasing emphasis on formal education and training as prerequisites for supervisory jobs at GM. The great crusade to make the foreman a "member of management" was beginning. Drucker did not seem enamored of the concept, and in the end it did not pan out.

The monotony of assembly-line work was another problem. Here Drucker was—and remains—unwilling to buy the simplistic proposition that rote work is willy-nilly awful and destructive and thus to be abhorred and abolished. He declares that a certain amount of monotony in the job is not only inevitable, it is necessary for most people. The opposite of monotony, he states (perhaps arguably), is insecurity. Nevertheless, the nature of the rank-and-file industrial job leaves a lot to be desired in giving the worker status and function.

And now Drucker offers a set of suggestions about how the vital attributes of the new order can be given to the worker. They boil down to some useful thoughts concerning the means by which the worker can be helped to see how his individual efforts fit into the larger scheme of things. For example, the worker who toils at one operation can be taken through the entire series of operations and shown the relation of his own contribution. Furthermore, the worker can be encouraged to submit suggestions about improvements to be made in the operation, and be rewarded for workable suggestions.

The worker cannot participate in the management of the corporation. Drucker makes no bones about this. But he can be given opportunities to become involved in the circumstances that are peripheral to his job. For example, he can take more responsibility for the "administration of the community services of the plant that are run for his benefit." Drucker sees workers "managing" such things as accident prevention programs, cafeterias, and the like.

Will these measures offer status and function? Realistically, Drucker calls them palliatives. But at the moment they seem to be about all he has got.

Wage rates should be dependent on productivity. Drucker saw this clearly, and he is unsurprised by the price we are paying now for wage systems that are not tied to productivity. But he did not blame wage problems entirely on the worker. He commented on management's seeming blindness to the fact that the worker is less interested in his hourly rate than in how much money he will earn in a year, and thus that he would understandably not be willing to talk about tying wage rates to productivity until his basic income was assured.

Drucker moves on—possibly with some relief—from the knotty problem of what the worker gets out of all this to certain other problems of the industrial society. Is bigness bad in itself? No. Bigness does more than improve efficiency. It contributes to social stability; a big business can subordinate temporary gains to long-range policies. Profit is not to be demeaned. The profit motive is not inborn in man, but it is the guarantee of survival for the corporation, and thus an essential factor in the society of which the corporation is such an integral part.

Do big corporations wield great power? Of course they do. But the lust for power is inherent in human nature. If it were not given vent in one way, it would find scope in another.

Finally, Drucker presents the "five pillars" on which economic policy of the new society must rest: full employment; definition of the desirable spheres of government action; a certain degree of protection for the individual against the vagaries of the marketplace; prevention of monopoly; conservation of human and man-made assets.

This is the posture of the corporation, the representative institution of the industrial society. Looking at it from the vantage point of today, one wonders in passing what General Motors got so upset about. But in the days just after World War II the corporation was not used to coming under such scrutiny. Attacks, yes, by labor leaders, proletarian novelists, and radicals of various sorts; but not searching examinations by those who were purported to be "conservatives" and thus "friends."

But, in the context of Drucker's broad philosophical scheme for a free and better world, *Concept of the Corporation* may be most interesting for what it does not do. It does not solve the problem of the "illegitimate rule" of the manager. It does not present any clear, strong plan for giving status and function to workers. The ideas about suggestion campaigns and committees to run the lunchroom are clearly inadequate to the task.

Drucker knows this. But he knows too that the industrial society, beneficial or not, is about to become a huge global reality. Perhaps it can yet be made to fulfill its bright promise. After all, the corporation must be managed; and if the craft of management is made strong enough, maybe this will be sufficient.

So Drucker turns to the next logical step in his unfolding picture of the new order. He begins to concentrate on giving managers the tools to manage well—not just so they can clear bigger profits, but so their skills can contribute to a free and better world.

3.

The Interpreter of Change

Future becomes present, and soon-to-be-past. And, says the eighteenth-century philosopher Vico, the past will be future again.

Much of Drucker's work points toward showing us the realities and possibilities of life. He combines past, present, and future on his palette as he paints the unfolding scroll.

In 1959 Drucker published *Landmarks of Tomorrow*. The book was important then. It remains important today. He called it a "report on the new post-modern society"—nothing more. He said it did not deal with the future, only the present. He declared that he was trying to understand rather than to innovate, to describe rather than imagine. But, while reporting, describing, and understanding, he speculated and imagined. And, inevitably, he innovated.

In *Landmarks* Drucker set himself three tasks:

- to explore the new view of the world, the new concepts, the new capabilities;

- to define the new frontiers that humanity would be obliged to penetrate;
- to probe to the present realities of human existence.

In order to describe the new view of the world it was first necessary to demonstrate the awesome velocity with which universally accepted truth is discarded or becomes incomprehensible. The concepts and disciplines that define and direct our lives today were, by and large, unknown fifty years ago. Drucker speaks of the great changes in biology, psychology, economics, linguistics. He points out a fundamental development underlying these movements and others. *Causality* is no longer the keynote. In the old days the great effort of the scientist and philosopher was to go back to initial causes—where it all began.

Now we are far less concerned with *cause* than with *purpose*. *Purpose* is the unifying thought. We assume a cause—Einstein said that God does not play dice with the universe. But we look for the purpose—not the reason for the existence of the universe, but the purpose of various realities within the universe.

We have come to accept the proposition that growth and change are normal elements of the world; and that things are constantly happening that we cannot at the moment understand or that we could have predicted. This seems an obvious statement; but Drucker goes back to show us that it was not at all obvious as recently as the 1920s, when permanency in all things was accepted as the norm.

This new reality affects our thinking in business and in life. We no longer look for the one right solution that will be fixed, statically, forever. We try to think more fluidly to cope with the fluidity of real events. But we don't really understand what is happening. For example, as the physicists find out more about the various sub-atomic particles, they keep exploding their previously held theories about matter, energy, and time.

We must accept the idea that knowledge does not come in a fixed number of packages, big and small. The old view was that education was a matter of getting and opening these packages. The more packages you opened, the more you knew.

Now it turns out that the more "packages" you open, the less you may really know. Some disciplines are adjusting to this fact better than others. Drucker felt that the medical fraternity was not responding well to the new reality. Young doctors were not as well taught as their ignorant predecessors. The reason? "Medical schools are still organized around the idea of disciplines as static bundles of knowledge." In the old days there had been at most six or seven such "bundles." Now there were at least fifty, and the number was rising.

All of this was confusing to the average man, and no wonder. He looked to scientists and academicians for leadership and clarity. What he was now getting was a babble of jargon. Here Drucker displayed his concern for language. A clear simple writer and speaker himself, he is infuriated by the erosion of language and style. And this is not just an annoyance. Effective communication is essential to society. When language is captiously subverted, communication stops.

No wonder, he said, that people are anti-intellectual. What we had to do was understand how disparate patterns of "physical, biological, psychological and social order" are meaningful as reflections of a larger unity. We needed a concept of the "whole" that would let us understand ourselves and what is happening to us, and thus give us more control over our lives.

Drucker did not use the term "interdisciplinary"—but here he was calling for the kind of exploration of reality that goes beyond the limits of parochial disciplines. Nowadays we are awash in "interdisciplinary studies." Perhaps we do not understand any better, but we can hope that progress is being made.

Under the old concept of fixed bundles of knowledge, the idea of research—particularly industrial research—was the cause of amused contempt. Why pay good money so that some crackpot can play with white mice in a laboratory? A great many businessmen held this view —and clung to it. They are not laughing today. Now we know that research is necessary. It is inevitably often wasteful, but if we accept the new reality that change, not permanency, is the way of the world, how can we do without it?

Drucker explores the problem of the relationship between pure and applied research. The hard-headed businessman and the practical citizen had always opted for applied research. Experimentation must be aimed at a definite purpose. Otherwise how could you know if it were worth the money?

But now we are finding that "pure" research was increasingly concerned with applications, and was having the greater impact; and "applied" research was becoming more and more related to the search for fundamental knowledge. Innovation is not a one-way street. It is a circular process. New knowledge is discovered. It is applied. In this process the need for the discovery of yet more new knowledge is uncovered. For example, the application of theoretical statistics to marketing problems showed the need for a new theory of consumer behavior, not based on statistics. So applied research shifts into pure research, and then back.

There had always been innovation. But in the past it had come as a bolt from the blue—"Eureka!" Today we were learning that innovation was not something to be left to the fates but, rather, an approach to industry and to life that could be made systematically and that would enable ordinary mortals to accomplish things previously accomplished only by extraordinary geniuses.

The acceptance of innovation as a constant and worthy objective can give mankind the power to break through historical roadblocks and solve traditional problems such as disease, famine, and poverty. The acceptance of innovation as a principle was in itself not enough to do this; but it was a necessary first step.

Along with scientific and technical innovation—and combined with them—would go social innovation. Industry—the corporation—would be an essential factor in the process of social innovation. Such innovation must be responsible. It would not aim at destroying the past, but, rather, building on the past.

Innovation involves risk. Drucker feels that the biggest risk in innovation is not that of failure, but of *success.* Prefiguring the widespread furor over the ecology (Rachel Carson did not publish *Silent Spring* until 1962), Drucker pointed to a "minor" example of what can happen when an innovation is successful. DDT was a great achievement, making it possible to control pests. But, unexpectedly, it was killing beneficial insects as well. Bird life was threatened and thus, in turn, were the flowers and trees.

So innovation called for more than the willingness to risk failure. It imposed the responsibility of success. Change was always coming anyway; but we have an obligation to see that man-made change does not make things worse in the very process of trying to make them better.

So innovation requires planning—not vast "five-year" plans but decentralized local planning. Centralized planning leads to chaos. Local planning might seem confusing. There would be conflict—between, say, the planning of a company and the planning of the community in which it is based—but we would have to accept the defeats and make free, decentralized planning work.

Planning takes organization. Automation is a good example of the organization of human effort. Teamwork was replacing individual effort. The thrust of the concept is to organize the skill and knowledge of many people and apply it as if it were being exerted by one man. Unskilled workers would be replaced by skilled ones, "one-man-bands" by specialists; but through planning and organization they would function as an organic unit.

The building of such organic units would demand the utmost from professional management. The manager is a specialist in harmonizing and maximizing the strengths of a disparate collection of specialists. He possesses enormous power. With it he must accept tremendous responsibility. We would have to recognize a new concept of organization ethics, involving self-respect, self-discipline, and humility. (Critics who view Drucker as a cold, amoral exponent of corporate power and profits, without regard to human welfare, overlook his

67

heartfelt insistence on the proposition that management must be conducted within an ethical framework.)

The new ethics would not be a matter of pious pronouncements. Its tenets must be ingrained in the management job, implanted there from the earliest moments of management training.

Of course the manager would want to get ahead. Of course he was subjected to great tension. But Drucker rejected the popular idea of the "organization man," a glib conformist who wears the right clothes and says the right things. The real manager, secure in his discipline, knows that his task involves risks and effective direction, not safety and uniformity. And the real manager welcomes that set of circumstances.

The new organization is based on the principle of human order in society. Its process is "human dedication, human knowledge, and human effort," devoted to the creation and satisfaction of human values. It is above all an information and decision system. Information and questions and ideas are generated by the people inside the organization as well as by the environment that surrounds it. Then somebody makes a decision, which is translated into effective action. All of this is *human* process, not the activities of machines or robots. The principle of organization is that of the man in society.

Society was changing. The middle class was becoming dominant. The worker no longer remained a proletarian. He joined the middle class, and espoused its tastes, aspirations, and way of life.

The middle class was now the class that does the work. We no longer had the stratification of "capitalists" and "workers." Karl Marx had been wrong in his prediction of the continuing growth of the proletarian class.

Of course capitalists had not disappeared; neither had the poor. But the entrepreneur now needed the organization; he had to act as a manager. And the poor were no longer the "masses"; they were isolated groups —albeit sometimes large ones—that were having problems moving into the dominant middle class.

There were enormous gradations within the middle class. But it was also fluid. An individual was no longer fixed by circumstances of birth or occupation; he could move, laterally and upward.

This was a free society—but the freedom could only be *freedom within order*. The individual could act voluntarily as an individual—but his activities should be within the framework of the organization: "He has to accept its reality, has to affirm its objectives and values, has to focus his values, knowledge and efforts on its needs and opportunities."

This view is central to Drucker's philosophy of the new order. The individual finds freedom and fulfillment only when he lives and works as part of a larger entity. Earlier Drucker had said that the corporation was the representative institution of the new society. The organization gives the individual a place in the world and a chance to use his abilities and live his life. In turn the individual accepts the basic purposes of the organization and harmonizes his individual actions with the overall ends of the group.

Drucker admitted that no organization came close to fulfilling this vision. He admits the same today. But he maintains that, confused and mismanaged as the new order may be, it still offers the best way for humanity, somewhere between imposed collectivism and unheeding anarchy.

There is always a dualism in Drucker, exemplified by his abiding interest in Kierkegaard's concept of man's simultaneous existence in time and in eternity. Man must be an individual and at the same time part of the whole. The whole owes certain things to the individual, and he in turn has responsibilities to the human order. If the balance is maintained, human life—always difficult—can be fulfilling. And one of the most important factors in keeping the balance is the continuing development of organizational insights and dedication to the disciplines and ethical imperatives of management.

What about Drucker himself? He is not a member of an organization, and maintains none—not even a secretary. He acts as a full individual. His answer would be that this is his role, and that he is functioning as an individual within the larger entity of the society as a whole. One may accept this proposition. One may reject it. Or one can see it as the kind of paradox that makes life interesting and individuals fascinating.

The development of the new order called for educated people. We were entering an age of knowledge revolution. In a few years everyone would be educated in a way that had previously been the province of a privileged few. But the revolution brought problems. Somehow money would have to be found for the new expanded educational facilities and for the teachers required by the new society.

Teachers must be paid more. They would be paid more. But—*for what?* The performance of a machinist can be measured. But who would measure the performance of the teacher, and what standards would be used?

We would have to develop a craft of teaching as we were developing a craft of management. Mass education would have to bring into play new tools of mass communication—radio, television, movies, the computer.

All this would cost a lot of money. To have the federal government foot the bill was undesirable in many ways, notably because it would inevitably impose federal control over what was taught and how it was taught.

Then, too, society would have to figure out the purposes of expanded education. "Education for what?" was the wrong question. Education is for some*body*, not some*thing*. The purpose of education would have to be the development of individuals who would be functioning members of the new society.

Here Drucker was posing problems that haunt us still. Education has become a battleground, and busing is only one of its segments. We are not agreed on the purposes of education. We frequently deplore the incompetence of those who teach our young. And, in localities around the country, we see an increasing movement toward "citizen participation" not just on the periphery but at the center. Organized groups demand that the layman have a say in educational policy. They are no longer willing to "leave it to the professionals." Teachers, now organized in unions, find themselves embattled with the communities by which they were once cherished—if, perhaps, underpaid.

As for the funding of education, we have only to look at the headlines. Everywhere voters are rejecting education budgets. Citizens denounce professional educators for wanting to solve problems by "throwing dollars at them." The educators retort that the citizenry is shortsightedly spiting the future of its children. More affluent communities look with fear at the movement toward equalization of educational expenditures throughout states—as against permitting the locality to call its own shots on the basis of property taxes.

The educated society, said Drucker, was becoming an accomplished fact. The frontier had opened up. For better or worse we were entering an era of mass knowledge. He stated the questions, offered his thoughts, and hoped that we would have the wisdom and ability to solve our problems.

How could everyone be given his fair share of the good things that the new society would bring? Drucker reviewed the problems, human and otherwise, that stood in the way of widespread economic development.

His solution is embodied in the observation that "the common vision of economic development means that the whole world is dedicated to a business civilization." The business enterprise is crucial in worldwide economic development. The ultimate goal of large business must not be profit; profit is not a goal but a necessity of survival. The goal must be the development of people.

A great problem in the realization of the dream is the shortcomings of government. Traditionally, government was assumed to have a monopoly on organized institutional power. But this concept was on its deathbed. Now other institutions, independent of government, were able to organize large numbers of people for cooperative effort toward joint goals. The corporation was the most prominent, though not the only, such institution in the field. These nongovernmental institutions had to function in harmony with federal, state, and local governments. This was not happening. Government had become a "swollen monstrosity." For all of its hugeness, it was unable to make policy or to get things done. Everywhere there was a proliferation of administrative agencies to control housing, transportation, and so forth.

71

But these agencies were beyond control. Drucker called them a cancer on the political system.

Perhaps, Drucker felt, the answer lay in new and enlightened political thinking. We needed a new political theory, attuned to the world of today. The old way of balancing special and regional interests was not working any more.

Enlightened political thinking should be a function of education. But political theory was sterile. In many schools political science was no longer taught. Modern government was in crisis around the world. Drucker could do no more than call for serious attention to the problem.

As to relationships between the areas of the world, Drucker focused on the failures of the assumption that the less-developed countries of the world would one day accept the methods and concepts of the West. As a matter of fact, he observes, the Western system has collapsed. There is nothing left to accept.

But at the same time, Eastern civilization had vanished. Japan, China, and India had tried to build industrial societies on non-Western foundations—and had failed. True, Western technology was spreading through the non-Western world; but this only compounded the problem. Technology is not just tools. It needs social and cultural foundations. The industrial approach cannot be imposed merely by the importation of a steel plant. Both West and East must seek a new world view.

Drucker rejected the idea that Communism lay at the root of the world's troubles. He minced no words about his feelings: "Communism is evil." But Soviet Russia and China and the Communists were aggravating, rather than causative, factors.

The "free world" should, as a start, give the highest priority to the development of education. Only an educated people could be equal to the problems facing society.

Government should understand its limitations. Private business would have to take on a major role in the shaping of the new order. And the individuals involved in business would have to develop a discipline and an ethics of management.

Finally, Drucker turned away from vast movements and institutions to take a look at the condition of the individual human being. He called for a return to spiritual values, and he observed that the historian "a century hence—should there be one to record our survival —may well judge the return to religion to have been the most significant event of our century and the turning point in the crisis of the transition from the modern age."

We need, he said, compassion—"the deep experience that the Thou and I are one." He urged that "only compassion can save—the wordless knowledge of my own responsibility for whatever is being done to the least of God's children."

Many Drucker-watchers come upon such eloquent tributes to the values of the spirit as strange, coming as they do from "Mr. Management"—the man who is capable of the most hard-headed pragmatic observations and analyses. This is a side of Drucker that is not easy to fit in with a large body of his work and with the conventional view of the man. Nonetheless, it is Drucker.

Indeed, throughout *Landmarks of Tomorrow* we see a number of varying aspects, all of which add up to the essential Drucker. We see him as the "great connector," drawing together disparate threads from history and philosophy to show us the world in a new light. We see, also, the observer who is skeptical to the point of cynicism, scornful of the pretensions of pundits and the obfuscations of alleged experts, puncturing sacred cows with detached (and yet somewhat joyful) accuracy.

Some of the recurring themes emerge to be blended with the whole: the emphasis on the need for education; the faith in the business organization as a molder of a better world; the urging of the development of management skills as a necessary corollary of the growth of the corporation; the insistence that automation is not just gadgets, but rather a new concept for organization of human effort; and the continuing restatement of the idea that the human being can fulfill himself as an individual at the same time he fills a role within a functioning organization.

This is Drucker, the conservative innovator, who sees the inevitability of change and the need to build on the past rather than reject it.

At the same time we see glimpses of another Drucker. The ultimate optimist, who can see beyond the problems that his own analysis poses to the solutions that he hopes and feels mankind can bring about. And this Drucker merges into the dualist Drucker, the advocate of an almost mystical Christian view of the world, who tells us that the new order that we, by ourselves, will create, will yet put us in harmony with God and eternity.

4.

Industrial Citizenship: The Dream That Never Became Real

The scene: the boardroom of Hamilton Manufacturing. The Executive Committee of the company is sitting in weekly session. First on the agenda is a financing plan designed to raise capital for an expansion of the small-unit assembly plant. The Treasurer will present his ideas. Then the Vice-President for Production will comment on how well the expansion will meet the needs he projects for the coming five-year period. Division heads will discuss the plan from their differing points of view.

There are other items on the agenda. Hamilton is encountering unexpected competition in an area it has dominated for a long time. The Director of Marketing has made a study of the situation and he has some proposals to make. And then there is the problem of retraining workers on the payroll and hiring new ones to handle the larger load that will be carried within the expanded small-unit facility.

The Executive Committee is doing what it is supposed to be doing: taking a long-range view of the future, setting policy, acquiring and collating input for top-level decisions.

At the same time, another group is meeting in a conference room nearby. This is the Plant Community Council of Hamilton Manufacturing. The elected chairman, a machinist, calls the meeting to order. Sitting around the table are lathe operators, secretaries, clerks, maintenance people, painters, finishers, quality-control inspectors.

....This body is an important governing unit within the Hamilton complex. It does not set company policy in the traditional areas of marketing, manufacturing, engineering, research, finance, and so on. But the council is an autonomous group that runs the plant community surrounding the Hamilton operation. The council and its leaders work with company management—but they make their own decisions and set their own policy within the sphere that has been designated for them.

Today the council's agenda covers a number of items. The proposed expansion of the small-unit assembly plant is a matter of concern. The council members will not be deciding whether to undertake the expansion and how to finance it. But they will consider the placement of workers within the new facility.

There are other considerations. Some of the council members are worried that management's plans do not adequately cover the need for worker safety within the expanded operation. Then, too, there is the question of working conditions—lighting, restrooms, recreation facilities. Does the expansion offer enough within those areas?

A council member is concerned about traffic and parking. The entire pattern of automobile flow around the plant should be rethought. It may be that the divisions of Hamilton Manufacturing should go on staggered working hours. The council will discuss and generate a proposal.

The problems ancillary to the expansion are not the only things confronting the Plant Community Council. The time is approaching when the health insurance program is to be renegotiated with the carrier. A sub-

committee will report on its recommendations for changes in the policy.

The Red Cross blood-donation drive will be conducted in two months. The Community Council was somewhat disappointed at the number of donors who turned out for the last effort. A fresh and more aggressive campaign will start within a week.

The Hamilton Suggestion Contest is going well. Suggestions are flooding in, and many have already been accepted, with suitable cash and stock awards being distributed. The Council runs this program, and there will be some talk about how to keep up the momentum.

And then it will soon be time for the workers at Hamilton to elect new members to the council. Some incumbent members have already indicated that they wish to continue; others will step aside. Plans must be made for orderly elections and transfer of power. This is a democratic process, and the Hamilton people take a deep interest in their representation, because they know that they hold in their hands the power to control many aspects of their lives that are related to their jobs.

Still another meeting is taking place. This group is the Management and Technical Governing Council of Hamilton Manufacturing. This body comprises representatives of the "industrial middle class" of the company—foremen, salesmen, engineers, technicians, designers, department heads, etc.

These people stand between the rank and file and top management. They do not make company policy; they do not work on the plant floor. They are a distinct entity in the social hierarchy of the enterprise. They relate to the groups above and below them; but they have their own concerns as well.

So this segment of the Hamilton organization is organized into a separate self-governing body, with control over many aspects of life at Hamilton Manufacturing. Unlike the rank-and-file council, the middle group's self-government is not established by a union contract but rather by delegation from the top.

The proposed expansion of the small-unit plant has ramifications for the Management and Technical Coun-

77

cil. For one thing, they are concerned about the specifics of the training program. The consensus of the body is that the imminent changes offer an opportunity to review and improve the entire spectrum of company training practices. A committee of this group is preparing a presentation on revised training. They will soon make their presentation to the Executive Committee.

At the same time, members of the middle group are thinking about how rank-and-file people will react to a number of the changes. This is a matter of utmost urgency; these people depend on the rank and file for performance. So it will be necessary to meet with representatives of the Plant Community Council to talk over the difficulties that might arise—in such areas as working conditions, safety, traffic—and come up with some solutions that the Management Council will then submit to the Executive Committee.

This group, central in the hierarchy, serves as a bridge between top management and rank and file on a broad range of subjects relating to the ways in which the Hamilton plant community functions. The group has its own areas of autonomy, and is democratically representative of the important elements of the company whose interests it espouses.

Three separate bodies—each autonomous in some aspects, each democratic to a certain degree, each functioning and making decisions about aspects of work and life at Hamilton Manufacturing.

And each separate group works with the other two to offer the most rewarding life to everyone connected with the organization.

The foregoing is the scenario for a dream. It is a representation of Peter Drucker's vision of the plant community, "which in an industrial society is the distinctive and representative social unit."

The concept of the plant community was a vital and inevitable development of Drucker's thought. He had proclaimed the end of Economic Man and the rise of Industrial Man. He had identified the corporation as the representative organization of the new order. But at the same time he had insisted that any workable social order had to confer "status and function" upon all its members.

But this status and function had to be real, not phony. It could not be done the way the Nazis did it, by giving portentous titles, uniforms and spurious mandates to every worker and peasant who joined the party. Every member of the new society would have to hold a real measure of control over his life and his destiny, and have some kind of voice in the organization of which he was a part. This would be the quid pro quo for his agreement to function in harmony with the objectives of the majority; and at the same time it would enable him to live and work as an individual.

How could this be done? Should the workers "own" the company, sharing equally in all policy decisions and profits? This was nonsense. Drucker had seen too many Marxist regimes trumpeting equality while maintaining a fiction of full participation. He did not for a moment take it seriously.

No. A corporation must be *managed*. And a central point in effective management is the location of authority for specific functions at the proper places in the organization. Decisions as to the long-range course of a company could be made only by those top executives who were charged with that responsibility.

So—what was left over for those who were further down on the organizational totem pole? Where would the middle and lower managers, the supervisors, the technicians, and the rank and file find scope for the "status and function" that was their due?

As Drucker examined the problem, he was pleased to find that there was quite a lot of potential scope. He put his ideas into a singular book, *The New Society*.

The New Society is a succinct, comprehensive picture of what Drucker thought the new world should be like, and what it was going to be like. In one sense it recapitulates the themes he had been developing for fifteen years. But *The New Society* does more. It brings together disparate threads of Drucker's philosophy and method, weaving them into a tapestry of the future. It elaborates, makes concrete, gives flesh to abstractions. It is, to a considerable extent, a blueprint for a made-over society, an industrial Peaceable Kingdom in which the management lion would lie down with the rank-and-file lamb, after which both would rise and work shoulder-to-shoulder for the joint good of the corporation, the society, and all of the individuals comprised therein.

Of course it never happened.

Drucker saw many things very clearly. His analysis of problems in *The New Society* is keen and articulate. His vision is fresh and breathtaking in its scope. Many of his propositions are as valid today as they were when he first uttered them.

But the plant community is not a reality. There is no typical corporate structure of top executives, middle-level people and rank-and-file workers, each happily turning to problems within their own scope, and each communicating and working with the others to build effectiveness on the job and happiness off the job. Rank-and-file relationships with top management are adversary relationships. The operative unit is not the plant community council but rather the grievance committee. Broad-scale decisions are taken at the top, with more or less effort to sell them down the line. Workers express and manifest little or no loyalty; through their bargaining units they go all out for everything they can get. "Everything they can get" does not relate to greater autonomy in running the suggestion program or the blood drive. They don't care about the suggestion program and the blood drive. What they want is more money and bigger benefits.

And the man in the middle—the supervisor, the technician, the engineer? He is truly in the middle—often rejected and mistrusted by rank and file, but equally unwelcome in the executive suite.

The plant community sounded like a good idea at the time. It still sounds like a good idea. But it did not come into being. The failure is not just incidental. It is central to Drucker's philosophy of a harmonious industrial society. It does not mean that Drucker was wrong in foreseeing the rise of Industrial Man and the supremacy of the corporation. He was right; and to read *The New Society* today is to see the world we live in in a useful and revealing light. But the coming of Industrial Man has not so far given us a workable world order.

Once Drucker thought of the plant community as his most important contribution. He regards its nonviability with sadness. Typically he does not spend much time speculating on what went wrong, or rationalizing his predictions. He is aware that many industrial thinkers point to the abortion of this concept as one of his great failures. For example, the distinguished industrial psychologist Douglas McGregor (quoted in *The Planning of Change*, by Bennis, Benne, and Chin) observed, "People today are accustomed to being directed, manipulated, controlled in industrial organizations and to finding satisfaction for their social, egoistic, and self-fulfillment needs away from the job . . . Genuine 'industrial citizenship'—to borrow again a term from Drucker—is a remote and unrealistic idea, the meaning of which has not even been considered by most members of industrial organizations."

Today the search for satisfaction, gratification and "self-fulfillment" is the name of the game. And there is no question that the quest takes the place of the job. To whole generations the job is something to be scorned, at best accepted as a necessary evil.

But this may be one of the major reasons why the new society is not working very well. Drucker has long felt that if status and function were not available within the structure—of which the corporation is the representative institution—the new order would have difficulty working. So there is considerable point in examining more closely the things that Drucker wished would happen, and why he wanted them to happen.

"In an industrial society," he said, "the only meaningful units of local government are enterprise and plant community." Traditional local governments were decaying. They could no longer serve the cause of freedom. "Only in a society where enterprise and plant community are autonomous local self-governments, and where they carry and administer social security, will freedom be strong."

Business—made manifest through its organ, the company—would be dominant in the new order. But this would not be "Capitalism" in the sense in which we have long considered it. *"An industrial society is beyond Capitalism and Socialism, transcending both."* (Emphasis added.) In 1950 Drucker concluded that the United States was very close to achieving the ideal new society. Bringing it about would require no radical changes in direction. Such concepts as the plant community, while new, would merely be the culmination of current trends. We have the know-how and the will—all that was necessary was the follow-through.

Yes, Drucker acknowledged, there were still problems. One problem lay in the bugaboo of *legitimacy*. He had long been concerned with the proposition that any government must be a legitimate government—a government that rules in the interests of its subjects, and grows organically from their needs and aspirations. Drucker had made no bones of this. No matter how benevolent or wise a ruler might be, if he was not legitimate he was not a good ruler.

Now the corporate manager was to be the ruler. This idea coincided nicely with Drucker's picture of the new order—except for one annoying difficulty: *the manager was not a legitimate ruler*. He did not represent the workers in the company. He did not even represent the stockholders. Stockholder ownership had long since become a fiction. True, this had happened because the stockholder had voluntarily and complacently abdicated his role, but that fact did not change the reality. Nobody had elected the corporate manager; he elected himself.

Worse, the manager could not rule in the interest of his "subjects." The corporation is a government, but "the main function and purpose of the enterprise is the production of goods, not the governance of men. Its governmental authority over men must always be subordinated to its economic performance and responsibility." The manager was not legitimate, could not be legitimate, as a ruler.

Political thought for twenty-five hundred years had postulated that any government must be legitimate. (Drucker did not, at this point, call attention to his own repeated insistence on this point.) Therefore the corporation was disqualified as a governmental body; or it was disqualified—that is, if the requirement for legitimacy were kept in force.

Perhaps at another stage of his thinking Drucker might have proceeded to the next logical step, admitted the insurmountable theoretical barrier to the achievement of his vision of the industrial society with the corporation at its center, and either settled down to make money as a consultant or set off on a different tack. But Drucker had invested a great deal of his life in the dream of the industrial society; too much, maybe, to permit it to come to grief over what, after all, was a theoretical consideration.

So he came up with a way around the problem of legitimacy; a way that, one observer is compelled to remark, owes more to ingenuity and the powers of self-persuasion than it does to rigorous logic.

To salvage his ideal Drucker declared: *"That the enterprise is not a legitimate government does not mean that it is an illegitimate one."* (Emphasis added.) Illegitimacy was bad—*if* the illegitimate ruler ignored the interests of his subjects and governed instead in his own interests. But the corporate management, while it was obviously not governing in the interests of the workers, was not governing in its own interests either.

What, then, was the interest in which managerial government was carried out? Drucker had the answer: "the economic interest of the enterprise and of society."

Drucker did not let it go at that. He admitted that, to the subject of the illegitimate government, the distinction was irrelevant. The worker's interest was not identical with that of the economic performance of the enterprise. There was no way to get around the problem. Worker ownership had failed miserably wherever it had been tried. A return to paternalism would not serve as an answer. No, the problem of legitimacy would remain. But somehow, through such developments as the plant community, the new order would have to be made to work anyway, in spite of this theoretical flaw. Drucker set out to find ways to make it work.

Looking backward from the luxurious pinnacle that

hindsight affords us, one can say, "Aha! Here is where he went wrong." The problem of legitimacy was not just a semantic trap or a vestige of traditional thinking. We see how the sharp and abrasive faults along which increasingly alienated segments of our society grind in opposition to each other, with occasional destructive tremors and the ever-present possibility of a shattering earthquake. We can say that much of this results from the increasing social and political supremacy of corporate enterprise, which is scorned as a legitimate ruling mechanism by workers, their children, and a vast portion of the society.

But Drucker was trying to forge concepts that would make for a livable world at a time when such concepts were hard to come by. Earlier he had acknowledged that two major problems in bringing this about were lack of legitimacy and the necessity for status and function. Now he felt that he had discovered the answer to status and function. He might have abandoned the whole effort because he did not come up with an equally plausible answer to the question of legitimacy.

However, he admitted that he had not come up with this answer. He did not try to rationalize the manager's legitimacy into existence—although he did attempt to minimize the consequences of the gap. As we contemplate the lack of workable alternatives to this view of a world order, we may well come to a more charitable opinion of Drucker's persistence.

The New Society laid down other basic premises for the coming industrial order. The idea of profit had to be accepted universally as being in the social interest. Profit is not a reward; it is the life-support system of the enterprise. A company needs profit to pay the current and future costs of staying in business. The quest for profit is its primary goal. To put it another and Darwinian way, "The law of loss avoidance must be the first law of the enterprise. For on its economic performance depends the very survival of the enterprise; and like every other institution the enterprise must put first its self-preservation."

The holder of stock in a corporation is, Drucker said, not an owner with property rights in the traditional sense. All he has bought is a claim to share in future income. He has made it quite clear that he is not interested in exercising the rights of ownership; he is perfectly happy to turn the burdens of running the enterprise over to the management.

There would have to be a new attitude—shared by management, workers, and union leaders—toward what the worker gets paid. The unions concentrated on wage rates and to hell with productivity. But what choice did the workers have? They would have to press for higher and higher wages as long as management placed its emphasis on wage rates while denying the workers guarantees of minimum income or maximum employment. But such insistence was placing the worker and the union in opposition, not only to the enterprise, but to society as a whole. Working together, unions and management must come to agreement on compensation methods that would be geared to productivity while affording the worker assurance of a basic income.

Only when this were done could we expect to see an easing of the worker's resistance to higher output and his hostility to profit. Workers now feel exploited. They are driven to rage when they think of the huge salaries paid to executives. Most of the justifications presented for big managerial salaries are nonsense—and yet they do have validity in terms of the hierarchical structure of the corporation. However, the worker is not to be blamed for his inability to see the logic in this.

In the new order, "the managerial attitude" would be part of the intellectual equipment of even the lowliest worker. The managerial attitude would enable everyone in the organization to "see his job, his work and his product the way the manager sees them, that is, in relation to the work of the group and the product of the whole." When this different and more responsible viewpoint was prevalent, the worker would be more understanding of such propositions as the necessity for profit and the justification for big salaries in the executive suite.

There are other requirements. The worker is "pathetically" eager to find out more about the company and his job: he must be communicated with. The position of the foreman or first-line supervisor must be defined and strengthened. "Bigness" and mass production cannot be thought of as evils; they are part and parcel of the new order, just as profitability is the sovereign criterion of the enterprise. There would have to be more emphasis on the "human resources" of the company. Profit-sharing plans would have to be devised in a way that would give the worker a meaningful share in the success of the enterprise, along with security against lack of success. And, above all, management would have to do a better job of managing. Only a few managements were handling their responsibilities adequately.

There was much to be learned, Drucker said: "The proper study of mankind is organization." But it would be worth the learning and the doing. The institutions themselves were not a stumbling block to effective and beneficial change; they were the medium through which change could be effected. Our problems were our lack of courage and vision in attacking the difficulties we faced in building the new industrial order.

Unhappily, *The New Society* has come true in many more of its grim aspects than in its hopeful ones. Drucker was perceptive about the viewpoints and the problems of the industrial worker, and his increasing alienation from the company he works for and the society of which that company is a representative institution. He put his finger on the consequences of continued concentration on the battle for higher wage rates, without reference to productivity or the survival needs of the enterprise. He probed with great insight into the anomalous position of the "middle" people in the corporation —the supervisors, technicians, and professional contributors who are neither management nor rank and file. He expounded with eloquence the necessity of involving all members of the corporation in its functions and goals. He spelled out with dispassionate accuracy the new and dominant role of the corporate manager, and at the same time pointed to the desperate need for better ways to prepare managers for their awesome responsibility.

But the developments that Drucker recommended and predicted have not come about. His feeling in 1950 that we were "very close" to the new society was optimistic to say the least. The grand ideal of the multilevel corporate institution—with each member being involved in the management of those parts of the operation appropriate to his involvement, and with each member deriving "status and function" from this involvement—remains on the drawing board of a quarter of a century ago.

How did Drucker—so perceptive in so many ways—miss the mark here? We may consider a few possible reasons. For one thing, at the time he wrote *The New Society* Drucker's experience of corporations *from the inside* did not extend far beyond the pioneering work with General Motors that had led to *Concept of the Corporation*. He shows a tendency to infer—with considerable enthusiasm—great meaning from events that he might now regard with more skepticism. For example, he refers to the truths about workers adduced from the General Motors essay contest of 1947, in which workers told their views of their jobs and of the company.

Drucker has never been an elitist in the conventional sense, nor an advocate of a highly stratified society. Nevertheless, one may find throughout his thought a consistent feeling that "everyone has his place"—with the corollary that the individual should accept his place and work to make himself effective and happy within that place. In the concept of the plant community he doles out pieces of responsibility and areas of concern to the strata of the corporation. Of course the top executives run the integral areas of the company concerned with earnings and profit—sales, manufacturing, design, and the like. These bailiwicks are beyond the purview of the lower-level worker. Drucker has given the latter another set of things to manage—the collateral functions surrounding the profit-making areas, such as fund-raising campaigns and social activities. Drucker rejects paternalism, but unhappily there are many who see considerable paternalism in this. The punch-press operator does not seem willing to settle for getting his kicks out of organizing the blood bank while a $100,000 vice-president derives his own sense of "status and function" from making cosmic decisions affecting the life of the punch-press operator and ten thousand other people. This is particularly true when a number of these big decisions turn out to be palpably wrong and when the rank-and-file worker—perhaps with lamentable bias—regards the vice-president as an overstuffed boob.

And then there is Drucker's natural optimism, which bubbles to the top even when all his realistic evaluations of the situation conduce toward a more pessimistic view. Drucker has said again and again that belief in the perfectibility of man has been one of the curses of civilization; but, while he does not claim that man is perfectible, he is often sunnily sanguine that man can be improved an awful lot if only the right kind of techniques are employed. By 1950 he was starting to modify the near-adulatory regard in which he held the corporate manager—he had now seen management close up—but he certainly still felt that the holders of management jobs were capable of doing immeasurably better than they had been doing, if only they were given the tools.

The New Society is not with us; certainly not in the healthy form for which Drucker worked and hoped. But it is worthwhile to ask the question: Is it too late to try to bring it about? Or, perhaps a better question would be: What choice do we have? We live in an industrial world. With all that opponents lament the development and wish it were otherwise, the multinational corporations bestride the world. Drucker, admitting that many of his earlier hopes have failed of fruition, still looks upon the organization as the framework within which a livable society can be built.

Maybe it is time for us to take a fresh look at the possibilities that lie within the realities with which we are surrounded. The corporation is, after all, at least one of the representative institutions of our day. Conceivably, with vision and skill, it can be made into the means of providing us with The New Society.

5.

The Tasks of the Manager

They say that before long the manager will enjoy the privilege of working with a computer terminal at his elbow. Confronted with a problem, he will simply crank data into the machine, and out will come the answer.

Given a choice, the average manager would like to have at his side, not so much a computer as a super-management expert; someone like Peter Drucker, or at least like the image of Drucker as super-consultant that exists in many executive minds. The manager could handle most chores on his own; but, when difficulties arose, he could turn to his mentor and obtain expert guidance.

Of course Peter Drucker does not do this. Even if you could afford to buy his time, you could not so involve him in the day-to-day tasks of management. For one thing he would not leave his study at Claremont to undertake the job. For another thing, it would bore him to distraction.

So the manager who wants answers from Drucker reads Drucker's books and articles and listens to his lectures when he can. This can be extremely frustrating. Most executives are looking for specific answers to the nitty-gritty problems that come up, day after day. They know they should be thinking big thoughts and taking the broad view, but nagging details keep interfering. So they want help in handling the recurring, mundane matters that make up their working lives.

It is hard to find this in Drucker. His books do not resemble the typical books produced for managers in great profusion. Within a Drucker book—even those that focus most specifically on the tasks of management—you do not find the kinds of chapter headings you find in a typical "how-to-run-a-business" book; headings like "Six Ways to Make Things Happen," "How to Change Bad Habits to Good Ones," "Ten Steps to Solving Problems," "A Sure-Fire Way to Organize Your Time," and so forth.

Drucker does not make it seem that simple. It is not that he is vague; he is quite specific. But he does not distill his message into convenient and catchy little nuggets that can be ingested with no effort at all.

Drucker is a stimulator. He tries to make people think, not give them substitutes for thinking. Moreover, he approaches management from a philosophical point of view. He places small, discrete activities in a larger framework. So you can't consult the index of a Drucker book and thumb the pages to a brief, specific "answer" for your current problem. He doesn't make it look that easy because he doesn't think it is that easy.

However, let's fantasize. Let's assume it were possible for a manager to work intimately with Peter Drucker, turning to ask Drucker about the problems that come up during his day. What would it be like?

Here is a scenario. It is not an actual picture of Drucker in action; this is not the way he works. It is rather a fictionalized version of how he might work in such circumstances. All of the comments and suggestions attributed to Drucker are drawn from things he has written or said.

The lucky manager who is about to work with Peter Drucker is called, unoriginally, John Smith. Smith is an executive; not the president of his company, but a man who hopes to achieve that stature. For the purposes of this exercise we can omit specification of the particular business Smith's company is in; management problems do not vary much in their intrinsic nature.

Smith ushers in his mentor. He meets a solid, somewhat heavy-set man who looks younger than his actual mid-sixties: square face, thick graying hair cut fairly short, deep-set penetrating eyes, full lips that tend to curve humorously. The voice is deep; the direction is clear and precise; the Viennese accent is noticeable but not obtrusive. Drucker's manner is, on the surface, grave and courtly, redolent of old-world charm, culture, and civility; but even the casual observer can see, just below that surface, a lively willingness to make the outrageous comment or dispatch the mocking thrust.

After brief greetings—Drucker is not by inclination a small-talker, although he can indulge in it with the best of them—Smith begins his day. He starts, as many managers do, by reading some correspondence and then calling in a secretary to dictate a few letters and memos.

Smith is having trouble with one particular memo. He asks Drucker for help. What is the point of the communication? Well, one of Smith's subordinates, Jones, is working on a project, and Smith feels called upon to give Jones some further directions. Jones does not seem to be progressing in the way he should. How, Smith wants to know, can he get his message across to Jones?

"What do you expect Jones to do? What are the objectives?"

Smith has a little trouble with this, but he explains that the objectives are to jack up production in a certain area while keeping a rein on costs. Sometimes Jones seems to miss the point.

"How does Jones see it?"

By this Drucker means, what are the objectives as perceived by Jones, and what contribution does Jones feel that he should be making? Smith replies, "Well, I assume we have the same objectives—to get the job done."

"And why do you assume that?" Drucker wants to know what Jones said when *he* talked about the project and about what was to be done. Smith finds it difficult to answer; they discussed it, sure, but it was pretty much a matter of Smith saying what should be done and Jones requesting some follow-up details about lines of communication and so forth.

Drucker says, "And now you are writing another memo to Jones to tell him the same things you told him before?" Smith allows that this, in essence, is what he is doing.

"How would you class this part of your job?" asks Drucker. "Under what general heading would it fall?" Smith notes that all Drucker seems to do is ask questions, but he dutifully tries to answer. The general classification under which this would fall is "communication."

"Forget it," says Drucker. He goes on. Smith is not communicating at all. He is sending something out, and it is unlikely to be received. Communication has to *start* with the recipient of the message rather than the emitter. Downward communication does not work. It is impossible for it to work. You can only send a message downward after *upward* communication has successfully been established.

So where does that leave me? Smith wonders. I'm the guy's boss; I'm supposed to tell him what to do. You are *not* "supposed to tell him what to do," counters Drucker. "Your job is to enable him to perform well."

How? First, stop trying to force information and directives down the pipe. Get the subordinate—in this case Jones—to initiate some upward communication; not about the weather or the ball scores, but about the job. Find out how *Jones* sees the job. Let *Jones* talk about the objectives.

Does this mean, Smith wonders, that he should permit Jones to say what is to be done and how to do it? Of course, replies Drucker, except that there is no "permit" about it. You will find that Jones will not only describe the objectives differently from the way you see them, but that he will very likely require more of himself than you are requiring of him.

Smith nods. "You mean I should *listen* to Jones." That's part of it, says Drucker, but listening by itself is not enough. What is necessary is that you and Jones establish a basis for exchange—the objectives toward which Jones makes a contribution. Then both of you talk about them. You will find that Jones will come up with many things you do not expect.

To get some real communication started, says Drucker, sit down and talk face to face with Jones—for as long as necessary—to establish the objectives. Ask him what he wants to do.

"But," says Smith—and to him this is the big question—"supposing after all this he decides on going a route that I don't think he should go?" Then, Drucker replies, you may end up issuing a command: "This is what I tell you to do." But at least then you will know that you are overriding his desires. You will realize that Jones has a problem; and so do you. The important thing is to set a basis for exchange. "There can be no communication if it is conceived as going from 'I' to 'You.' It works only if it is from one member of "us" to another.

"All right," says Smith. "I will stop trying to get the point across to Jones by writing him memos, since, as you say, we don't seem to be getting anyplace with it anyway. I'll try to set up a meeting with him. But that takes time, and where the hell am I going to find it? I don't have the time to do the things I should be doing now."

So they begin to talk about how Smith spends his time. Smith is ready for this. A month ago, when the day with Drucker was first set up, Drucker asked Smith how he spent his time. Smith began to try to describe it; "Well, I start with the correspondence, that usually takes an hour a day, and then of course there are the meetings. . . ." Drucker interrupted; "Do you have a log of your time?" No, said Smith. Drucker responded that, if Smith was relying on memory to say how his time was spent, he did not know how he was spending it. Drucker said, "Make a log of your time; the method you use is not important. But make a record."

Now Smith has a record; imperfect, but it is a record. Drucker takes a look at it, remarking, "As you've probably realized, your time is not your own. The manager's time belongs to everybody else."

One thing has already struck Smith. His initial guesses as to how he disposed of his time were wildly off target. For example, he spends a lot more time in meetings than he thought he did. He puts in more time talking to people on the telephone than he would have expected. He spends less time working out decisions than he believed; in fact, it takes some effort to figure out exactly when he *does* formulate decisions.

They begin to discuss the time log. Smith has already spotted some obvious time wasters: "You'll note that I eat lunch out almost all the time. Just looking over the record I see that there is often no point in it, just a habit. Thinking it over, I realize that I could get more done on many days if I just grab a sandwich and work through. I have more time to work, and, there are no interruptions."

Drucker nods. Then he notes that, during this period, Smith has been working on a report. It's important. Drucker asks, "How much time have you put in on it?" Smith says, "When you add it up, I've spent about nine hours on it." How much time does the report warrant? Well, at least nine hours, Smith figures. How far has he gotten on it? Not as far as he would have liked.

Now, asks Drucker, what's the longest single chunk of time that you put in on the report? Smith considers; "Thursday afternoon I was able to spend a full hour working on it. I had hoped to spend more, but a couple of calls came in and I got onto something else."

Drucker shakes his head. This is not the way to do it. "It's pointless to approach a task that should take eight or ten hours by giving it small dribs and drabs of time. You just get started and then you stop. The next time you turn to it, you have to 'tool up' again. But you waste the 'tooling up' time when you don't give yourself a substantial span in which to be productive. All you wind up with is some squiggles on paper. If you can lock the door, disconnect the phone, and spend, say, five or six hours without interruption, then you have a pretty good chance to at least come up with the 'zero' draft—the version that should come before the first draft. From then on you can work in smaller installments, rewriting and editing."

Smith agrees. "But you have to free yourself up for that first big chunk," he adds. Drucker says, "Yes. It's essential. Every executive needs to be able to dispose of his time in reasonably big chunks. Otherwise you are constantly wasting it. For example, I see that on a typical day you met at different times with twelve different people, sometimes for no more than five minutes. To spend a few minutes with people is just not productive. You say hello and just barely begin to get into something, and then you break it off. By and large, to have much of an impact in an important conversation, you must give yourself an hour. If you think you can get away with less, you are just kidding yourself."

Smith gets the point. One of the first principles in using time productively is to consolidate it into the biggest chunks possible. Of course, as Drucker has already pointed out, he is to a considerable extent at the beck and call of others. The demands of others on the manager's time do not diminish as he gains more power; they increase. But the manager's ability to call the shots and consolidate his time increases as he goes up the ladder—if he is not too sunk in habit to do something about it. Drucker gives a couple of examples; pack all necessary "operating work"—informational meetings, phone calls, routine reports—into, say, two days a week instead of having them strung out through the calendar. Cram vital discretionary time together until you have at least a full day of it; and then see if you can't sometimes work at home on that day, away from the "drop-ins," the trivial phone calls, and the temptations to "just take care of one or two little things" before getting down to serious work.

But there are still problems. Smith says, "It's all very well to talk about consolidating time, and I haven't been giving enough thought to that, but there are still too damn many things for me to do. Just look at what I have to do today. I have five different locations around the country to check. All that takes time."

Drucker is unimpressed. "Suppose you didn't do it?"

Smith doesn't quite get it. Drucker reiterates: "What would happen if you didn't do it?"

Smith shrugs. "I have to do it. These people are expecting me to get in touch with them."

Then Drucker points out that the number of things in a manager's day that need not be done at all is truly amazing. Many executive schedules are festooned with activities that never would be missed. He presses Smith on the telephone calls, and finally Smith admits that if he did not make them, there would be some puzzlement and momentary confusion, but the answer is that, basically, nothing would happen.

"The obvious conclusion," suggests Drucker, "is to stop doing it."

Okay, agrees Smith. There *are* some things he might cut out—he can see that. But his plate is still filled to overflowing. All right, says Drucker: the next question is, "Which of the things you're doing could be done by somebody else?"

Smith nods knowingly; "Yeah, I see what you mean. I should delegate more. I realize that."

Drucker shakes his head. He is not interested in sermonizing on "delegation"; managers are always being exhorted to be better delegators, and no one seems to listen. "I have done my share of the sermonizing," he notes. The reason that nobody pays much attention is that the customary idea of delegation makes no sense. The manager is told to let someone else do part of "his" work; the more of "his" work he is able to fob off on a subordinate, the better he is as a manager. Wrong, says Drucker. A manager should do his own work, he will have to get others to do anything that they can handle. So let's not get into a complicated discussion of the complexities of "delegation" as if it were an abstruse and delicate part of the management art; just figure out what others can do and have them do it. It's that simple.

Now Drucker puts his finger on another part of Smith's schedule. Three key subordinates present him with biweekly summaries of certain processes. "What about the time that's being wasted there?"

Smith smiles. "That's not a time-waster. The three

96

guys boil everything down to one page each, and I just glance over it. Takes a few minutes."

"What do you get out of it?"

"Often, not very much. Occasionally there's something that merits some follow-up. But it's not a big deal. I don't waste much time on it."

"I was not," says Drucker, "talking about just *your* time being wasted. *You* don't spend much time on it. But how much time do these key men spend in summarizing and boiling down something that you don't consider to be a big deal?"

Smith doesn't know. He hasn't thought of it that way. Drucker points out that the manager should not be cavalier about wasting the time of others. If it's not a big deal, cut it out. Even if you're in doubt about it, cut it out. If you miss it, you can always put it back in.

There are other points. Year after year, November brings a kind of saturnalia of wheel-spinning while Smith's subordinates try to iron out last-minute details in the budget proposals. Often they are waiting for one another to complete phases of the work, and Smith is waiting for all of them. Drucker observes that recurrent time-wasters are sloppy and not to be condoned. There are other symptoms of sloppiness and disorganization. Smith seems to spend a disproportionate amount of time straightening out conflicts between people in his department. If people are bumping into each other, the department may be overstaffed. Finally, one prime indicator of bad organization and time wasting is a proliferation of meetings.

Drucker and Smith sum up a few simple points about the handling of time. Consolidate it. Eliminate some activities. Be conscious of wasting the time of subordinates. Look for the telltale signs of time-eating organizational foulups: recurrent crises, conflicts, too many meetings.

"Well, talking about meetings," says Smith, "I have one coming up now." Drucker goes along as an observer.

After the meeting they review what happened. "Did you think the meeting was a success?" Drucker asks. Smith says, "We covered a lot of points, got a lot of things out on the table. People had a chance to get things off their chests."

"And what happened?"

Smith shrugs. "I guess not much."

"What was supposed to happen? What was the purpose of the meeting? Did you expect a report? Decisions? Answers? Was the idea to make it clearer to everybody what each was doing?" Smith says that he supposes the purpose of the meeting included a little of each. You "have to have" meetings to find out what needs to be done.

Drucker insists that this is not good enough. A meeting takes time and effort, not only Smith's but everyone's. The purpose should be thought out and spelled out before the meeting is called.

Drucker says, "The manager who calls the meeting should state, at the outset, the specific purpose and contribution it is to achieve. Obviously, to state the purpose he must know the purpose."

Smith acknowledges that he didn't do this—and that no doubt this lack contributed to the rambling nature of the session. He decides that, on future meetings, he will establish the purpose beforehand, call the meeting only if there is sufficient need for it, state the purpose and keep on the track, and not let things degenerate into a bull session.

"And, at the end," adds Drucker, "go back to the original statement and summarize conclusions in relation to it. When you follow these practices you will find yourself calling fewer meetings, which can be nothing but an advantage. Meetings will be more sharply focused. Furthermore, they will be shorter. Meetings that drag on and on are not only wasteful, they are demoralizing."

There is one other observation about the meeting that Drucker offers. He prefaces it with a question: "John, who directed the meeting?" Smith says, "Why, I ran it." Drucker points out that, at the same time, Smith also engaged in discussion, bringing up ideas and debating the comments made by others. "You can either direct a meeting and listen for the important things being said, or you can be part of the meeting and talk whenever you want. You cannot do both. To think you can is to diminish your effectiveness in either capacity. But the important thing is to focus the meeting on *contribution* right from the beginning."

Over lunch, Smith gets to talking about his difficulties with certain colleagues and subordinates. "We just don't seem to hit it off. We're not on the same wavelength." Drucker asks for specifics. Smith gives examples of misunderstandings and bad feelings of lack of co-operation. He winds up by saying, "Maybe it's me. Maybe I ought to go and take some sensitivity training or something."

Drucker remarks that it would be worse than futile for Smith to subject himself to the kind of activity that is often lumped under the heading of "sensitivity training." He says that Smith is worrying about the wrong things. "You seem to feel that the problem is that warm, friendly feelings do not exist between you and them. You're starting at the wrong end. If the relationship is not productively *work-focused*—if it doesn't produce results and accomplishments for all concerned—then all the warm feelings and pleasant words in the world are meaningless. They are worse than meaningless, they are phony—a facade for wretched attitudes."

Drucker says that, in his experience, two of the leaders who enjoyed the best "human relations" were Alfred P. Sloan and George C. Marshall. "Neither, so far as I know, ever took a charm course." They inspired loyalty, devotion, and sometimes true affection. But they didn't worry about "human relations"; they took them for granted.

"A lot of managers," says Drucker, "feel that they must establish 'rapport' first and then the work will go easier and better. That's the wrong end to start at. Take this one man you mentioned, Brown. You've been trying to become more friendly with Brown, but it doesn't seem to work. Forget about that for the moment. Why don't you sit down and figure out what you can contribute to Brown to make him more effective on the job—and what he can contribute to you in the same way? Something may even occur to you right now."

Smith says, "Well, Brown needs certain kinds of information fast from our operation. I know that. I'd like to sit down with him and work out a way for him to get the information, but we can't seem to get together on an amicable basis to work it out. After all, I want his cooperation too."

Drucker sighs. "It has to start someplace. You think you know what Brown wants. The difficulty is talking to him. Well, don't talk to him. *You* make the arrangements to get him the information he needs. Then tell him what you've done and ask him if the procedure is really helpful, and if not, how he would like it changed. You and Brown don't have to be smiling and clapping each other on the back while you're doing this. It's a job-oriented discussion. You are trying to do something that will enable him to make a greater contribution. Why? Not because you are desolate without Brown's friendship, or because you hope he will remember you in his will, but because maximizing contribution wherever you can is your job. It's what you are paid for. When you do your job in this sense, the kinds of relationships you want will come. They are a corollary of contribution."

Smith agrees that this makes sense. He notes that the term "contribution" has come up several times. He knows it's important, but he wonders exactly what Drucker means by it.

Drucker says, "Let me respond—as you have noticed I often do—with a question. What do you do in this company that justifies your salary?" Smith answers that he runs the so-and-so department, that he has so many people working under him.

Drucker smiles. "That's the way most managers answer that question. And yet, you know, it's the wrong answer. That's a description of the situation within which you are placed. It says nothing about what you *do*, or why the company should pay you money. You're focusing on your authority—and the man who focuses on authority will always be a subordinate, no matter what title he carries."

Where should the focus be? On commitment and contribution, not on downward authority or rank or job title. The manager who has the proper focus will answer, "I'm responsible for opening up new and profitable markets," or, "I have to give the president the information he needs to make the right decisions."

It is natural for us to be highly conscious of our specialties. But an executive can become the prisoner of his own background and narrow skills. The concept of contribution requires that he relate what he does, and what his particular operation does, to the entire organization and its purpose. Every move, every plan, every policy should have its rationale within that broader framework.

Smith looks bored and skeptical. "Do you mean every time I tell a guy to fly to the coast and inform a division of a policy change I have to first go through a big philosophical dialogue with myself about the overall purpose of this?"

Drucker explains that this is not quite what he means. "However, if your general frame of mind is attuned to the importance of contribution, you will automatically fit actions into the larger framework. For the successful manager it becomes second nature. Your organization, like every other organization, needs to obtain results today and to develop people for tomorrow. If you are contributing one hundred percent to each of those objectives, then you are a superb executive. You probably also do not exist, because no mortal can contribute one hundred percent. But you can look for the areas in which your contribution can be increased."

They seek an example. Finally they hit upon a young subordinate, Green. Smith has mentioned that Green is a source of concern. He is bright and has ideas. But he is not tactful. "He rubs people the wrong way; including me. If there were just some way to get the benefit of his brains without having to come in contact with him, that would be perfect."

"What are you doing about it?"

"I've moved him into a spot where, frankly, I don't have to see him that often. He can still be productive."

"But not as productive as he might be," says Drucker.

"True," answers Smith. "But I realize he's too valuable a man to lose. So we're trying to help him strengthen his interpersonal skills, enable him to get along with

101

people better. We've sent him to some seminars, and there are other things we can do."

Drucker doesn't want to hear any more. "This man is paid to perform, not to please you. I assume he has considerable talent, since you are going to so much trouble and expense to try to get him 'straightened out.' So your job is to ask, 'What does he contribute?' —not 'How does he get along with me and with others?' By shunting Green off on a side track you have cut down on his capacity to contribute. At the same time you are failing in your responsibility to contribute to him."

"But I have to have a team. Green is not a team player."

"You have to have performance, not a team. If you are lucky enough to find somebody—like Green—who is excellent in at least one major area, thank God for your good fortune, grab him, and get the most out of him. If you have to put up with tantrums, put up with them. And show by your example that other people should do the same. Forget about trying to compensate for weaknesses. Look for strength and build on it."

"You mean we shouldn't try to improve Green's ability to get along with people?"

"Well, in the first place I doubt that you will get very far with the method you've chosen. Even though it has become very popular, I am of the old-fashioned school that feels you do not enhance your relationships with people by attending a seminar. In the second place, you have obviously tried to work around Green's strengths by putting him in a job where he doesn't come in contact with you or anybody else. This is a corporation, not a club. To try to build against weakness frustrates the whole purpose of an organization. You seem to be looking for a 'team' on which everybody looks and lacks like everybody else."

Smith says, "You have to admit that an organization works better when the people in it all have something in common, can talk with each other, like and respect each other."

Drucker replies, "I admit no such thing. The whole point of an organization is that you can maximize one man's strength and compensate for his weaknesses someplace else. So the people should be different, not all the same. You shouldn't be blind to Green's inability to get along with people. It's a problem. But you have him on the payroll because he has brains, not because he is supposed to act as a social director. Concentrate on strengths. When you hire for strengths that complement and reinforce each other, then weaknesses don't mean so much."

Smith goes on to talk about a job he is trying to fill. "I'm having trouble, and it surprises me. The way we have worked out the job description, it doesn't seem to be too demanding. But the last guy we had in there fell apart completely after six months. And now I'm seeing a lot of people who have interesting backgrounds of various kinds, but nobody who fits the job. How can I find the person I need?"

Drucker says, "If you go on looking for someone to fit a job, it may take you forever, depending upon how detailed the description is. To me, the effective executive starts with what a person can do rather than what a job requires. In interviewing a lot of people you are giving yourself a wonderful opportunity to look for strengths. But you're wasting the opportunity by blinding yourself to the strengths of the applicants and simply running a comparison test, seeing if any of them fit into the outlines of the job. You say the job should be easier to fill because you've made it small. This is a commonplace practice—to make jobs small. And I think it is utterly wasteful of human resources."

Smith says, "I think I see where you're heading."

Drucker says, "Don't think of yourself as 'having a job to fill.' You need some more strength in the organization. Look for strength. Concentrate on what someone can do, not what the job description says. And when you find strength, bring it in; even if you have to change the job requirements. They should be changed anyway. A job should be big and demanding, not reduced to bite-sized bits."

As the afternoon wears on Smith grapples with some tough problems. At last he leans back and says, "No doubt about it. Making decisions is the hardest part of my job. For instance, I have to decide on one of three plans to use in this area, and I can't get the facts that will help me make the right choice."

"You know, John," says Drucker, removing his eyeglasses and gently massaging the bridge of his nose, "a decision is rarely a choice between right and wrong. At best it's a choice between 'probably right' and 'probably wrong'—but usually it is simply a matter of picking among several courses of action, none of which is any better than the other."

Smith manages a tired grin. "You mean we should just flip a coin?"

"Oh, no," Drucker responds. "Even if that were no worse a method than any other—which I don't admit for a moment—what would you and I do for a living?"

They talk about the decision facing Smith. Drucker starts by commenting on Smith's complaint that he can't get enough facts. "Most advice on decision-making starts that way. 'First get the facts.' That is facile nonsense. You don't start with facts; you can't. You don't even know what facts are, not relevant facts, because you have no yardsticks for relevance."

"So where do you start?"

"Where it is logical. With opinions."

"But I've always tried to stay objective, to keep opinions out of the process."

"John, it is a human impossibility, so stop pretending that it can be done. Start by forming an opinion. Ask people, not for the facts, but what they think. At least you'll begin to get a sense of what they feel the decision is about."

"How do I know if those opinions are worth anything?"

"You don't. But you insist that the people you ask join you in spelling out what needs to be tested, so that a reasonable test of the opinion can be made."

For the next step, Drucker advises the collection of alternatives. Alternatives come with dissent—so the manager must encourage it. "A cardinal rule in decision making is that you don't make a decision until there is disagreement. If everyone agrees, you can't tell what the

104

decision is all about. Maybe there's no decision to be made at all. So get disagreement."

"And how do you figure out which alternative is right?"

"There's that word 'right' again. When a man disagrees with you, don't immediately ask 'who is right and who is wrong?' You are likely to give yourself the better of the bargain on too many occasions. Admit that the other fellow has some intelligence. Admit that, given his intelligence, he has reached a different conclusion from yours because he sees things differently. Why? Find out about the reality that he sees. It may be closer to the truth than the reality that you see."

"And then what do you do?"

"Why," says Drucker, "you choose a course of action. But, before putting it into execution, pause a moment. Ask yourself if it is necessary to make a decision at all. You always have the option of doing nothing—and, although we often see undue emphasis on decisiveness for its own sake as a favorable trait, doing nothing may often be the best thing you can do. Having decided to do something—if that's how you decide—think about who is going to do the work and how you will get them to do it. If you run into real problems with that portion of your thinking, perhaps you have the wrong answer after all. Decisions are not entire of themselves. They have to be executed. But, when you are satisfied with all this, go ahead and execute your decision."

"No matter how big a risk is involved?"

"John," says Drucker, "risk is what it's all about. We hear a lot of talk about techniques that 'minimize' risk or even 'eliminate' risk. Nonsense. To try to eliminate risk is not only futile, it can be harmful. The bigger your job, the greater the risks you should be taking. The idea is not to try to eliminate risks, but to take the right risks."

The day is about over. Smith tells Drucker he has learned a lot; he asks if Drucker will summarize the important points about the manager's job. Drucker answers that this is what they have been talking about. How would Smith describe it?

"Well, you seemed to be saying, consolidate time. Concentrate on contributions, my own and others. Focus on strength instead of weakness. In making decisions, start with opinions, get dissent, pick the alternative that seems best. And don't be afraid of risk."

"How does it sound?"

"It sounds like common sense."

Drucker beams. "That's exactly what it should sound like. If you would like to refresh yourself on any of it, read my book *The Effective Executive*. And remember; we hear a lot of talk about the manager of the future. But the important man is the manager of today. He must know his craft; and he must be able to function."

Soon afterward, Drucker says goodbye. Smith sits looking at the door. Then he says to himself, "He didn't mention one damn thing that I didn't know already. So why the hell haven't I been doing them?"

6.

Management by Objectives:
How a Concept
Comes into Use

Peter Drucker has seen a great many of his ideas gain general acceptance. But sometimes in practice they don't come out quite the way he envisioned them.

"Management by objectives" is the dominant concept in management today, and it has been for some years. The term was introduced by Drucker in *The Practice of Management* in 1954, and he is recognized as a leading pioneer of the concept.

This idea is thought by a good many people to be the most important and influential concept Drucker has ever generated. Richard H. Buskirk of the School of Business Administration, Southern Methodist University, says: "His emphasis upon the results of managerial actions rather than the supervision of activities was a major contribution for it shifted the entire focus of management thought to productivity—output—and away from work efforts—the inputs."

Management by objectives was a natural development in Drucker's thinking. He had described the new order of Industrial Man, and identified the corporation as the representative entity of that society. He had outlined the concept of the corporation in philosophic terms. Corporations must be managed. The manager was the key individual in this vision of the future. Therefore, the next need was for a strong central principle by which management could be conducted to meet the requirement of the new world.

Drucker comments, "I didn't invent the term 'management by objectives'; actually Alfred Sloan used it in the 1950s. But I put it in a central position, whereas to him it was just a side effect."

Drucker sketched the broad framework of the concept. Since the mid-1950s there have been numerous books and articles on management by objectives. Accepting the principle, managers and academicians have refined it, applied it to a wide variety of situations, and debated many of its implications.

What is it? At this point we are faced with a distinct split between the idea as Drucker conceived it and as others have promulgated it, and the way it is often thought of in practice. In his *Management by Objectives*, George S. Odiorne, Director of the Bureau of Industrial Relations of the University of Michigan, gives this definition:

In brief, the system of management by objectives can be described as a process whereby the superior and subordinate managers of an organization jointly identify its common goals, define each individual's major areas of responsibility in terms of the results expected of him, and use these measures as guides for operating the unit and assessing the contribution of each of its members.

This principle has come into such wide acceptance that the reader who comes upon it for the first time might well say, "Of course. Is there any other way to run a company?" There were other ways, and there still are. In first talking about management by objectives, Drucker was responding to the inadequacy of an older idea of management that concentrated on processes rather than goals. The old-time manager was expected to learn the ins and outs of the business and to keep people busy. His operative question was, "What am I supposed to do?"

Management by objectives shifts the focus to goals, to the purpose of the activity rather than the activity itself. Instead of asking, "What do I do?" the manager is led to ask, "What is the objective toward which we are working?" Under the concept, the manager is held responsible for results rather than for activities. It is no longer a matter of how well he understands the machinery or how many meetings he holds or what volume of correspondence he is able to turn out but, rather, how his activities pay off in terms of the objectives of the organization.

In practice, however, we often see the concept of management by objectives translated totally into a formulation that might be called "bottom-line management," or management by results. More and more an upper-echelon executive holds himself aloof from what is going on beneath him. He figures that his responsibility lies in hiring somebody to do a job, telling him the "bottom-line" results that are expected, and then rewarding the subordinate if he delivers or firing him if he does not deliver.

This bastardization of management by objectives has had some unfortunate consequences. One obvious one is that organizations are not run well. But there are other elements of fallout. The executive who knows that he must deliver or else is apt to be an extremely insecure fellow. He deals in abstractions rather than concrete entities; he finds less and less pleasure in his work; and he is subjected to greater tension.

Another offshoot of management by objectives has been the notion of the transferable manager. According to this view, the superior manager is so involved with broad-gauge objectives—to the exclusion of details about how they are to be attained—that it does not make much difference what kind of company he works for. So we have seen numerous examples of top executives taking on big jobs in industries with which they are unfamiliar.

The idea that a manager who has mastered his craft

can carry his attaché case into any situation and be a success is often attributed to Peter Drucker.

Drucker realized in the 1950s that management by objectives was susceptible to this kind of misguided application and warned against it. Always conscious that people are the vital resources of an enterprise, he cautioned that the bottom line should not become an obsession, and that managers should not subject the organization to pressures approximating those in the Mindanao Trench in the quest for results. His fears have been realized in no small degree.

Recently, he commented: "The most important thing in management by objectives is not management but *objectives*. Frequently they're forgotten. It may be all right to hire a man and then promote him and leave him to sink or swim—if you know the objectives. Nine times out of ten you don't. So a manager doesn't work out, and the Peter Principle is cited. I have very little use for the Peter Principle. If you put a man in a spot and he's unable to do the work, you've made a mistake. He has not been promoted beyond his competence, he has been put in the wrong job. Ninety percent of the time the Peter Principle is a dangerously all-consuming alibi by an inferior executive."

But what Drucker means is more complex: *"I do not maintain that a manager can just move from one company to another and be equally effective. I'm not saying the opposite either; perhaps what I'm saying is more complicated.*

"A good many managers can learn to be effective in a different environment, but not by transferring from one company to another. That's why it's so important to examine the question of whether to work toward a promotion or go to a new company.

"Look at the reasons why so many promotions fail. Here is John. John was such a good salesman we made him sales manager and in six months he is a burned out stick. His boss invokes the Peter Principle. But there are two reasons actually. One is that the man has been put into the wrong job.

"But there's a more important reason. The man who got the promotion acts on a very plausible assumption.

110

He says, 'I got the promotion so I must have been doing something right as a salesman; and therefore what I did that made me a successful salesman is the right thing to do now that I'm a sales manager.'

"This is usually the very worst thing to do. The manager who moves into a new environment had better stand back and see what the new job requires. And this is very difficult to find out by yourself; almost always you must be told by somebody else."

Drucker underscores his point:

"When I was a very young man I had been a securities analyst with a small bank and they made me secretary to the partners. The senior partner—a wise and wonderful old man—was, I knew, not in favor of this. For three months he was very courteous, but he didn't really say anything. Then he called me in. 'Mr. Drucker,' he said, 'You know that I was not in favor of you coming here.'

" 'Yes, sir, I know that.'

" 'But,' he said, 'You know, I didn't realize how stupid you'd be.'

"I answered, 'I've worked my ass off.'

" 'Look,' he said, 'If we had wanted you to remain a securities analyst we would have kept you where you were. We brought you in here as a junior partner, and you are still doing security analysis. Isn't it about time you thought through what the new job requires?'

"If he hadn't said it, I would not have realized it.

"The same is true of moving from one company to another or from Manufacturer's Trust to United Hospital. After three months, when you understand a little about the organization, stand back and ask yourself, What does it really require? What are the few things I could do on this new assignment that would make a difference? If you do this, you have a chance. If you don't do it, you have no chance.

"It's not a matter of transferring skills—except for accounting, where skills are the most transferable, the most detached from the operation. If your field is, say, personnel, you cannot come in and apply the fourteen principles of good personnel management. You'd better look at the organization and figure out what they expect from you and what you can contribute.

"Your skills remain the same; but the new balance is not the same. The emphasis is different, the relationships are different. You must think through your contribution.

"So I believe in the ability of a seasoned and gifted executive to become capable of functioning in a number of environments, but not by merely transferring his skills."

But the principle of management by objectives is still not only a valid one; it is *the* working principle by which an organization must run and control its operations if it is to be a viable entity in the industrial age. True, we may see certain reactions against the extremes of the bottom-line obsession, counseling a return to process orientation rather than goal orientation. And not only in business management; in a great many places. Concentration on results places great pressures on human beings in every area of activity. At the risk of wandering afield, one is tempted to cite recent developments surrounding the act of sex. Time was that sexual performance was totally goal oriented, and this concentration was reinforced in fact and in fiction by the notion that performance—and, somehow, character —was to be judged by the achievement of stable erection in those instances where it is appropriate and orgasm in all instances.

The recent work of Masters and Johnson, among others, discloses that such goal orientation can place so much pressure on the individual that the result is no performance at all. Now the tendency is to move back to a more process-oriented approach: massage the feet, kiss the back, and so on. This Drucker would not object to at all. It is process, but process in harmony with progress toward a clearly defined goal.

In spite of sporadic reactions, management by objectives is here to stay. It is an eminently sound principle, when applied properly. It is worthwhile to reexamine the essentials of the concept as Drucker sees them.

There is no one single objective for any organization.

However, at the same time there should not be a profusion of objectives, big and little, hoarded in every nook and cranny of the enterprise. Objectives must be set up in every area where performance and results directly affect the prosperity and survival of the business.

Drucker says, "We can't start talking objectives until we know what they are. The things we desire are not objectives. Corporations and institutions alike mistake good intentions for objectives. Health care is a good intention, not an objective. Nothing operational follows from it. When you do not figure out the real objectives, you substitute procedure for thinking."

Many businessmen might say offhandedly that they have one objective: profit. Drucker does not accept profit as an objective at all in the sense in which he talks of objectives. Profit is a necessity for survival. It is the wherewithal to pay the cost of today and tomorrow. Since objectives must conduce toward survival, profit is involved in objectives. But profit is not primarily what management by objectives is all about.

Organizational objectives must grow out of a thorough knowledge of what the business is and what it should be. Specific targets, not abstractions, make it possible to make specific assignments.

Objectives, Drucker says, should enable us to do five things: organize and explain the whole range of business phenomena in a few general statements, test these statements, predict behavior, gauge the soundness of decisions before they are made, and enable businessmen to analyze and improve their performance.

There are eight areas in which objectives should be set: market standing, innovation, productivity, physical and financial resources, profitability, manager performance and development, worker performance and attitude, and public responsibility.

Who sets the objectives? As the years have passed, Drucker has become more and more convinced of the importance of pushing the task of objective setting as far down the organization chart as possible. Take, for example, the goals that are to be set up for subordinate managers.

The objectives of the individual are a function of the

objectives of the larger unit of which he is a part. For example, the objectives set for the district sales manager are defined by the contribution that he and his salesmen should make to the sales force as a whole. Higher management has the authority to approve or disapprove the goals. But the development of the objectives is part of the manager's responsibility. He participates fully in setting them. "Indeed," says Drucker, "it is his first responsibility."

The idea is not to give the manager a "sense of participation"—real or phony. A manager has responsibility by definition. He must understand the purpose of management by objectives, know the goals of the unit of which he is a part, and have the judgment and integrity to generate goals for himself that fit the concept.

Having set his own goals, the manager gauges his performance against these goals. Obviously he needs sufficient information and coherent enough controls to do this. The measurements don't have to be highly quantitative; it is folly to try to reduce a management function to a series of tiny components, each of which can be reduced to numbers. However, the controls must be "clear, simple and rational."

So when Drucker talks about management by objectives he is not talking about mere "bottom-line" management; and when he discusses controls he is talking largely about self-controls. As Drucker points out, there has been a great deal of stir over the concept of management by objectives. An entire body of literature has grown up to explain and apply it. A great many companies have adopted a policy of management by objectives.

However, there has been far less acceptance of Drucker's corollary—*self-control*. The leaders of industry are willing to go along with the concept of objectives; but only a handful have followed through by giving the manager the means of controlling himself.

It is necessary, says Drucker, to do both. In accordance with his lifelong emphasis on building on strength, he declares that "What the business enterprise needs is a principle of management that will give full scope

114

to individual strength and responsibility, as well as common direction to vision and effort, establish team work, and harmonize the goals of the individual with the commonweal."

"Commonweal" may seem a peculiar word in this context. Its dictionary definition is brief and to the point: "the public good; the general welfare." But the term, and the approach that it conveys, is highly appropriate to Drucker's vision. He is not talking about a way to run a business; he is talking about a *philosophy*. And his philosophy emphasizes freedom. Within this concept, the manager decides to act because he recognizes the objective task, and the objective task demands that he act in a certain way. Management by objectives and self-control convert "objective needs into personal goals. And this is genuine freedom."

Drucker never loses sight of the potential for the public good that rests within the organization in general and the corporation in particular. Corporations must be managed; not only according to a set of pragmatic rules, but within a philosophical framework that conforms to the role of the organization in the industrial society. Drucker has seen the concept of management by objectives applied as a better way of getting results. He regrets that the other element of the concept—self-control—has not been given much more than lip service. But he is still hopeful.

7.

Problem or Panacea: Drucker and the Computer

"I've never had any problem with the computer. Computers sit up and say please when I come near them. . . . I treat it just like a big adding machine."

"I have known a hell of a lot of companies to worry about where the money would come from to meet the payroll, but I have never known a single one that had any difficulty paying it out. Yet for this they now have a computer."

"The main impact of the computer has been the provision of unlimited jobs for clerks."

"The computer is a moron."

Peter Drucker's attitude toward the computer frustrates both the computer's greatest advocates and its severest critics. Drucker has never looked at the onset of electronic data processing as a mechanized miracle that would solve all problems and bring the millennium to fruition upon earth. At the same time he has not joined the doomsayers who cringe with fear before the winking consol, crying that the computer will enslave us all.

Drucker views the computer and its acolytes with

indulgent skepticism. He admits its capabilities as a means of making it easier to translate intelligence into effective action. The computer is a part of our future, no question about that; but it is only a tool. Tools can be overestimated and misused. This one has been. For manager and layman alike, exposure to Drucker's thoughts about the computer is refreshing, reassuring, and useful.

Drucker reminds us of the stunning miscalculations of the experts that served as an obbligato to the introduction of the computer and that contributed so much to its relative lack of impact on our lives. In the early 1940s the pundits were saying that the big applications of the new development would be found in science and in warfare. There was little consideration of the role the machine would play in business, government, and education. A vast market-research study offered an interesting conclusion: at the most, the world market would be able to absorb one thousand computers by the year 2000. The utterances of those who said that practically any business of any size would have a computer were dismissed as the babblings of people who have been reading too much science fiction.

Now, of course, more than 150,000 computers have been installed throughout the world. They may not be accomplishing what the dreamers had hoped, but they are in place and running. The development brings to mind the exclamation by Lord Melbourne, the salty Whig who was Prime Minister of Great Britain when Queen Victoria came to the throne, who pointed out that "what all the wise men said would happen, has not happened; and what all the damned fools predicted has come to pass."

As it became evident that computers were being spewed forth in much greater numbers than had first been envisioned, the prognostic pendulum swung with great velocity in the other direction. No longer were the commentators acting like the villagers in the early scenes of a monster movie, cracking rustic jokes about the doings of the crazy scientist in the old house on the hill. Now there were forebodings of catastrophe. The scientists had created an ogre that would devour many

117

of us and reduce the rest of us to slaves. There were the kinds of mutterings that precede the advance of the townspeople—each bearing a flaming torch—up the mountain in the penultimate scene of any self-respecting Frankenstein film.

The computer would throw masses of people out of work. The first victims would be middle managers. In a few years there would be a president at the top of the organization chart, and then the next boxes would represent foremen and supervisors. All the in-between work that had previously been done by human beings would now be taken over by electronic marvels. *Harvard Business Review* asked, "Is middle management obsolete?" and answered with a definitive "yes."

"At exactly that moment," says Drucker, "the tremendous expansion of middle-management jobs began." Since then middle management has grown three times as fast as total employment; and this growth has closely paralleled the spread of computer use.

However, this is by no means to say that the proliferation of computers and middle managers is an altogether healthy development. Drucker sees a generation of managers who have become transfixed by the mystique of the computer: its speed, its massive memory capacity, its awesome computational ability. And he sees these managers becoming slaves to the computer—although not in the sense envisioned by the predictors of doomsday. Drucker points out that the glamor of the machine has led too many managers into a basic error in reasoning. They get the new toy, and then—instead of using it to save their own time—they expend their time in the quest for new things for the computer to do. This is, of course, a losing game, because the computer can do jobs faster than human beings can devise new jobs to provide it with. The objective is to keep the tool in operation. The manager forgets that the work does not exist for the sake of the tool; the tool exists to do the work.

One of the malignant byproducts of this frantic search for things for the computer to do is that the machine spews out endless scrolls of information that the manager does not need and cannot use. He would be best advised to throw it away. But that is not in human nature. Instead, the executive does his best to keep up with the computer's output. He kids himself into thinking that this indigestible mass of information—because it has been disgorged in his in-box by an infinitely sophisticated (not to mention expensive) modern marvel of technology—is of enormous value and is making him a far better informed planner and accurate decision maker. Russell W. McFall, Board Chairman and President of Western Union, remarked, "There are days when I think we spend all of our time slicing data with a razor blade and dishing it up with a shovel."

So Drucker looked past the garish advertisements for the wonders of the computer and saw a harried human being sitting behind a littered desk staring hopelessly at an incomprehensible printout. He takes note of the forecasts that the new device would have the most profound effects on management strategy, policy, and planning, and remarks that on none of these has the computer had the slightest impact whatever.

The computer can—and has—been of great value in the factory. It puts back into manufacturing a measure of the flexibility that was removed from it by the onset of mass production. Before the computer, a change in process required the stopping of the work, with inevitable costly delays. Now a machine tool run by computerized "numerical control" can make the changes instantaneously. Drucker attributes the upsurge of the shipbuilding industry in Sweden and Japan to adroit use of the computer in turning out ships of great diversity from standardized parts. Here is where the machine has been at its best.

But the manager is not a standardized part. Drucker does not feel that the computer has served the manager very well, mostly because neither the manager nor anyone else has made proper use of the new technology. By now the computer people know this too. Isaac L. Auerbach, president of an international firm offering consulting services on computers and information systems, observes that three things went wrong in computer development. For too long it was controlled by mathematicians and engineers who were not use oriented. Manufacturers did not sell solutions; they sold hardware—and the customer bought hardware. And most users failed to plan their systems, methods, and procedures so that the computer could do the job it was entitled to do.

Drucker remarked in *Technology, Management & Society* that, as of that time, we had a wonderful gadget but we did not yet have an information industry. We were busy trying to get the gadget to learn tricks, such as "the asinine attempt to have the computer speak English, which it cannot do." The main impact of the device thus far had been to create unlimited employment for clerks.

So the computer is not a mere gadget; but it is not the apocalypse either. It can be of great value—if we use it in a way that brings out its value. Drucker has some thoughts on how this can be done.

We must, he tells us, get an intellectual grasp on what the computer means. We have the hardware; now, as he says in *The Age of Discontinuity*, what we need is a "conceptual understanding of information." There is no use in railing against the computer. It is here. It works with punch cards; but it does not turn human beings into punch cards. No, "the computer, for those who understand anything about it, is emancipation for the individual. The purpose of the computer is to enable us not to spend time on 'controls,' but to use the time for tasks that require perception, imagination, human relations, and creativity. . . ."

These tasks are, in particular, the ones that young people—the most vociferous opponents of the computer —profess to be the paramount ones for the individual and for society.

The computer is not a maker of concepts, or a thinker. It is, indeed, a moron—a big calculator. But herein, according to Drucker, lies its strength. When the computer is seen as nothing more than a better tool, it fits into a perspective and enables us to do certain things with it.

For one thing, the computer—with its memory and its powers of manipulating large numbers—makes it far more possible than before for the theoretician to test theories and verify his hypotheses. But the computer remains the tool, not the thinker. It was Einstein, not the telescope or calculus, who gave us the theory of relativity.

Implicit in Drucker's thinking here is the warning that the scientist, like the businessman, can become overly intrigued by the capabilities of the computer and confuse facility with accomplishment. (In this context I recall a recent conversation between a physicist and a scientifically trained interrogator. The physicist was expounding on the properties of "quarks" and the wonders of subatomic particles. The questioner asked, "And are you sure that there is objective reality there, and not just readings on instruments?" The physicist admitted that he could not be certain, but that there was an implicit pact among the members of his scientific fraternity to act on the assumption that objective reality underlies the readings.)

There is now a great barrier between the ordinary human being and the full fruits of the computer. This is the presently necessary (or assumed to be necessary) step of "programming." Drucker considers this an abomination. It is "unspeakably clumsy, slow and expensive." And, he feels, it will soon be eliminated. Here he draws an analogy with music. "In music, the difference between East and West is that many centuries ago St. Ambrose invented notation." Before then, the only way to describe a tune was in words—and this is the way it is still done in the East. But this is clumsy and inaccurate, and it makes the job of composition immeasurably harder.

Drucker draws the picture of a day, not too far distant, when the individual will have direct access to the computer, without having to have his questions and thoughts translated into computer language by a programmer. The manager will use a simple console at his desk. Indeed, extrapolating from this, the child in school will punch into the computer the input of his choice —and use the machine as it should be used. No reason why not, Drucker tells us; seven-year-olds can learn musical notation in two weeks.

But liberation through the computer will not come

unless we are in the frame of mind to make it come. The manager should first ask, Does this gadget enable me to spend less time controlling, and more time on the important things? If the executive is reading more stuff, not less, as a result of computerization, then something is wrong.

The second test is that the computer should enable the people in the organization to do more of what they are getting paid for doing. Now it has the opposite effect. An abundance of useless data provides multiple temptations to get off the track, and powerful excuses for doing so.

For example, salesmen and sales managers should be freed as much as possible from paper work. Not only are they the worst people in the world at clerical labor; it takes them away from doing the things that are their only reason for being on the payroll. So the computer should be used to ease the reporting function in the sales area.

But—is this an exalted enough use of the computer? Computer experts will protest that it is not. But Drucker is unperturbed. He would say to them, "Never mind, my boy. If you want to do technically demanding jobs, go back to the university. You are on my payroll." Such jobs would no doubt cause an EDP impresario to bridle in indignation, but Drucker does not care. Maybe it could be said "a little more nicely. I long ago learned not to be nice, because people do not hear it when you hint."

But Drucker does not suggest that the function of the computer stop with handling the payroll and credit functions, or following an order through the plant. (He remarks, however, that while everybody says he is already doing such mundane tasks on the computer, he has yet to see it really being accomplished.) Drucker says: Master the mundane. Apply the computer to the lowly clerical things. Then get started on building an information system.

Information is energy, he says. He compares information to electricity. In this conceptualization, the computer is like the central power system. Time was that factories had their own power systems; now they draw electric power from a separate facility. In the same way, he speculates, the time will soon come when companies will not have their own individual computers, but will rather draw their informational "energy" from huge centralized sources. The world will be dotted with "knowledge utilities." Time-sharing will spread to make the individual-company computer as rare as the individual-company steam generator.

Drucker is very taken with this analogy between information and electricity; it is an interesting fancy, one that appeals to his writer's mind. One can go overboard on an analogy, and it may be that Drucker is too captivated by this one. But his provocative ideas about the computer and information make great sense, and are worth the closest attention of both manager and non-manager.

We must, he says, learn to make knowledge productive, in business and in society. Knowledge must be used and challenged. We don't use our present knowledge nearly well enough and, as our access to knowledge continues to expand, the lack of fully productive application of it will become more critical.

This does not mean—as some think it should mean—putting computer people in the top echelons of the organization, business or otherwise: "As to the EDP function being placed on a higher level, that's a lot of bullshit. I decide whether I want a washing machine. It's the mechanic's job to keep it running." The technician remains a technician, no matter how awesomely powerful the machine he tends. Drucker's urgent message is that the new technology must be brought closer to the ordinary man, not placed at a greater distance from him.

Information will become cheap and more abundant. Answers will be found to the problems of storage and transmission of information. At the same time, answers must be found to the ethical questions surrounding the capacity of the computer to invade the privacy of the individual. Privacy is not merely a right; it is a social need, and the existence of means of breaching it does not make that need any less important.

As—assisted by the computer—we move more deeply

into the age of knowledge, we will grow to be more at ease with it. The first industrial revolution substituted skill for brawn. Now we are substituting knowledge for skill. Knowledge has become respectable—but it was not always so. As recently as the 1940s, Drucker points out, General Motors "carefully concealed the fact that one of its top three men, Albert Bradley, had a Ph.D. It was even concealed that he had gone to college, because, quite obviously, a respectable man went to work as a waterboy at age fourteen." The degree was an embarrassment.

Experience will become a far less important factor in management. This will be hard for the older manager to accept. Very often all he has going for him is experience. But now a very young man can pick up everything he needs to know with great speed. He doesn't have to attend the "school of hard knocks." Young people will be better able than older ones to take on demanding jobs because they have not been conditioned to have responses that are no longer appropriate. We will see people promoted to top jobs who "we wouldn't have thought old enough, a few years ago, to find their way to the water cooler."

And, as we use electronics to make knowledge work for us, we will get better at doing business and living life.

Drucker, with all of his animadversions on the computer, is not really an enemy of the device. He just does not assign to it supernatural powers—or even any powers at all beyond the ability to calculate very quickly. This makes it a potentially valuable tool—but that is all it is, a tool. It is not an ogre, swallowing jobs and people. And it is not the universal answer to all our problems. It is a gadget that will serve us well if we don't lose sight of what it can and cannot do.

8.

The Problem of
Executive Stress

If anyone can be identified as the "inventor" of the modern manager, that individual is Peter Drucker.

Having elevated the corporation to the eminence of a predominant political and social entity as well as an economic one, Drucker identified the manager as the key figure in the new society. He then set out to help to perfect the craft of management. His ideal manager —at least the one whom he envisioned in his early conceptual thinking—is a person (or, let's be candid and say "a man") who must handle awesome responsibilities, and who brings to the task equally awesome qualities of discipline, intellect, and creativity.

But Drucker is like a Pygmalion whose Galatea— though beautiful—has developed a severe tic. For many years, professionals and laymen have been talking about the awful stresses under which the high-powered executive must try to function. A great deal has been said and written—in fact and fiction—about the emotional consequences of the management burden. Managers worry; they work too hard; they neglect their wives and children; they cannot relax; they take the job home with them; sometimes they crack up; they drink too much; they collapse; they die early.

Like almost any other artist or inventor, Drucker tends to minimize or deny the flaws that observers claim to find in his creation. He dismisses the popular picture of the "organization man" as a caricature and a stereotype (although he does not go so far as to say it is altogether without validity). Nevertheless, there is ample evidence that the managerial role places exceptional strain on the manager—more, often, than he is able to handle.

The factors involved in this need not be belabored. Drucker is familiar with them; he has had a lot to do with bringing them into being. For one thing, we can take a look at the responsibilities Drucker says the manager must be able to assume. It's not just the task of making a profit; that's only the beginning. The manager must be conscious always of his role as conservator and developer of the organization's human resources. When the careers and lives of men and women are placed in your hand, you are, willy-nilly, "playing God." That can be enough to make anyone nervous.

Drucker emphasizes the paramount role of knowledge in the new society. The erstwhile manual worker has been upgraded to a skilled worker. Operations that were formerly performed by muscle and sweat are now done with brains. Not only is the manager the principal "knowledge worker"; he is also responsible for devising the methods by which all work is upgraded to brain work.

And then there is the social responsibility that Drucker assigns to the corporation and the managers who run it. Admittedly he is unable to offer a clear-cut formula that the executive can use to devise the proper mix of profit-mindedness and social responsibility. He concedes that the moral problem is a real and a prevalent one. As the voices of the ecology activists and the opponents of super-business continue to rise, the split becomes even more troublesome. This is another source of stress.

In helping to develop the craft of "pure" management, Drucker has contributed to a situation in which the executive may find himself functioning in an environment of abstractions, only tenuously rooted in the real world. Drucker, as we discuss elsewhere, maintains that he has never claimed for management the status of an art, nor has he advocated that a manager who has mastered his craft is then equipped to move from company to company, from industry to industry, without reference to what the company makes and sells.

He is correct; but Drucker has been *interpreted* as being a proponent of the "floating manager" concept. In recent years we have seen a spate of management activity that is founded on this premise. Many other business thinkers—prominent among them the leaders of the American Management Association—have given impetus to the notion that a "pure" manager can pack his attaché case, move into a totally alien organization, set up shop, and ply his art with success and profit. There is less emphasis on this proposition today, mainly because there have been too many instances in which it has not worked out. However, it was in great vogue, and it still happens. And the manager who simply makes plans and decisions in an environment remote from the real world is not just an ineffective manager. He is in danger of becoming a sick manager. The plethora of abstractions combined with the paucity of concrete realities weigh him down and add to his emotional burden.

Allied to this last phenomenon is the practice of transferring managers from one location to another as if they were so many pins on a map. Drucker disapproves of this; but it is fair to say that the prevalance of executive transfers is an organic development from the elevation of the manager to his position of supreme importance. A corporate chief executive, attuned to the message that it is vital above all to have the right manager in the right spot, wants to move his top people around to get the most out of them. But the life of a corporate nomad, we are finding, takes a toll on those who live it.

All—including Drucker—agree that the manager must motivate those who work for him. But who motivates the motivator? Subordinates too know all about the exhortations that the executive is responsible for motivation. Frequently they seem to take the attitude: "Okay, motivate me. You're getting paid for it." The boss who spends time and energy trying to come up with the right combination of motivational factors to apply to his people depletes his psychic reservoirs, sometimes to the extent of exhaustion and neurosis.

The manager's family suffers from the fallout resulting from his workload. Dr. Benjamin B. Wolman of New York is a psychoanalyst whose patients include many executives—and their wives. His comment is typical of many: "I have a case now—the wife of an executive. A charming and accomplished woman—but she is being driven berserk by the fact that her husband has absolutely no time for her. She is faithful; she will not have an affair with the milkman. Her husband comes home with an attaché case. He works or he falls asleep. She sees him as a tenant, not as a husband."

We might mention just one other problem that the manager faces: that of job insecurity. Drucker has remarked perceptively that the loss of a job means more than just economic deprivation. It is a loss of status and function. The individual is cut off from society. But Drucker seems here to be talking about the lower-level worker. With the manager he is tougher. What happens when a manager is not delivering? "If the man has been with you only five years, you fire him; that is easy." If the manager has been around longer than that you must treat each case with compassion but also realism. In Drucker's lexicon, management is a demanding priesthood; if you can't reach the objectives, you are through.

Of course it is true that many executives boast of the tension under which they labor. They consider it a badge of accomplishment. As Erich Fromm has said, we tend to treasure our neuroses, because they are peculiarly our own. Nevertheless, whether you are proud of it or not, excessive tension is bad for you. It can kill you.

Drucker can seem pretty cavalier about all this. He tells people who are unhappy with their jobs to get other jobs. He maintains that those who are not up to the demands of executive life should find something else to do. When he does touch upon the strain of the managerial tasks, he tends to talk about it in terms of organizational difficulty rather than human tragedy. He is cool, remote, untouched. Typically, in his monumental *Management: Tasks, Responsibilities, Practices,* he discusses jobs that are "widow-makers." If a job has defeated two good men in a row, it should be restructured. No tears are shed for the "good men" who have been destroyed.

This dispassionate approach to the personal problems of managers—as well as those of workers in general—has done much to bring Drucker under attack as being cold and unfeeling. But the late Abraham H. Maslow criticized Drucker for "inhumanity" in a different context, one that is more germane to our topic. Maslow's argument centered on the advocacy by Drucker of Douglas McGregor's "Theory Y"—the proposition that workers do not have to be driven, that they do not have an ingrained dislike for work, that they will work better when given freedom and responsibility. Maslow pointed out that the demands of freedom are very great, and that not everyone by any means is up to them. The "inhumanity" that Maslow referred to was Drucker's fancied lack of concern for the weak and the vulnerable people who *needed* direction in their jobs and would be ruined if forced to take on responsibility and the rigors of self-discipline. As Drucker points out, Maslow felt that the world was not peopled by adults: "It has its full share of the permanently immature."

Maslow was critical of the limited amount of freedom and responsibility that Drucker and McGregor proposed to give to the worker. But how much more of that "dangerous" freedom does Drucker propose for the manager? The manager is the eternal point man, always exposed, always on the alert for dangers ahead of him and behind him, never able to take it easy, lest he slip up on some part of his demanding job and lose out to a rival.

The freedom and responsibility that Drucker demands for his ideal manager are absolutely necessary if that manager is going to be able to do the kinds of things Drucker insists that he do. But the price can be high.

It is being paid every day in the psychiatrists' offices, bars, bedrooms, and sanitariums of America.

The stress of management is not something to be brushed off with references to myths and stereotypes; nor can it be remedied by the restructuring of "widow-making" jobs. The fact is that many executive jobs are widow-makers, not because they are designed poorly, but because of their intrinsic nature and the immense pressures to which they subject even the strongest of men.

There would appear to be good reasons behind Drucker's failure to acknowledge this. One principal factor that we may cite is the comment that "he has never met a payroll." Peter Drucker has never worried as a manager. He has never experienced the endless meetings, the formidable paperwork, the recurring interruptions and the executive-suite jungle fighting that confront so many managers every day. His placid existence has never been penetrated by the sharp fear of losing a job, or the angry humiliation of having lost one. Yes, teachers get tired and frustrated and bored and disillusioned, and so do writers, consultants, and even philosophers—but not in the same way as the manager does. The organization man may be a caricature, but his wounds bleed nonetheless.

Middle age is the time of crisis for the manager. He has struggled hard. He has achieved much. But it is a rare executive who feels that he "has it made." Although his experience and ability have grown, the anxieties that go with the job have grown as well.

Harry Levinson—Visiting Professor of Business Administration at the Harvard Business School and President of the Levinson Institute—is acknowledged as one of the foremost commentators on executive stress. In his influential book, *Executive Stress,* Levinson cites a study—conducted by Lee Stockford of the California Institute of Technology—which underscores the prevalence of the problem. Stockford's survey of 1,100 men shows that five out of six of those in professional and management positions undergo a period of frustration in their middle thirties; and one in six never fully recovers from it.

Levinson identifies a number of the factors contributing to executive malaise: the intertwining of life and career; the continuous threat of defeat; the increase of dependency on specialists; denial of feelings (for example, the inadvisability of getting close to those whom one manages) ; a constant state of defensiveness in the pursuit of success; an awareness of the decline of physical capacities.

The creativity of the executive does not decline at an early age, but it does change form. It becomes less passionate, more analytical. The manager who is growing older is frequently bored. He does not enjoy the political infighting that he once indulged in with great zest. And, he finds himself more frightened (though he seldom admits it) and more angry; angry, for example, with the "younger generation." He has not been able to develop as close a relationship with his children as he would have liked; but he is severely wounded when his children turn away from him. He often wonders what he is doing and why he is doing it.

What can he do about it? Levinson's recommendations are detailed and useful. For the purposes of this chapter I will, however, merely summarize the general headings under which they fall. The manager must, first of all, face up to the fact that there is such a thing as middle-age crisis. He must act: talk things over with his wife to redefine their marriage contract; make a formal effort to find and cultivate new friends, with a particular emphasis on developing companionship; and he should become involved in "some on-going activity of social value which has enduring purpose."

In his business life, the executive should "be exercising a different kind of leadership and dealing with different organizational problems." Ideally, he will become a resource for others in the organization.

Organizations should, says Levinson, do far more than they are doing to build programs that minimize stress and get the most out of aging human resources. He knows of no organization that does this effectively now.

If attention is paid to the problem, and thought is given to ways of coping with it, middle age can be a renaissance, for the manager and those around him.

These, in brief outline, are Levinson's views. Does Drucker have anything to contribute?

If Drucker never gave a thought to the human calamities that result from the stress of management, we could simply say that he does not think about those things, and concentrate on his concepts, his projections, and his analyses. But Drucker does think about these things. He rarely goes on about them in public; he does not see this as his role. But, when invited in conversation to talk about some of the darker aspects of the executive life, Drucker has some comments, some insights, and some advice.

He sees the increasing degree to which a lot of managers fail to get any pleasure out of the job as they get older: "There is an enormous number of middle-aged people who have retired on the job. Take the case of a man who, at age twenty-nine, gets the job he wanted: director of market research for a certain toy company. By the time he is forty, there is damn little about market research that he doesn't know. Even the jokes he tells are stale; he is bored silly. And this is true, even though business is the least eroding environment, because it has the most flexibility. We can move a market research man into product planning; if he is astute enough he will work to move himself into another and more congenial job. There's no problem about that. But the young professor who became a specialist in the French Revolution can never move out of the French Revolution, no matter how hard he tries, unless he is a very great man."

While maintaining that business has great flexibility to offer a manager a change of scene or occupation, Drucker recognizes the factors, internal and otherwise, that militate against that solution: "The market research man should get out of that company if he is stuck. He should have gotten out a long time ago. He knows he isn't going to be vice president of marketing. He knows he should leave. He wants to leave—and yet at the same time he doesn't want to. He's paid pretty well, and he has his stock options, dubious as their value may be today. So he's forced into one of the four degenerative diseases of executive middle age. He takes to the barroom. Or he takes up with a girl. Or he goes to an analyst. Or he begins to play around with refined techniques. He applies reverse regression analysis to basically meaningless data. This may be reasonably harmless, but it greatly cuts down his usefulness because nobody can understand him any more. He is bored and disinterested. He begins to sit out his last twenty years on the job. What he needs is repotting. He might still go elsewhere. But he is locked in, to the pension plan, the routine, the 7:42 out of Scarsdale."

This is the plight of the manager who begins to lose hope and drive as he sees that the success he sought will not be his. All executives want success, recognition, and promotion to bigger things. Or do they?

"No, they don't. The man we are talking about may fall into that category; let's say he does. He has been working toward becoming vice president. But he doesn't really want the job. He wants to be offered the job, but he doesn't really want it. That's probably why he has stayed so long. On the surface he could tell himself that he had a good chance for the promotion. But inside him he knows always that he can't make it. It may be that in his company the vice president of marketing always comes out of the sales line. Or it may be that the marketing vice president is not much older than he is, and an unlikely candidate to be unseated. The man we are talking about sticks in that situation because he really does not want to get the big job."

Middle-aged managers who have lived only for the job begin to lose their zest. "Their inner resources are not very great. They have not developed them; they have put everything into the job. The job does not become exactly a bore, but it is no longer a challenge. The manager has learned, or thinks he has learned, that the smart and safe thing to do in the organization is to be as invisible as possible. If you expose yourself you are in danger. Taking risks is the only way to get ahead, but it is also the one sure way to get into trouble. So the manager goes through the motions. If the company has a new fad every three years, he learns to parrot the current party line. They know damn well

133

that, while human relations may be the big thing today, in two years it will be cost reduction or something else. So what's the point of trying to do anything? They stop learning."

What happens? "The crisis of middle age is a normal, human crisis. You reach your forties and you realize how few of the things that you set out to do at twenty have actually been done. Erikson has been writing about the identity crisis of childhood. Believe me, the identity crisis of middle age is a far more important and serious one. And then you experience a setback. Nobody goes through life without them. But when you are at this point in life, and you don't have the inner resources, you are very vulnerable. When you make the organization your life, you are defenseless against the inevitable disappointments. You are passed over for a promotion. Or that plan you worked on so goddamned hard for three years is turned down by top management. Or—and this is very common—old Jim, who has been working next door to you for fifteen years, is being transferred. It may seem trivial but it's not."

One way in which the manager can prepare to minimize the effects of this kind of experience is through planning. "Take a little control over your career. I don't mean the kind of career planning that says by age fifty-one-and-a-half I'll be executive vice president. I've always considered that as silly as can be. Incidentally, I knew only one man who did it, and he frightened me when I was nine years old. We did our homework and played together. One day we played 'What are you going to be when you grow up?' And we were saying firemen, or policeman—except for Gustav, who said, 'I am going to be Professor of Islamic Studies at the University [of Vienna].' It scared me spitless, because somehow I knew that Gustav would carry it out. And he did carry it out. The only change in the plan was brought about by Adolf Hitler. Since Gustav was half Jewish, he did not become Professor of Islamic Studies at the University of Vienna, but rather at the University of Chicago. He was a great scholar. But he is the only one I know who could do it that way. If anyone had told me at even age twenty-nine what I would be doing now,

I would have laughed. This kind of 'career planning' makes very little sense.

"I am talking about career planning in the sense of: What do I have to learn, what are my strengths, how can I build on them, where do I belong, do I really belong in this company? One must take the responsibility of asking oneself these questions from time to time, and acting on the answers. You will make mistakes. But if you make them early enough they will not endanger you. They are not irretrievable. I feel that young people in particular do not sufficiently concern themselves with what they have to learn in order to be more effective on the job and in life. It is not so much a matter of specific skills as the ability to read and write and speak. You do not prepare for a particular job. You build your strengths so that they stand you in good stead when you need them."

There is something else, even more important. "Develop a genuine, true, major outside interest. Not a hobby, a genuine interest, which permits you to live in a different world, with different peers whose opinions are meaningful to you. The most extremely successful case of this was Walter Leaf, an English banker at the turn of the century who was head of what was then the largest English bank and who wrote one of the best books on banking ever published. Leaf also happened to be one of the great Homeric scholars. When he died in 1927, both groups appeared at his funeral—the scholars and the bankers. The scholars found out for the first time that their beloved colleague was a banker. The bankers learned to their astonishment that Walter Leaf was the man who conclusively demolished the theory that the *Iliad* and the *Odyssey* were written by two different people. He had lived in two different worlds and kept them separate, and had excelled in each. A very happy man, I should imagine.

"One does not have to go this far; but one needs a true outside interest, not just water-skiing. It not only develops your strengths; it helps to protect you against the inevitable shocks."

Business organizations should be more tolerant of the manager who develops an outside interest; indeed, they should encourage it. "The older organizations have learned a few things. Look at the Catholic Church, or at any army. They have learned not to discriminate against the man who has a genuine, true, major outside interest. It did not do General [Archibald] Wavell [leading British commander in World War II, who defeated the Italians in East Africa and liberated Ethiopia; Field Marshal and later Viceroy of India] any harm to be known as a fairly good minor English poet. In Sears Roebuck it would kill you. It does not do you any harm in a church career to be known as a first class authority on medieval art. Too many organizations take a dim view of this. They feel that it leads to divided loyalty and diminished application to the job. On the contrary, it makes a man a better manager and saves him to continue on the job."

Management should foster the development of outside interests—and it should create the atmosphere within which the manager periodically examines his career goals and himself. "This is particularly important with young people. It's very hard for them to raise these questions —what do I have to learn, what are my strengths, where am I going, do I really want to get there—by themselves. The boss should force them to ask these questions, help them think it through. He has a responsibility to do so."

The manager who has developed a real outside interest may, in the end, want to turn to it as his major occupation when and if business palls on him. "It happens, but not often enough. I know a banker, a fine executive, who found that he was getting bored with it. It was the same, every day like every other day. So he left banking. He has done fund-raising work for hospitals, and now he took over a big hospital. He was not trained in formal hospital administration, but he knew all the things he had to do. A hospital, like a bank, is a big machine. For years he had been building the bank machine, oiling it, repairing it, adding to it. Now he sets out to do the same things with the hospital. He knew how to put in an accounting system, he knew how to set up a cost system, he knew how to organize. The level of demand on him is less than it was at the bank, but he is doing a superb job, one that's needed, and he is blissfully happy. A different setting and different values. A fresh and rewarding career."

This is Drucker's advice to the manager on how to avoid the alienation, the boredom, the diminishing effectiveness and the danger of degeneration that are part and parcel of the executive career. At the same time it is his answer to the question of finding a way to offset management tension.

It may not be the answer that is to everybody's taste. It is vintage Peter Drucker. It contains no panacea, no magic formulas. It does not tell the manager that his tensions and stresses mark him out as something special. Drucker is firm in his feeling that there are problems of stress in all kinds of work, and that the manager has more opportunity and greater resources to handle them than does his counterpart in, say, education.

Moreover, Drucker does not advocate relaxing, doing less work. On the contrary, he talks of doing more. He is not interested in hobbies. By "another interest," he means a second career, with challenges, risks, and hard work. Here, says Drucker, lies the opportunity to use a wider variety of intellectual muscles; to avoid falling into the trap of becoming overly committed to one job, one company, one career; and, as an ultimate resort, to provide an alternative means of making oneself useful, making a contribution.

It all seems to come back to the concept of status and function. A weekend golfer does not achieve status and function in his off-the-job activities; but the man who works seriously at making himself into a superior golfer may do so. But the real achievements are those that come when a manager chooses and works at an outside interest that faces him with real challenges and gives him the chance to win the recognition of people whose opinion he respects.

In sum, this is not markedly different from the prescription offered by Harry Levinson.

Peter Drucker does not offer to the harassed manager any easy way out of his dilemmas. He offers, instead, more work; but work of a different kind. It is certainly a far better answer than the barroom, the extracurricular bedroom, the analyst, or the slide into miserable on-the-job retirement.

9.

Drucker and the Concept-Makers

The man who comes up with a new management concept can be sure his words, written and spoken, will receive a warm and remunerative reception. This is true even if his "concept" is not a new concept at all, but merely a catchy reformulation of ideas originated by others—or even if it is just a gimmick.

Belief in magic did not die out with the druids and the alchemists. Businessmen still believe in magic, but today the magicians are called consultants and "management thinkers." The expert who offers a new formula draws executive attention as if he had energized a powerful magnet. For a while the novel incantation will be intoned in a thousand executive suites.

Potions for instant success come in various sizes and levels of sophistication. There is the basic vaudevillian approach, usually popular with salesmen and sales executives. Over the remnants of thousands of lunches and dinners, marketing people used to listen to Jack Lacey extol the potency of the "Hot Button," or Elmer Wheeler exhort that they "Don't Sell the Steak, Sell the Sizzle." Wheeler's "Sizzlemanship" resulted in dozens of books and articles and a full itinerary of star billings and meetings and conventions. All there was to "Sizzlemanship" was the gimmicky arrangement of a few words, but this did not deter a generation of marketers from listening to the message over and over again.

The vaudevillian approach has gone the way of the joke about the traveling salesman. It is not completely dead, but it is on its way to join the more traditional form of this entertainment. Management has become more serious. The sales manager of yesterday is the marketing vice-president of today. The manager still wants panaceas in the form of "concepts," but they must be articulated in more portentous and scholarly fashion.

With the growth of this trend, the management academician has come into his own. His objective is to enunciate a principle that seems new and useful. If it is new enough, and useful enough, and packs enough magic, he will achieve instant stature. If there is really nothing behind his formulation, it will fade away to be consigned to the dustbin of management fads—but not before a considerable amount of satisfying and profitable attention. Business is complex and tough; businessmen never tire of hearing and reading about things that may enable them to see a little more clearly and be a little more successful.

The big thing is to come up with a concept that catches the imagination—and come up with it first. Although Peter Drucker has never been a retailer of fads or panaceas, he has been a very important figure to the concept artificers of the past thirty years—because Drucker's work, imaginative and iconoclastic, has provided a motherlode of thought within which members of the management academia quarry for the nuggets that will make them rich and famous.

Perhaps the deepest and darkest mystery that has confronted managers in this century is that surrounding the problem of how to make people work effectively. The concept-makers have clustered around the banner of motivation for many years. There has been an immense amount written and spoken about how to motivate people, a vast reverse pyramid growing from a relatively modest basis in fact.

For more than two decades, for example, practically all of the courses, lectures, and treatises on motivation of workers stemmed from the celebrated "Hawthorne Experiment" conducted in the late 1920s by Elton Mayo and his Harvard Business School associates at the Hawthorne, Illinois, plant of the Western Electric Company. The essence of the Hawthorne effect lay in the following sequence. First, workers were given better working conditions: brighter lights, more pleasant surroundings, and so on. Their production went up. Then the improvements were taken away. Production continued to go up. Then conditions were intentionally worsened and the work was made more monotonous. Productivity continued to increase. Workers remained fresh and satisfied. Why? The answer lay in the fact of the experiment itself. Workers would produce—*as long as someone was paying some attention to them.*

The Hawthorne Experiment served as a meal ticket for business academicians, training directors, and a whole congeries of experts for more than twenty years. As a source, it began to wear thin. As this vein appeared close to being mined out, the pundits looked around for another Golconda. They found it in the thinking of Peter Drucker.

Not that there had been strenuous efforts, continuing up to the present time, to generate panaceas from other sources. No possibility seemed too tenuous to stand a chance of becoming a management fad, particularly if it were simple to grasp and articulated in language that was easily understood. The advertising executive Alex Osborn found himself proclaimed as a new corporate prophet when he began to explain, at some length and with some diversity, how creativity could be unleashed through the medium of "brainstorming." For a while, boardrooms resounded with the shouting of wild ideas, untrammeled by critical comment. But brainstorming soon came to be regarded as somewhat lacking in substance, even as business panaceas went, and it quietly subsided into the discard heap.

New concepts continued to shoot into the corporate

firmament. And the creation of a concept meant the assurance of a career. The author of some new formulation could quit his job in business or the university, set up his own organization, and go around the country preaching the latest gospel and running workshops designed to enlighten the faithful. In the 1960s one of the most intensely discussed new tools for executive development was the "management grid." Developed by Robert R. Blake and Jane S. Mouton of the University of Texas, this proposition made no strides in the furtherance of management theory. However, it packaged some things that were already known in a novel and intriguing way. The "grid" is a rectangular framework on which managers are rated from very low to very high in their concern for people and their concern for production. At one corner would be the boss who does not give a damn for humanity but who goes all out to get the job done. At another corner would be the executive who is all-consumed with the establishment of rapport but who will let productivity lag because of his sympathy with people. A 1/1 would be the lowest rating. A 9/9 ranks the executive as optimum in his concern for production and for personnel.

The grid itself is simple enough. However, it gradually gave rise to a complicated structure of exercises and techniques designed to push managers toward the optimum corner. The grid was on the lips of all "hep" managers a few years ago, and it still lives in many quarters. Concrete results are somewhat difficult to find. Nevertheless, Blake and Mouton were able to embark on a new career of conducting seminars and workshops involving the grid. Indeed, they have since expanded the grid approach to include other areas of human endeavor, such as marriage.

Drucker, willingly or otherwise, has contributed the basic thinking that has been translated by concept-makers into the catchiest and most prevalent dogmas of modern enterprise. He is, of course, thoroughly identified with the concepts of management by objectives and multinational corporations, which are considered elsewhere in this book. In a general way he is regarded as the man who started the trend toward the consideration of management as a craft in itself. But he is usually overlooked in allocating the credit (or the blame) for a number of popular ideas that have influenced modern management; nevertheless, a strong case can be made for his paternity.

Incidentally, it is worth pointing out that Drucker's liveliness as a source is by no means restricted to the business area. *Future Shock* was a best-seller and became embedded in the American lexicon. It owes much to the thoughts expressed in Drucker's *Age of Discontinuity*. The discovery, a few years ago, by political pundits of the "New Majority" was anticipated in Drucker's essay *The New Politics*, published in 1966. Here Drucker commented on the trends that have culminated in the establishment of a metropolitan society, anchored by a "new majority" of the educated, employed middle class. More recently, the political commentator Kevin Phillips, in his book *Mediacracy*, has discovered the "knowledge industries" and the "knowledge workers," who are generally better educated and more liberal than the public at large, and who have been gaining ascendancy in our society. Drucker has been talking about the knowledge worker for a good many years, notably in *The Age of Discontinuity*—although he credits the coinage of the term "knowledge industries" to the Princeton economist Fritz Machlup in Machlup's book *Production and Distribution of Knowledge in the United States*.

But, leaving these episodes aside, we may concentrate our examination of Peter Drucker as a prime source for conceptual material on two exceptionally influential formulations in the area of getting people to work more effectively. One concept is the "Hygiene Theory"; the other is "Theory X and Theory Y." Just about any manager today is familiar with both concepts; and there was a time not long ago when no self-respecting specialist in corporate behavior could bear to see the sun go down unless he had said "hygiene factor" and "Theory Y" at least once.

The "Hygiene Theory" is attributed to Dr. Frederick Herzberg. Herzberg published his concept in 1959 in *The Motivation to Work*. This book had two co-authors, Bernard Mausner and Barbara Snyderman, but their names have not survived prominently in connection with the idea. "Hygiene" has become synonymous with Herzberg.

What is the "Hygiene Theory"? It is a widely influential proposition devoted to determining the things that impel people to work more effectively. It is based, according to the authors, on a large-scale experiment involving two pilot studies and then a major project. The major study was conducted within nine varying business concerns in Pittsburgh and involved the interviewing of a "sizable group of people in each company." The interviews were subjected to intense analysis and cross-checked with other data and psychological literature.

Herzberg's findings constituted a bombshell within the hermetic world of motivational research. He stated that the study had identified two sets of conditions that affect a worker. One set of conditions has the power to satisfy. These he called "motivators." The most important motivators are: achievement, recognition, the work itself, responsibility, and advancement. All of these factors are intrinsic to the job.

Herzberg defined another set of conditions affecting the worker—and it is this second finding that has given prominence and bite to his theory. These other conditions he terms, variously, as "dissatisfiers" or "hygiene factors." These are factors that have only a negative effect. When they are absent, or deficient, they cause the worker to be dissatisfied. But they cannot satisfy, and—no matter how abundantly they are provided for the worker—they cannot motivate him to do a better job.

The leading hygiene factors are company policy and administration, supervision, interpersonal relations, working conditions, and *salary.*

It was this last finding that provided the real dynamite. Herzberg was saying that money is *not* a true motivator. If you do not pay a man enough, true, he will become unhappy. But, above a certain point, you cannot motivate him through dollars, no matter how many you pay out. Salary, like the other hygiene factors, is not intrinsic to the job, but, rather, peripheral to it.

This proposition gave such new impetus and direction to the motivational movement as to turn it into a new subindustry. For the businessman—let's face it—it was welcome doctrine. Businessmen like to keep costs down, and the hygiene theory gave solid academic underpinning to the notion that more money did not buy better performance. The average manager was happy to embrace a theory that offered a rationale for keeping the lid on payroll costs.

Industry behaviorists seized upon Herzberg's concept as the avenue of approach to fresh answers to the age-old questions revolving around the need to get workers to perform better. There was renewed emphasis on such ideas as "job enrichment." Psychologists looked with concern at what they saw as the boredom and emptiness of so many jobs, and tried to find ways to motivate people through application of recognition, opportunity for advancement, and the other beneficial factors cited by Herzberg.

Of course there have been dissenters. Some find the theory too broad and simple. They talk about the *perception* of salary as varying widely with individuals and with job classifications. For example, young Madison Avenue copywriters—steeped in instant cynicism—regard the salary check as the only form of acceptable recognition. They are not striving for more money because of what it will buy, necessarily—after all, how many stereos can one own—but because it is a stamp of achievement to make more than somebody else, and to make more than you did last year or in your last job. Can salary, in this sense, be so conveniently classed as a "hygiene factor" that lacks the true power to motivate?

Efforts to follow through on the theory by conferring additional responsibility and "making the job more interesting" have met with cynicism on the part of workers. The industrial psychologist—convinced that Herzberg is right—maintains that, although the worker may say, "I work strictly for the buck," he is really impelled to do a better job by nonmonetary factors. But in a great many cases the worker does not seem to act in the way that the theorist says he should act (a phenomenon that has received ample and caustic attention from Peter Drucker).

Nevertheless, the Hygiene Theory has become vastly popular and influential. Dr. Herzberg was elevated to stardom on the business lecture circuit. He regaled management audiences with words that were eminently popular. This was not a chalky pedagogue who mumbled about "universes," "control groups," and "continuums." This was a down-to-earth business orator who drew laughter and applause by proclaiming his abiding faith in the "KITA" principle (Kick-in-the-Ass).

In the context of an examination of Peter Drucker, the point in raising the subject of Herzberg and the Hygiene Theory is that Drucker very definitely articulated the cardinal tenet of the theory years before Herzberg promulgated it.

In neither *The Motivation to Work* nor his later book, *Work and the Nature of Man*, does Herzberg cite Drucker as a source. Drucker makes a mild observation on this fact in a footnote in his recent and massive *Management: Tasks, Responsibilities, Practices*. He reviews with approval Herzberg's central finding, and then observes "This was first noted in my book, *The New Society*."

The New Society came out in 1950, nine years before Herzberg's *The Motivation to Work*. But even at that Drucker is understating the extent of his priority. In *The Future of Industrial Man*, Drucker focused on the inadequacy of salary as a motivator. He observed that "economic satisfactions are only negatively effective in society and politics. The absence of economic satisfactions creates severe social and political dislocations. But their presence does not by itself constitute a functioning society." A page later he compares economic satisfactions to vitamins, commenting that their absence creates deficiencies, but their presence does not provide calories.

Of course in this book Drucker was not writing about matters that lay strictly within the area of business and management. He was grappling with the philosophic, economic, and political problems of the larger world,

146

seeking to define a social order that would make the world fit to live in after World War II. His observations on the failure of money to satisfy appear within the context of his projection that minimum economic security would be an accomplished fact in the postwar democracies of the West, and that there would be equal distribution of the basic necessities regardless of income. Later, in *The New Society* and other books and essays, Drucker drew more precise attention to the application of this principle to the working man.

Nevertheless, his early articulation of the principle could not have been more clear. Of course he did not mount a broad-scale research project and interview hundreds of people. He did not buttress his observation with elaborate charts and tables, nor did he enter into extensive exposition of the methods he used in coming up with the idea. He merely stated it as a proposition that had become evident to him.

We have a tendency to dismiss ideas that are put forward clearly and without fanfare. If the concept is not surrounded by a zareba of jargon—if, instead, it is stated simply and positively—we seem to feel that it can't draw very much water. We judge contributions by weight and density rather than by simplicity and soundness.

Several people, working independently, can come up with identical findings without ever having had an inkling of what the other was doing. There is said to have been a case in the 1920s of a man in a remote Siberian village who worked for years on his original idea and finally invented the bicycle. And this indeed is the case with reference to the Hygiene Theory. Asked about Drucker's statements that seem to anticipate the theory, Herzberg responds that they are not familiar to him. He points out that they "have historic precedence in wisdom writings." However, he did not read the books in which Drucker made them. Herzberg's formulation stems directly from research and evaluation of job attitude survey findings and his post-doctoral studies at Public Health School of the differences between ameliorative medicine and corrective medicine.

"Theory X and Theory Y" is a perfect label for a

management concept. By itself it does not mean anything, but it is vaguely scientific. It is intriguing. It is easy to remember. And it constitutes a kind of jargonistic shorthand that makes the person who says it instantly identifiable as an "insider," one who is up-to-date with the latest thinking. A problem comes up in the personnel area: a manager nods knowingly and murmurs "Theory X." This stamps him as the man with the latest insights and answers.

This is not to say that the late Douglas McGregor was primarily interested in public-relations packaging when he coined the term. McGregor, a highly respected and thoroughly liked professor of management at MIT, had something he felt was important in providing a better way to manage human resources. It turned out that his concept was—and is—useful and valid. Nevertheless, McGregor could not have been unaware of the value of presenting an idea in a few catchy words.

McGregor articulated his concept in *The Human Side of Enterprise.* The essence of his proposition is that there are two theoretical assumptions relating to the management of people. Executives deal with subordinates according to one assumption or the other.

The traditional assumption—which McGregor styled "Theory X"—is that the average human being has an inherent dislike of work and will avoid it if he can. He prefers to be directed, avoids responsibility, has little ambition, and wants security above all. Because of this human characteristic, the worker must be controlled, coerced, and threatened in order to get him to make an adequate effort.

Theory X, said McGregor, was the way most bosses dealt with people. It led to "carrot-stick" management. And it was not a good way to manage. It was time to reformulate assumptions about human nature.

In place of Theory X, McGregor suggested Theory Y. This formulation states that working is as natural as playing or resting; that people want to work and achieve; that the average human being learns, under proper conditions, not only to accept but to seek responsibility; and that the intellectual potentialities of the average worker were only partly utilized. Therefore,

148

says Theory Y, external control and the threat of punishment are not the only ways to bring about effort: "Man will exercise self-direction and self-control in the service of objectives to which he is committed."

McGregor's book proceeded to give various justifications for the concept, and to show how it could be applied in such areas as appraisal and salary administration, staff-line relationships, strategy and planning, management development, and so forth.

"Theory X and Theory Y" was a sensation. *The Human Side of Enterprise* was widely bought and read. There were sequels, including, inevitably, a series of McGregor motivational films on the concept. Business teachers, motivational consultants, and training and personnel executives seized immediately on "Theory X and Theory Y" as a new way of looking at boss-subordinate relationships and a new framework on which a system of workable relationships could be built. The message took a little longer to get to line managers, but it arrived with impact. The new concept caught on with a vengeance, and Douglas McGregor was an instant star in the motivational firmament.

Where did "Theory X and Theory Y" come from? According to McGregor, it began with some questions about management raised by Alfred Sloan during a meeting of the Advisory Committee of MIT's School of Industrial Management, and was first fueled by a grant from the Alfred P. Sloan Foundation. (This is interesting in light of the distaste, ranging up to hostility, expressed by Sloan and his GM colleagues for the ideas that Drucker had put forth in his *Concept of the Corporation*, based on an analysis of General Motors.) McGregor remarked in the preface to *The Human Side of Enterprise* that he was "not an experimentalist." He added, "It is completely impossible for me to acknowledge individually the help I have received in evolving the ideas presented here." In the "References" following a number of the chapters there are mentions of a few of Drucker's books and articles, including *The Practice of Management*—but not *Concept of the Corporation* (an omission that may be understandable in light of the auspices under which McGregor worked). There are a couple of glancing references to Drucker in the text. One reads: "The concept of 'management by objectives' has received considerable attention in recent years, in part due to the writings of Peter Drucker. However, management by objectives has often been interpreted in a way which leads to no more than a new set of tactics within a strategy of management by direction and control." And, in the conclusion, McGregor notes, "As Peter Drucker has pointed out, the modern, large, industrial enterprise is itself a social invention of great historical importance. Unfortunately, it is already obsolete." (This point is made in *Concept of the Corporation*.)

Drucker has said, looking back on McGregor's book, that "McGregor conducted no original research. He acknowledged freely in his book that he had developed no new ideas but had formulated the ideas of others (and especially those I had put forth in three earlier books)." Whether or not McGregor's words and references constitute such a sweeping acknowledgment as that is, perhaps, a matter for speculation. Drucker—who expresses high regard for Douglas McGregor and for "Theory X and Theory Y," has always been relaxed and generous about the use by others of ideas he has originated.

For there seems little doubt that Drucker was an early and perceptive exponent of the proposition that is central to McGregor's concept. To cite just two examples, we can look into a couple of his works that predate *The Human Side of Enterprise* by some years. In *Concept of the Corporation* (1946) he says: "The second great lesson of the war was that it is not really true that the worker is happy and contented if he gets nothing out of his work except the pay check, or that he is not interested in his work and in his product. On the contrary, he yearns for a chance to know and to understand as much as possible about his work, his product, his plant, and his job." Then, in *The Practice of Management* (1954), Drucker lays out some principles about how the enterprise must learn to employ the worker as a "whole man," and concludes: "The basis for these concepts is clear: it must be the assumption that people want to work. We cannot make the assumption that they do not want to work. . . . To assume that people do not want to work would make the job of managing worker and work totally hopeless."

Of course, in the affairs of men, there is such a thing as coincidental generation of ideas. Charles Darwin learned this phenomenon firsthand. Darwin had labored for twenty years, painstakingly developing and documenting the theory of natural selection that was to change the world. Then, one day, Darwin received a letter from a naturalist and traveler, Alfred Russel Wallace. Wallace, who knew nothing of what Darwin was working on, opened by saying that, during a period of contemplation in the South Seas, an interesting idea had come to him. The letter then proceeded blithely to outline the entire theory on which Darwin had been working for so long. Thunderstruck, Darwin hurried to confront his friends with the problem. As a result of all this, Darwin's paper on evolution was read before the Linnaean Society the same day as Wallace's. Of course, Darwin's work—buttressed by a profoundly detailed experimental and theoretical structure—will live for all time. Wallace's instincts led him to the same conclusion, but his name is little remembered today.

However, what we see here is not a Wallace-Darwin effect. Other thinkers may have conducted elaborate projects to come up with the same concepts as Drucker —but the difference is that they did this *after* Drucker stated the ideas.

Perhaps there is a more apt analogy. In Mozart's operas you will sometimes hear an exquisite piece of music that lasts but a few bars and is never repeated. In *Don Giovanni*, for example, the scene in the Don's palace is threaded by a minuet—but the minuet is just background music to other things that dominate the scene. Nevertheless, this minuet is one of the most beautiful tunes ever written.

Offenbach was called the "Mozart of the Boulevards." But Offenbach knew his limitations. He wrote two or three outstanding airs, and they recur again and again. The well-known "Barcarolle" was first used in an operetta about Rhinemaidens, which was a flop; Offenbach hung onto it and used it extensively in *The Tales of Hoffman.* Similarly, you meet the famous can-can music under many different guises in the works of the French composer.

A very few people have the ability of a Mozart, to be so fruitful of ideas and tunes that they simply toss them off, caring little that others then seize upon the ideas and make careers of them.

Drucker has been an unprecedented generator of ideas in the area of work and institutions. His thoughts have been turned by others into stature, money, and fame. To Drucker this seems to matter little; he always has more tunes.

Indeed, the reader of this book who looks over the appendix, "The Sayings of Chairman Peter," is likely to find a number of original ideas that can—and no doubt will—be adopted and exploited by others. In this fact lies one of the most significant aspects of Drucker's influence.

10.

Drucker the Consultant

The ubiquitous consultant seems to be involved with more and more aspects of our lives.

Businessmen and corporations began to fuel the consultancy wildfire after World War II. Before then a businessman might occasionally bring in an "efficiency expert" to help with some specific problem, usually one dealing with a complex area of operations. Now we have consultants who study the business and the people in it from top to bottom, and offer advice for substantial fees. At last count there were more than two hundred "management consultants" listed in the Manhattan telephone book.

The consulting industry is self-perpetuating and self-proliferating. For example, when people as well as machinery and processes began to be regarded as appropriate subjects for the consultant's ministrations, there was a vast infusion into the area of academics representing outside disciplines. Foremost among these were the industrial psychologists. Industrial psychologists started to apply clinical techniques—the Rorschach "ink blot" test, for instance—to the task of determining the capabilities and potential of people on the payroll. Such applications might uncover neuroses, but this was not the principal aim. The prime beneficiary was not to be the subject of the testing but rather the employer, who paid for the studies and who received information about the people who worked for him.

But why stop there? The employer was interested, too, in the emotions, preferences, and abilities of people whom he was considering for employment. So a thriving subindustry in preemployment testing grew up.

From here it was a natural step to the notion that a consultant might be best qualified to find the best possible individual to fill a job, particularly a management job. So there arose the booming practice of the executive search consultant, commonly called the "headhunter." The headhunter is not primarily a psychologist, although lay headhunters make use of psychological applications and industrial psychologists engage in searches. The headhunter is the fellow who is hired by the Acme Company to find a vice-president of marketing, does the best he can to obtain an idea of just what the Acme Company is looking for, and then locates the ideal (or its closest possible facsimile), usually in another company. Headhunters don't ordinarily come back to their clients and recommend that the man for the job happens to be a fellow who is presently "at liberty." To this, the client is apt to respond, "What am I paying you for?" He wants the headhunter to bring him the head of someone currently working for another company.

And so the headhunter has become a familiar part of the management scene. An executive who has never been approached by one is not likely to want to admit it. By now everyone knows the approach. The first contact follows a euphemistically formal pattern as rigid as that prescribed for the courtiers of Louis XIV. The headhunter calls and says, "We are at present conducting a search to fill a very important position in the marketing area (or whatever it is). Your name has been mentioned to me as someone who might be able to help me in locating a suitable candidate for this impor-

154

tant position with one of the outstanding firms in the world."

There is a pause. The manager receiving the call then says, "I can't think of anyone offhand; but, you know, if the job is everything you say it is, I might even be a little bit interested myself." Another pause. Then the headhunter, with a simulation of sincerity that would not disgrace an Olivier or a Billy Graham, says, "Oh? Gee, it never occurred to me that *you* might be interested! In that case perhaps we might have lunch and talk it over. . . ." And they take it from there.

You have consultants who tell which people to put in which jobs; you have consultants who tell you whom to hire; you have consultants who tell you who "is not working out," you have consultants who go out and find the replacement for the person who is "not working out." During the economic downturn—as a fine example of resourceful adaptation—there developed a branch of consultancy that tells the businessman how to fire a person. (These consultants designate themselves as "out-processors.")

But of course the consulting trade revolving around the hiring and use of people is only part of it. There are consultants for everything—nowadays, not just in business. Today we have consultants who tell us how to save our marriages, do the housework, talk to the kids, perform the act of sex. There is not much in life for which you cannot hire an expert whose task it is to tell you how to do it better.

Peter Drucker is by far the best-known individual management consultant in the history of the profession. Most consultants are corporate entities. The business in need of counseling hires a firm—Booz, Allen or McKinsey or Cresap or any of the myriad others—and the consulting firm assigns a group, probably under the leadership of an associate of the firm. Individual members of consulting companies become well known; but they still work as part of a team. In most cases star performers from consulting companies do not become widely recognized in their own right until—as often happens—they "go over to the client side" and take top executive jobs with corporations whom they formerly advised.

Drucker has always been on his own, the "lone wolf" of the consulting profession. He works with no team; he does not operate out of an office; he has no organization and no "front." The prospective client picks up the phone and dials a number. He reaches Peter Drucker or Doris, his wife. And, like as not, the prospective client is turned away with a courtly refusal before he even gets to the subject of the fee. Drucker travels to keep up his international governmental practice; but, in most cases, business clients must now come to him. Nevertheless, the demand for Drucker's services seems, if anything, to have grown in recent years. But the demand far exceeds the supply.

Consulting was once his principal activity. Starting with the monumental General Motors assignment in the mid-1940s, Drucker worked with many of the principal firms in the country and the world. He was at the crest of the wave of the demand for consulting services.

And why not? Drucker's work has contributed in enormous degree to the proliferation of consulting services. By developing the craft of management into a distinct discipline, he was able to show businessmen how little they really know about management—and how much they need assistance from the outside.

Businessmen hire consultants because they have problems that need solutions, and they lack the strength and specialization on the payroll to deliver these solutions. That's one reason, and it would seem to be the overwhelmingly logical one. But there are other reasons, some of them far less logical, that have made consultants in general—and Drucker in particular—both necessary and rich.

Belief in magic did not disappear from the human equation when our ancestors stopped painting themselves blue. We still believe in magic; or we'd like to. The kind of magic we believe in has changed as our needs have changed.

The magician is someone who makes things happen in ways that the layman does not understand. The more complicated things become, and the more difficult the problems we face, the more we yearn for the outsider with the magic wand who will intone the right incantations and make our problems go away.

Business is immeasurably more complicated than it used to be. To a greater degree than is likely to be admitted at a meeting of the President's Club, corporate leaders have come to rely on the latter-day counterpart of the magician: the consultant. Of course this fellow does not come around with a bone in his nose and a stick with feathers on the end; he carries a briefcase and dresses in the approved "Man of Consequence" executive style. But he brings a kind of magic with him. He is expected to come up with the answers. To do this he practices his own brand of magic. His implements are charts, reports, printouts. His mission is to make things better.

This is not to say that a consultant can get by on sheer front. Consultants do deliver, every day, and for perfectly good reasons. The well set-up consulting firm has specialists who are able to bring far more expertise to bear on business problems than are the managers within the structure of the client company. Furthermore, the experienced consultant has seen most problems before; he has a background on which to call. The line manager has not had anything like the same amount of experience in dealing with certain kinds of difficulties.

But, beyond this, there is a mystique to consulting. The consultant is not just an individual who visits your company to do a specific job. He is, in a way, a measure of the client company's success and standing. If your company has arrived, you should be able to hire the best consultant on retainer. He is of great substantive help to you, no doubt about that; but, in addition, it is considered no bad thing for a board chairman to be able to say, over lunch with one of his peers, "Yes, we had McKinsey make a study on that for us two years ago." The businessman who does not bring in a battery of august counselors on a regular basis is not envied as being a lucky man who does not have problems. Other businessmen know damn well that he has problems, and they conclude that he lacks the resources and/or sophistication to hire the approved magicians to take care of them. When one listens to corporate executives dropping the names of consultants who have and are serving them, one realizes the degree to which chicness influences their use. There are fashionable consultants just as there are fashionable society doctors. They do a good job; but, in addition, their retention bestows a certain cachet on the patient.

Peter Drucker became, to a host of businessmen, the preeminent fashionable consultant. And this was somewhat strange, because Drucker has never played the mystique of consulting to the hilt as many others do. He would often seem anxious to point out that what he was doing was really very simple, nothing that could not be done by the client if it had only occurred to him.

Of course this is not really descriptive of the contribution that Drucker makes to a client. "Less is more" said Robert Browning in *Andrea Del Sarto*, and that legend later became identified with the style and approach of the great architect Ludwig Mies van der Rohe. The client who brought in Peter Drucker as a consultant without knowing much about the way Drucker worked probably got less than he expected in some ways—and immeasurably more in the ways that really counted.

He certainly got something different from the ordinary run of consultants. For one thing, he got a counselor with a distinctly different point of view. Most consultants tend to be somewhat complimentary, perhaps even reverent, toward the clients they are serving and toward management as a profession. Not Drucker; he has never minced many words about his opinions of the way most businesses are being run. He remarks that he is often thought of as more of an *in*sultant than a consultant, and this sobriquet does not bother him a bit. In an essay in *Peter Drucker: Contributions to Business Enterprise* —a series of tributes to Drucker—John F. Gibbons of Pace College describes himself as recalling to Drucker the remark that "no more than about three to five percent of American businesses are really well managed." Drucker's reply is characteristic: "Did I put it that high? I must have been in an optimistic mood."

The client cannot expect backslapping congratulations from Drucker. Another thing he would be unwise to anticipate is painstakingly detailed blueprints for the revision of procedures. Drucker paints with a broader brush. He does not consider himself very gifted in the operational area; he is surprised at the influence he has had on this facet of management.

Here is Drucker, talking about his approach: "The contribution I make to a client is basically to be very stupid and very dense; ask simple, fundamental questions; demand that you be thoughtful with the answers; and demand that you make decisions on what's important. I feel very strongly that a client who leaves this room feeling he has learned a lot that he didn't know before is a stupid client; either that, or I've done a poor job. He should leave this office saying, 'I know all this —but why haven't I done anything about it?' "

Naturally there is a lot more to it than that. The simplicity of the conversation between Drucker and the client is deceptive. Drucker does his homework thoroughly before talking with the client. He absorbs a great deal of detail about the company.

And he follows up: "The greatest contribution I make isn't what happens in this room. It's when I sit down and write him a letter, a week or two later. Sometimes the letter is one page, sometimes it's fifty pages. And that's the greatest contribution I usually make."

As one talks with clients who have been served by Drucker, certain principles of his consulting approach emerge. They are individualistic, growing out of his personality and philosophy, and yet—as he says—they are simple enough to be applied by any manager on his own, without benefit of a third party.

Drucker *simplifies*. He cuts through to isolate the one or two problems that are most critical and about which something can be done. At any given time a businessman is faced with a multiplicity of difficulties. At the moment that he talks with a consultant, there may be a couple of dozen problems, large and small, on his desk. Some have arisen recently; others are of long standing.

The manager who is engulfed with these matters is not in a good position to step back and look at the situation objectively. He may assign more importance to a new problem that impinges sharply on his consciousness than he does to a problem that has been around for a long time and to whose dull ache he has made some adjustment. So he insists that the consultant address himself to the new problem—even though the new problem may be of considerably less importance than the old one, and indeed even though it may grow out of the long-standing difficulty.

Now, any experienced and capable consultant will find out as much as he can about the situation. He is apt to see that the prospective client has his priorities mixed up, and that the real contribution would be a full-scale attack on a difficulty that is not uppermost in the businessman's mind at the moment. The consultant will say this. But if the client insists, the consultant faces a dilemma of his own. He wants to perform effectively and ethically but he needs to eat as well. In many cases such a confrontation is resolved by means of an interior compromise made by the consultant. He avers that he will deploy his resources to solve the problem that the client wants solved; at the same time he makes a determination (which he may or may not express directly, according to the circumstances and the personality of the client) that he will try to clear up the problem that he feels to be the most urgent.

Drucker does not make this kind of compromise. To him the identification of the problem is not a preliminary to the conclusion of the deal. It may be the single most important thing the consultant can do for the client. In fact, it may be the *only* thing the consultant can do for the client. And Drucker does not envision himself as "doing" things for the client. Rather, he serves as a stimulant and catalyst that enables the client to see and ultimately do things for himself.

So Drucker simplifies. He puts an order of priority on problems. He says, "Let's not talk about twenty-four problems. Let's figure out what you really want to do, and see if it makes sense."

Drucker focuses on the consulting *objective,* not the means of attaining it. Some consultants become well-known for their specialization in a particular approach to helping a client—intense analysis of operations, the amassing of copious volumes of information, "sensitivity training" for executives, a currently popular new concept in management, or whatever. This is natural, given the economics of the consulting business. The problems do not change, but new ways to attack those problems come along. Some are useful, some are mere fads. The consultant who latches on to a new approach that captures the imagination of prospective clients and receives good publicity will be in demand. It is the kind of treatment that draws the business, not the rate of cure.

Drucker does not concentrate on any one method. He is wary of current fads. Since his mission is to help the client to see things that are already before him and do things that he is already capable of doing, Drucker uses the mix of approaches that strike him as being most handy to the task. To hear Drucker tell it, his method is predominantly Socratic. He describes himself as sitting back and asking "stupid" questions:

What do you really want to do?

Why do you want to do it?

What are you doing now?

Why do you do it that way?

Those who have enjoyed Peter Drucker's services will tell you that this is by no means all he does. It is true that he employs the "simple question" approach to great effect, but this does not exhaust his repertoire. He will on occasion deliver lengthy and detailed analysis of divisions and operations, replete with facts and statistics. The facts and statistics are not important to him; he will not slave for hours to make sure they are right. Sometimes if the right statistic is not available he will make it up. (The client or listener who tries to write down a string of numbers and percentages cited by Drucker is wasting his time. They are not the gist of what Drucker is saying, and they may, in themselves, be wildly misleading.) Drucker is trying to do nothing more than to make people think. His "analyses" are often the equivalent of a writer's creation of miniscule detail to give verisimilitude to a bold design. Purists will—and do—object that this is not scientific. This is probably true, but for Drucker it works.

Or, Drucker may take any one of a number of other approaches to achieve his end. He may call a group of managers together and harangue them with the fervor of Knute Rockne addressing the old Notre Dame football team between halves of a game that is being lost. Or he may concentrate on one individual and deliver what may seem to be a harsh critique of performance.

In all of these methods, and in others employed by Drucker, the particular nature of the approach is not nearly as important as the objective he wants to reach. And that objective is the creation of new ways of looking at the problem that will enable the client to see where he is going wrong and to spot what he can do to go right.

One client, describing a long and fruitful relationship with Drucker, says, "We could always rely on him to give us an insight that we had not seen before, and to guide us from insight to solution. To do this he took every conceivable tack. Sometimes he would just do nothing. Just listen. Drucker has a way of listening that makes you think, really think, about what you're saying. Whatever he does, sometimes you are aware that you are witnessing a performance, but what a hell of a performance, and what an effect!"

Drucker uses a variety of methods to get through to clients and to make them think. However, there are approaches that he rules out of bounds. Some of the concepts that achieve popular currency among managers and consultants he dismisses as harmless but ineffectual gimmicks. There are other approaches that he sees as being potent, but as doing more harm than good. For example, he is highly dubious about sensitivity training in and out of management.

In talking over the "sensitivity" or "T-group" approach, he says, "I'm one of those people who believe that one is not entitled to inflict damage on the living organism. I do not believe in dissection of the body while it is still alive. The casualty rate is unacceptable. Even those who push this kind of thing admit the casualty rate is 10 percent. Imagine that you had a drug that would be useful in preventing cancer—but which had 10 percent damaging, irreversible, permanent side effects. How long would it stay on the market?

"As a matter of fact I think the casualty rate [on sensitivity training] is much higher. And I haven't seen the improvement. For most people these sessions may be just a harmless emotional binge. But for a significant proportion—the weak, the lame, the defenseless, the shy, the vulnerable—this is a very dangerous thing. It gives the wolves a chance to go in and tear the lambs to pieces. And there are others, who don't start out as wolves, who acquire a taste for it. I am deeply opposed to these things. If we applied the FDA rules to psychotherapy there would not be one prescription on the market. They all have casualty rates that are not acceptable. Maybe in the hands of masters like Doug McGregor—people who would keep tight control—it could be all right, but there's no way to keep unskilled people from running it. In the hands of the typical practitioner sensitivity training is like letting children play with razor blades."

Drucker does something else as a consultant. Consistent with the principles he has long espoused, he concentrates on maximizing strength instead of minimizing weakness. The natural tendency of the consultant is to concentrate on weakness. Weaknesses are the reasons he is called in. They are the obvious flaws that he gets paid to correct. He knows that he will be judged more on the short-run plugging of holes (even if the plugging job is transitory) than on the long-run development of strengths. So naturally he goes after the weaknesses, even if what he does may be no more than a cosmetic job, or in any event less productive than the maximization of strong points.

Drucker focuses on strength from the outset. He says, "Let's not talk about what you can't do. Let's talk about what you want to do and what you have the capability of doing." The client must be doing something right now. When he fixes his eye on what he is doing right, and figures out what makes it right, his next decision is whether to concentrate time, money, and effort on getting the most out of his strength, or instead devoting his efforts to correcting his weaknesses. He cannot give the same effort to both jobs. Drucker's inclination is to guide in the way of riding the strengths rather than bucking the weaknesses. Here, he feels, is where the most can be gained. No organization is perfect; weaknesses will always be there; but they become insignificant when strengths are fully exploited.

The whole thrust of Drucker's consulting approach is to concentrate on the future, not the past; strength, not weakness, people, not systems. He emphasizes objectives, strategies, contributions. He demands that the right, simple questions be faced—and answered. And he works on the assumption that the answers are already there.

As in all of his manifestations, there are pros and cons about Drucker as a consultant. Charles David Flory, himself for many years a distinguished business counselor, says of Drucker: "I find him interesting. I have read some of his books; I'm neither critical nor overly excited. I have consulted in the same companies that have used his services; the results are about average for competent consultants.

"I agree with much that he says. . . . His emphasis on ethics and the philosophical is a much-needed point of view in American society today.

"But, isn't he shocked? Many managers have never heard of him; others quote him without knowing what he is saying; and his most ardent supporters wave the Drucker flag as if it were the alpha and omega of management."

Long-term Drucker clients tend to border on idolatry. Frank Rooney, president of the Melville Shoe Company, Harrison, New York, is an outspoken fan: "He's the greatest thing that ever happened to me."

Drucker has been working with Rooney and Melville since 1961. Rooney says, "I didn't go to the Harvard Business School. I have a feeling that spending time with Drucker is more worthwhile."

Rooney recalls that, when Drucker was on the East Coast, he would meet with Melville's managers as much as six times a year—a day at a time, spaced through twelve months. With Drucker's move to Claremont, and his diminution of travel, the contacts have become scarcer. But, to Rooney, Drucker's ability to contribute has not been reduced at all: "He has a brilliant mind; you know, it's hard for me to believe that he's never really been in an operating position. He has a terrific understanding. He cuts through quickly, picks up the situation easily. He is just one hell of an adviser . . . always worth his fee, which is, I think, $1,000 a day now."

Sometimes Drucker would meet with Rooney alone; at other times division heads were brought in: "They would just sit there with their ears open. They had great respect and admiration for him."

In working with Melville, Drucker rarely got involved in specific questions of operation. His concentration focused on broader questions of organization and management philosophy: "He kept urging us not to build a lot of superstructure, to remain thin at the top. . . . You know, he does pontificate a bit; sometimes he'd go on and on and you'd think, we're wasting time—and then, all of a sudden, my God, the lights would go on!"

In the end, like many of Drucker's clients, Rooney views the relationship and contribution as a personal one: "Whatever success I've had is probably due more to him than anyone else I can think of."

Such accolades are not garnered by many consultants; and never with the breadth and scale with which they come to Drucker.

Robert Townsend, former president of Avis and author of *Up the Organization*, recalls how he worked with Drucker:

"It was when I was with American Express. When a problem came up, I would write it up laboriously, in great detail, as if I were explaining it to my twelve year old son. Then I'd outline the solutions as I saw them.

"I'd mail this to Drucker, saying, 'Read this and give me half a day' (which was all I could afford). Then I'd book a room at the Union League Club. I'd shut off the telephone—pull it out of the wall if necessary; Drucker is an impulsive phone-call taker.

"He'd sit on the bed and we'd talk for five hours.

It was marvelous; some of the best half-days I ever spent. This is how Drucker is most useful."

*   *   *   *   *

Here is Drucker, early in 1975, talking about his consulting work:

General Motors was the first big client. After that they came in fair numbers. Chesapeake and Ohio was a good client for three years. In the early Fifties I worked with General Electric. The basic structural design for their great decentralization project had already been completed, for the most part, when I went there. The architect of the GE plan was Harold Smiddy, a very extraordinary man. After GE there were many clients. The late Fifties and early Sixties is when I worked with the greatest number of companies.

My consulting work has changed quite a bit over the years. What I do now I would not have done twenty-five years ago; I would not have been qualified for it, or the means to do it did not exist. In GE, for example, I would work on a specific project, let us say the definition of the service staffs, their organization, relationships, structure, work assignments, and so forth. Typically I would work with a small GE task force. I have never had any staff of my own; I refuse to have a staff. The contribution I make to a client is to help his people to learn something.

Today I do not do the kind of thing I did at GE. That's too much like work; I don't work any more in that sense. I work differently now—although the consulting work is still very important; seventy days a year.

Occasionally I visit a country which I had better not mention, because while I've been working with them for years, officially I don't exist. Public opinion will put up with neither American advisers nor unofficial cabinet members. This takes days of preparation; it's very hard work. I'm always accused of being far too radical. In the Sixties I kept telling them that their problem would be jobs, jobs, jobs, jobs; that the population explosion would certainly mean that they would have an enormous number of young people much better trained than their parents, and with much bigger expectations. I say to the president, I fully understand why you have to take a very socialist stance in public, but I hope you realize that the main purpose of this is to enable you to do terribly conservative things in private. And I back it up with facts and figures. He may not like it greatly; he may even choose not to hear it.

International consulting is interesting but it can be depressing. There is not one competent government in the world today. It's frightening. For several years I have been playing with the idea of a book called *Can Government Be Saved?* When I was in Salzburg a few years ago, the Austrian prime minister Bruno Kreisky asked about my next book and I told him the title, "Can government be saved?" Kreisky gave me a long level look and said—not smiling, in dead earnest—"Do you really think it's worth trying?"

Look at the programs pursued by any major government in the past fifty years. Every program, except for warfare, has achieved the exact opposite of its pronounced goal.

There are many businesses in which I am a permanent part-time unofficial member of the management. However, I work with people, not with organizations. When the management changes, I go out. I don't want to be part of the mortgage.

The opportunity to work as a part-time member of the management is really the answer to why I like smaller companies. This is easy to do in a small company. It's not impossible with the big ones; recently I sat down for a day with an old friend who is now chairman and chief executive of a giant; I've known him for twenty-five years. We talked very freely about the structure of his office and his relationships. But I know his company very well, which made it possible for me to clear up a few things that were bothering him.

By and large, however, this is more fun to do with a

medium-sized company. Whether it's more productive, I don't know; but it's more fun. It's also easier. You can sit down with a small group and make decisions. A big company doesn't work that way; it can't.

And of course there is the matter of my working in my home. The head of a large corporation may stop off and see me on his way to Japan, but it's no big thrill. Others do not have the time to come here, or certainly to bring a team here. There are large clients whom I see when I go to New York for other purposes.

But for at least some smaller businessmen, coming out here can still be fun.

A great deal of my consulting involves a day or two. I would say that five days per year with a company is very active involvement. When the total spent with any one client is kept down, I am able to see more people and get more variety. In 1974 I spent a total of forty-three consulting days, within which I was able to include great diversity: typically, a trip to a Latin American country, then a day with a university, three days with a fairly large manufacturer near here, one day with a Canadian appliance firm, four days with a small service company, two days with some people from Germany, several days with state and city governments. It makes for a nice balance. I try to keep the total of my consulting and speaking days at 100; otherwise I would never have time for writing.

* * * * *

Drucker operates without staff of any kind. One of the ways he manages to keep down demands on his time is by use of printed mail-back cards. One reads:

MR. PETER F. DRUCKER

GREATLY APPRECIATES YOUR KIND INVITATION

BUT REGRETS THAT HE CANNOT ACCEPT

ANY SPEAKING ENGAGEMENTS FOR THE TIME BEING

Another goes like this:

MR. PETER F. DRUCKER

GREATLY APPRECIATES YOUR KIND INTEREST,

BUT IS UNABLE TO:

CONTRIBUTE ARTICLES OR FOREWORDS; COMMENT ON

MANUSCRIPTS OR BOOKS; TAKE PART IN PANELS AND

SYMPOSIA; JOIN COMMITTEES OR BOARDS OF ANY KIND;

ANSWER QUESTIONNAIRES; GIVE INTERVIEWS: AND

APPEAR ON RADIO OR TELEVISION.

Most of those who get in touch with Drucker seem to take this sort of turndown in good part. Not all. One journalist in a nearby city asked for an interview and received the latter card. He sent it back to Drucker with a hand-written addendum: "And Mr. ————— regrets to declare that he will never again review a Peter Drucker book or mention a Peter Drucker article or refer to Peter Drucker in any way, shape or form."

* * * * *

No matter how many invitations or offers he turns down, Drucker continues to be in lively demand. Today he seems more responsive to requests for consulting work from abroad than those generated within the United States. He assesses his foreign practice with the same kind of prideful self-deprecation that he likes to apply to his American work:

I work with institutions in other countries much as I do in the United States. I say, let's think through what you really want to do, and then let's do it in your context. Of course I have already found out something about the context.

For example, in Japan the American occupation had done absolutely insane things, because it had imposed an American pattern without looking at Japanese social habits. I just sat down with some people, said, "What is it you want to do?" and we looked for the best pattern we could establish within a Japanese context.

In Canada and other countries I work the same way.

In Canada the first objective was to discover the problem with the civil service, which was not working well. It became clear that civil servants simply could not move up through the ranks. They would run into blocks. Each agency was separate; only at the very top could you go from one agency to another. The level of frustration was incredibly high. The only way to get around it was to get yourself transferred to an embassy or the World Bank or something like that for a spell and then come back.

Not everyone by any means could do that. Here were talented people ready for big jobs, and they were bottled up.

My contribution was, as always, to say let's think through what is needed and right and then worry about how we can do it. Let's not worry about all the things we can't do. Let's decide right at the beginning that a commission like this can bring about one change, not 196. What is the one thing we want to get Parliament to adopt? We have a 50–50 chance with one thing; we have no chance with a hundred things. (That's why the Hoover Commission has no impact. Everything it proposes makes sense, but at last count there were 2,849 proposals.)

So we built a personnel management role into the structure, with a transfer mechanism. It didn't work very well, but it worked.

I always ask, "What's the one thing you want to do?" In Mexico they call me "Señor Una Cosa."

I will be sitting down with the Japanese to talk about university reform. I know what needs to be done, but they're not going to buy it. Not yet. It's pretty radical.

That the Japanese students riot is not something to marvel at. It is amazing that they don't tear the joint down and burn it up. The conditions are horrible, and to the perplexity and dismay of the anti-McCarthyites, I don't mean just the physical conditions.

Two prestige universities in Japan, Tokyo and Kyoto, form a monopoly. They are really bad universities. I would break that monopoly up. What is needed is a reform of the faculty board. I would abolish the system of the "Herr Professor" and create true faculties. They aren't going to like it—but it's now possible to do it.

As an example of the situation now we can take Keio, which is the best private university. It calls itself the Japanese Harvard. Before World War II Keio had 1,400 students. It has grown to 48,000 today without adding a single lecture room or a single chair in the library; and attendance at lectures is compulsory.

Conditions in a Japanese university are unspeakable. It was wise to decide not to put all the money into buildings, but they have overdone it grotesquely. And then there are the "Herr Professors." One very famous one wrote a wonderful book on industrial organization. He did no research; that would be beneath his dignity. He copied the German books on the subject and he did it rather well. This professor taught the one course at Tokyo University that was compulsory for everyone—introductory economics. Twenty years ago, when this was going on, there were 18,000 students. The professor, who was an insomniac, gave the course at 4:30 in the morning, on a suburban campus reached by no public transportation, in a lecture hall jammed to at least twice its capacity. And attendance was taken carefully.

Twenty years have made a difference. Something that extreme could not happen today. However, it's still bad. Until very recently you could not incur the displeasure of the professor because it was your only way of getting a job. In applying for a job, it is the height of rudeness to ask a question to which a possible answer is no. So you needed a middle-man. The professor was the middle-man. Now they have instituted entrance examinations. It's greatly undermined the power of the professor, thank God.

Living conditions at the universities in Japan are horrible. And, though the tuition is minimal, they are very expensive. To file for permission to take the en-

171

trance examination, you pay $500. To sit for it, you pay another $500. Of those who file for the examination, 10 percent are admitted. Ninety percent forfeit their deposit. Only one out of two hundred passes the examination. But everyone pays the fee; that's how the Japanese university is financed. They have no tuition fees; of each 1,000 applicants who all pay a median of $750, only 20 are admitted. So you get $750,000 for twenty students.

Japanese employers figure that college graduates have a monopoly on all managerial and professional jobs. If you don't go beyond high school, you are a manual worker. If you get a college degree, you are a professional administrator. This is a designation of status, nothing more; employers don't assume the kids have learned anything. But there's no possibility of circumventing the system.

I didn't like the Mexican land reform. I sensed that it came at the worst possible time; my Mexican friends were all convinced that, since Mexico had achieved a good surplus, food prices would continue to be low. I was not a bit convinced. But the thing had to be done politically.

However, the ultimate political effect was worse than no land reform. Up until the moment of the actual land reform the campesinos all believed that everything would be all right if only the land were distributed. The Mexican problem wasn't land, it never has been; the Mexican problem is water, and one of the things I've learned is that social revolution doesn't produce rainfall. I said to my Mexican friends, 'What you need is ten inches more rain in the north and less rain in the south, and I don't know any social revolution that's going to bring that about.' They didn't like it a bit; and anyway, the land reform had to be done.

Mexico's food production dropped 70 percent in three years, and Mexico again became a heavy food importer, and the poor campesino scratching out a little corn and beans on his small tract was worse off than before.

* * * * *

Drucker the consultant. Informality. Men sitting around in a room, talking. No team of experts, no elaborate charts, no computer printouts. Just talk about people, problems, relationships, structure, the future.

It may not look very scientific. It is the way Drucker has always done it.

11.

The Role Drucker
Has Not Filled

No matter how much a man has accomplished, it is always possible to point to things that he did not do.

Drucker's preeminence as the analyst of institutions and the architect of the craft of management is almost universally accepted. In recent years the edifice for which he drew the plans has been subjected to wave upon wave of bitter assault. Business, the free enterprise system, and the concept of profit are all under fire. There are many who feel that Peter Drucker is uniquely qualified to organize a cogent and effective defense.

Drucker does not conceal his opinions of the merits of the attacks. But he has not been out in front in the effort to fight back. In seeking the reasons for the omission we may be able to find out something about the man.

The waning days of the Weimar Republic produced a rare panoply of intellectuals: Erik Erikson, Hannah Arendt, Erich Fromm, and Herbert Marcuse to name just a few. When Hitler came, they left Germany, or at least the fortunate ones did, while there was still time.

They differ widely in personality and discipline, but they share a combination of piercing intelligence and intellectual boldness that endures in its influence on the world far beyond the "thousand-year-Reich."

Drucker—younger, not nearly as well known—left Germany during the same period.

There are parallels between Drucker and Herbert Marcuse, although Drucker was born twelve years later. Both left Germany, came ultimately to the United States, entered academia, and exerted enormous influence in their respective fields. Both were unhappy with the state of things, convinced that the world would undergo fundamental changes. Both were students of power and the institutions through which power is exerted.

From the vantage point of today, however, we find that the similarities are washed out by the obvious differences. Marcuse the Marxist; Drucker the Conservative. Marcuse the wild man of the campuses, Drucker the sage of Claremont. Marcuse the Peter Hermit of the youth revolution, Drucker the Nestor of the establishment. Marcuse the abomination of the businessman, Drucker his patron saint. Marcuse the destroyer of the free enterprise system, Drucker its guardian and explicator.

The differences in what the two men have come to represent are so enormous as to make them seem diametrically opposed. But the underlying similarities in background and area of interest offer a tantalizing field of speculation about what might have happened if these two had actively confronted each other as representatives of opposing forces. It seems, as they say in boxing, like a natural match-up.

Why didn't it happen?

Some men seem natural opponents. John Kenneth Galbraith and William F. Buckley enliven the lecture circuit as cordial enemies, debating the respective merits of their economic viewpoints, but clashing also over a wide constellation of social issues. Fifty years ago there was no certainty that Clarence Darrow would confront William Jennings Bryan over the question of evolution, but when they came together in Dayton, Tennessee, at the "Monkey Trial" the confrontation was so satisfyingly inevitable as to constitute what playwrights call the "obligatory scene."

Some potential adversaries seem like "naturals"—but they never join battle. When Senator Joseph R. McCarthy was riding high in the early 1950s, embattled liberals looked around for a saviour. Many thought they had found their champion in a young congressman from Massachusetts. This budding Galahad was attractive, intelligent, witty, liberal, wealthy, and Catholic. To make his credentials perfect, he was a war hero. But this Achilles stayed in his tent. John F. Kennedy's eyes rested on other things.

When Herbert Marcuse was urging a generation on to destroy civilization, Peter Drucker was placidly teaching his classes, advising his clients, giving his talks and writing his essays and books on management and the industrial society. This was the very industrial society that Marcuse and his followers were putting to the torch. Nobody who knew Drucker, or who read his work, had any doubt about where he stood. But many felt he should be in the vanguard of the counterattack. After all, the corporate society under fire was in many ways Drucker's invention. He possessed the depth, the background, the strength and the skill to mount powerful responses to the onslaught. But Drucker chose to do no such thing. It may be interesting to seek the reasons.

Peter Drucker has certainly not always played it safe. The circumstances of his departure from Germany testify to that.

As we have seen, it was Drucker's conservatism and the strong Christian underpinning of his approach to society and government that made Drucker decide to oppose Nazism and to leave Germany in 1933.

When Drucker arrived in the United States in 1937, Marcuse was already there. Ever since they have gone their separate ways—teaching, writing, consulting. Drucker was building his massive philosophical construct of the industrial society, clarifying and rationalizing the system and instructing practitioners of management in how to make it work. Marcuse was array-

176

ing his insights and energies against the moment of all-out assault on Drucker's system.

Both were concerned with freedom. Elsewhere in this book we discuss in some detail the philosophy of Peter Drucker. Here, briefly, it can be noted that Drucker yokes freedom with responsibility, sees man within the framework of the Christian ethic, considers it essential that the individual find status and function within a working society. Marcuse maintained that no one was free and rejected the traditional verities as hypocrisy and oppression.

Both were concerned with institutions in general and with the corporation in particular. Drucker postulated the corporation as the representative institution of the society. He had come to this point logically. In *The End of Economic Man*, his first book in English, he had described the destruction of the structure of civilization that had served for centuries. In *The Future of Industrial Man* he had called for a new social order but had presented few particulars to accompany his sweeping philosophical and historical analysis. In *The New Society* he had given flesh to his vision of man finding fulfillment by finding his place within a rational industrial society. In *Concept of the Corporation* he had explored in detail—and for the first time—a business organization as a social entity, not just an economic structure. And in *The Practice of Management* and subsequent books he took the next logical steps of outlining the ways in which the corporation—this "representative social institution"—could be managed successfully.

Marcuse looked at the corporation as the embodiment of repression. The system represented by the corporation was "managed by totalitarian controls and sustained by obscene violence." The society stifled the true needs of the masses. Worse, it permitted no erotic sublimation. Still worse, it gave its slaves a spurious feeling of well-being that sedated them well below the flash point and made revolution difficult if not impossible.

Drucker had said—some years earlier—that there was "never a more efficient, honest or dedicated group than the professional managers of American corporations." Marcuse looked upon these same individuals and saw

177

something different. These people were running the world, he said, moving its money, allocating resources, manipulating its people. "Who elected them?" he demanded.

Here Marcuse struck a nerve. Drucker had come to the conclusion that the corporation would be the linchpin of the new society. But from the beginning, one of the foundations of his philosophical approach had been *legitimacy:* "No society can function as a society unless it gives the individual member status and function, and unless the decisive social power is legitimate power." And again, "No illegitimate ruler can possibly be a good or wise ruler."

Legitimacy—the right to rule—recurred continually in Drucker's early writings. The old order was gone, and the need for a new order was clear: "We must try to develop . . . a new, free and equal noneconomic society on the foundations and from the premises of an existing economic society." Conserve what was good from the traditional, and then build on it.

But the new society would be an industrial society. The corporation was the functioning unit. Managers ran the corporation and thus the society. But who owned the corporation? The concept of entrepreneurship was fading, and the notion that a corporation was owned and controlled by its stockholders was a pleasant fairy tale. The key men in the new society were the managers, and they were not owners or representatives. *Who had elected them?*

Drucker never really solved the problem of legitimacy. His compromise rationalization is summed up in his conclusion, "That the enterprise is not a legitimate government does not mean it is an illegitimate one." Nevertheless, the legitimacy of managerial surpremacy has continued to trouble Drucker. He, however, was willing to seek justification for the role of the manager. Marcuse, on the other hand, was telling his troops (in line with his advocation of "methodological use of obscenities" to subvert the "linguistic universe of the establishment") that it was laudable to address these managers as "motherfuckers"—they were not, after all, fathers, but rather men who had committed (in some unspecified way) "the unspeakable Oedipal crime."

Peter Drucker has always been an orderly, logical thinker and a lucid speaker and writer. He seeks to clarify, rationalize, build. Marcuse gives little thought to these things, dismissing them as conceits of the repressive establishment. Reading Drucker is a pleasure; reading Marcuse is drudgery. For example, Marcuse opens *Counterrevolution and Revolt* with the statement: "The Western world has reached a new stage of development: now, the defense of the capitalist system requires the organization of counterrevolution at home and abroad. In its extreme manifestations, it practices the horrors of the Nazi regime." There follows a litany of barbarities: massacres, torture, religious wars. And the paragraph concludes with the astonishing observation: "The new composition of the Supreme Court institutionalizes the process of reaction. And the murder of the Kennedys shows that even Liberals are not safe if they appear as too liberal."

Drucker would dismiss this as incoherent nonsense, which it is. But it has nevertheless been very effective nonsense, although short-lived. Marcuse's demagogic philosophy helped to impel hundreds of thousands of young people into revolt against the "system," send stealthy bombers to destroy universities and businesses, reduce segments of a society to chaos. And while, of course, there were many who rose to denounce Marcuse and point out his divergences from reality and common sense, there was not a figure of real stature who was able to put a cogent case for the industrial society.

Herbert Marcuse, as a Marxist, harbored for a long time the expectation, or at least the wish, that the working classes would rise and throw off their chains. As the years went on and this did not take place, Marcuse gave up on the workers. He concluded that they had been mesmerized by the affluent society's control of the media and the channels of distribution. The worker, in Marcuse's view, was now hopeless as a potential revolutionary. He had been hoodwinked into thinking that he was well off, so he was willing to bear

179

his enslavement. Indeed, he did not even acknowledge that he was a slave.

Drucker, too, has long been concerned with the working man. He had hoped that the worker would find status and function in the new industrial society. He conceived the hope that workers would come more and more to own the companies they work for. Through the machinery of vast pension plans, this is happening. However, Drucker said in an article, "The Mirage of Pensions" (*Harper's*, February 1950), that pensions would have no effect on industrial relations, although the workers of America now own America in a brand-new (and very exciting) pension-fund socialism. Drucker has always maintained that this would not foster the "management attitude" among workers or help to make them happier. As noted in another chapter, he developed the idea that workers could be given scope in the running of the "plant community," leaving the job of management to trained managers. This, he admits, never went anywhere.

But Drucker is still concerned about the alienation and frustration of the workers, still hopes that ways can be found to alleviate the situation. Marcuse never understood the worker, developed a disdainful contempt for him, and turned away, to place his chips elsewhere —on the young, the blacks, the "outcasts."

Drucker, being a conservative, wants to conserve. He wants to keep what is good in institutions and build on it. Marcuse preaches destruction. To him, political or social action within the "system" is merely supportive of the system. Drucker maintains that man must function within social institutions. To Marcuse, the destruction of all institutions is the precondition for freedom.

Both men comment on the marketing aspects of society. Drucker is not a partisan of Madison Avenue or of the "marketing concept." He says that the necessary function of marketing has been distorted by faddists and glib incompetents. But Drucker, of course, stays with the proposition that a business must sell its goods.

Marcuse laments the fact that, today, happiness is not *true* happiness. People have been *sold* on the idea that they are happy, and so they no longer want to be free. This spurious happiness consists in the satisfaction of false needs "superimposed on the individual by particular social interests in his repression. If the worker and his boss enjoy the same television program and visit the same resort places, if the typist is as attractively made up as the daughter of her employer, if the Negro owns a Cadillac, if they all read the same newspaper, then this assimilation indicates not the disappearance of class, but the extent to which the needs and satisfaction that serve the preservation of the establishment are shared by the underlying population."

Drucker would find much to agree with in the foregoing paragraph—but his conclusion would be different. Drucker would feel that these are healthy developments. Marcuse sees them as instruments of repression. They are manifestations of institutions. And, since *any* institution is incipiently totalitarian, the manifestations must be rejected and the institutions they serve must be destroyed.

As for religion, Marcuse is so scornful of it as the opiate of the people that he scarcely bothers with God. But Drucker struggles with the riddle of man's existence and the question of the dichotomy between corporal existence and the life of the soul. In his essay on Kierkegaard, Drucker considers Kierkegaard's answer that "human existence is possible only in tension—in tension between man's simultaneous life as an individual in the spirit and as a citizen in society."

Kierkegaard, says Drucker, "expressed the fundamental tension in a good many ways throughout his writings —most clearly and centrally when he described the tension as the consequence of man's simultaneous existence in eternity and in time. He took his formulation from St. Augustine; it is the intellectual climax of the Confessions. But Kierkegaard gave to the antithesis a meaning that goes far beyond St. Augustine's speculation in dialectical logic."

Kierkegaard and St. Augustine are a long way from Berkeley and Kent State; a long way from GM headquarters in Detroit and the Vega plant at Lordstown. But Drucker has always maintained his own tension, coping with Caesar on the one hand and God on the other. He comprehends fully the failure of organized religion, but he finds much worth saving in the concepts of Christianity: "The great majority of the institutions of present-day society which make life tolerable for the masses owe their origin to these religious forces, because they are not built on the collapsed concept of Economic Man." In the 1930s Drucker looked forward to a new and different relationship between man and eternity, which could "become successful only after the routine of the churches has been destroyed or in other words, after persecution or social revolution has rendered impossible the maintenance of the outward institutions."

Of course Drucker's plus is Marcuse's minus. Since vestigial forms of religious observance "make life tolerable for the masses" they must be destroyed. Otherwise the revolution may never come.

Marcuse believes in the perfectibility of man. No measure is too extreme to impel man toward the perfect state. Guerrilla warfare, sabotage, obscenity, destruction of all things beautiful, even physical filthiness ("unsoiled by 'plastic cleanliness' ") —these are measures to advance mankind toward the new and happier day.

Drucker's view is darker and more nearly follows the traditional Christian doctrine of man: "The only basis for freedom is the Christian concept of man's nature: imperfect, weak, 'dust unto dust'; yet made in God's image and responsible for his actions." Since Drucker does not presume that man will ever attain the ideal state in this life, he need not indulge in hatred and killing to try to attain nirvana.

It is interesting in considering these two, the conservative and the revolutionary, to contemplate the rhetoric of negativism and rebellion. For example:

"The danger of the masses lies, not in revolution, but in apathy, cynical indifference, and despair."

"The debate between capitalism and socialism is meaningless. Both equate property and power."

"Capitalism has been proved a false god because it leads inevitably to class war among rigidly defined classes."

"That capitalism is doomed seems to be a commonplace, and it is correct. . . ."

"The fact that the standard of living and of consumption of each class is reduced proportionately less than that of the class immediately above, lends economic substance to the substitution of non-economic for economic rewards. This negative economic consumption is the greatest and the most potent social satisfaction in the noneconomic society of totalitarianism. And it will continue to satisfy the masses until and unless they cease to believe in the ideology of the non-economic society altogether. The collapse, if it comes, will be a moral and not an economic collapse."

"The new society . . . will again try to realize freedom and equality. . . . Economic equality will become possible when it has ceased to be socially all-important and when freedom and equality in a new sphere will be the promise of a new order."

Some samples of revolutionary rhetoric. None of it is drawn from Marcuse; it is all Drucker.

In terms of seeing clearly the inevitable destruction of the old order, Drucker is by far the more revolutionary thinker. Untrammeled by the Marxian-Freudian set that imposed tunnel vision upon Marcuse and his ideological associates, Drucker was able to take a cold look at what was really happening to society and draw the inevitable conclusions. Armed with superior knowledge and incisive intellect, Drucker penetrated into the future to discern the end of a way of life that had lasted for centuries. It was not easy or painless, but Drucker looked and spoke about what he saw.

For Marcuse the destruction of the old order was a matter for celebration. Chaos is the fertile soil for the Marxist flowering.

But this ready-made answer was not possible for Drucker. He had looked at this version of the millennium: "Marxism stands and falls by the promise to overcome the unequal and unfree society of capitalism and to realize freedom and equality in the classless society . . . Instead of establishing the true freedom, the socialist state would produce a genuinely feudal society, though the serf would be proclaimed the beneficiary."

Think of the possibilities of debate between Marcuse and Drucker. Consider the precision and flair with which Drucker might have put the case for the industrial society. Drucker's case would lack the simplistic assurance and all-out fervor manifested by Herbert Marcuse, but it would have the advantages of articulateness and logic. Drucker knows that there are things seriously wrong with the civilization, but he is able to make a powerful argument that enough of it is right to be worth preserving.

But this tempting vision has never become a reality.

The question is not whether Marcuse is an Odin or a Loki. The question is why Peter Drucker has never taken the field actively in defense of the system he has done so much to erect.

Why not? For one thing there is the matter of taste. When one vies with the Marcuses of this world, he must be ready to wallow in filth. Drucker's disdain for folly leads him to ignore it. He would simply not feel that a gentleman of any culture and civilization should involve himself with the linguistic atrocities and intellectual horrors of the radical movement.

But also—let's face it—Drucker has always shown a heavy tendency toward analyzing situations and stating principles rather than working actively to make something happen. ("I am a poor doer and manager.") His influence has been enormous, and is felt well beyond the boundaries of the executive suite. But his ideas have carried more by the strength of their relevance and power and the lucidity of their expression than by the strenuousness of their advocacy. Peter Drucker lays out the strategy and gives you the tactics to execute the strategy; he does not do it himself. He is a writer, a thinker, and a consultant; the attributes that go into these disciplines do not make a man an activist.

Drucker's message on business and profit does not seem always consistent. At times he counsels businessmen to respond by adjusting their own attitudes. He appears to feel that business regards profit within a framework distorted simultaneously by smugness and guilt. He urges that we must "stop thinking of profit as a reward. There are no rewards; only the costs of yesterday and tomorrow."

At other times Drucker seems to dismiss the idea altogether that business is under attack. He says that "hostility to business exists only on the front page of the *New York Times*, with other fabled monsters."

But in still other moments he expresses the feeling that, while the drive for profit may not be altogether noble, it is an inevitable and relatively harmless facet of the darker side of man's imperfect nature. This was expressed in *Concept of the Corporation*: "If we eliminate the profit motive, the result will not be the equal and peaceful society of the millennium but the emergence of some other outlet for man's basic lust for power." (Drucker once observed that, if the Depression had started a little later, Walter Reuther might have wound up as president of General Motors. In the same vein, we might speculate that if things had gone somewhat differently in the early days, Peter Drucker might well have been a formidable opponent of the free enterprise system.) Even as "Mr. Management" he certainly does not always sound like a staunch supporter of corporate enterprise.

Marcuse's audience is the young. Drucker is concerned about young people, and he has been for much of his career a teacher. But he prefers an audience with a few years on it. One manifestation of this preference lies in his lack of high regard for the conventional graduate school of business administration. Drucker says that management education is a clinical discipline, like medicine. He prefers to talk about management to people who are actually involved in it. And he professes what may be an overly complacent feeling that young people will think, say, and do many strange things, but that maturity will bring with it heightened responsibility and a sense of reality. (Late in the 1960s he was still viewing campus revolt as media-inflated panty raids.)

Drucker is not good in adversary proceedings. He is not a good debater and does not enjoy it. The idea of taking on Marcuse would have seemed to him fruitless. Nor does he think debates accomplish much beyond their possible entertainment value.

Another reason that Drucker has not been seen in the vanguard of counterattacks against the vandals who would tear down the system may be found in his resigned feeling that Marcuse and those who share his views are unpleasant but inevitable blemishes on the corporate state. "Marxism stands and falls by the promise to overcome the unequal and unfree society of capitalism and to realize freedom and equality in the classless society. And it is because it has been proved that it cannot attain the classless society but must necessarily lead to an ever more rigid and unfree pattern of classes that Marxist socialism has ceased to be a creed. . . . Since *criticism is its only* function, socialism as a social force is necessarily *dependent* upon the *existence and validity of capitalism*. Socialism can weaken the belief in capitalism; it cannot replace it. When capitalism disintegrates, socialism ceases to have any validity or justification." (Emphasis added.)

So the highly vocal Marxist is an emasculated carper, who has no more function but to complain. He is a kind of strident canary in the mine shaft, whose continued shrill calls serve no purpose but to proclaim the continuing existence of the establishment he attacks.

Drucker never expected that the student rebellion would make much difference to the vast majority of young people, or that it would have lasting effects on the universities or society. He feels that he has been borne out in this feeling.

Indeed, Marcuse, writing in 1972, is seen to be backing energetically away from his most extreme ideological and emotional salients. The philosopher of campus radicalism appeared resigned to the fact that the revolution was not coming. He proclaimed that the "first historic period of the movement," the period of joyful and often spectacular action, "has come to an end." Marcuse now makes a feeble attempt to equate the period of protest with the Age of Enlightenment that set the stage for the French Revolution. A few years back he had been insisting that we were *in* the revolution.

Moreover, Marcuse was now wagging his finger at his followers and urging strange codes of behavior. No more advocacy of violence, sabotage, obscenity, and filth as techniques of reform. Now the message was startlingly different: "Do one's thing, yes, but the time has come to learn that not *any*thing will do. . . ." And even more: "The standardized use of 'pig language,' the petty bourgeois anal eroticism, the use of garbage as a weapon against helpless individuals—these are manifestations of a pubertarian revolt against the wrong target. . . . In the society at large, pubertarian rebellion has a short-lived effect; it often seems childish and clownish."

Childish! Pubertarian! *Petty bourgeois!* The most dedicated of Marcuse's followers gaped at the sudden change in direction signalled by these dicta. But it was not really so sudden, nor should it have been unexpected. The young were turning away from the excreta and the obscenities and the bombs, and Marcuse was stirring his aged limbs to take up a new position at the head of his veering troops.

Drucker, smiling blandly in his peaceful retreat in the shadow of the San Gabriel Mountains, would likely observe with some satisfaction that irrational rebellion burns itself out, and that even septuagenarian radicals can achieve some measure of maturity.

And yet—a lot of damage was done, and we still have the scars. The vehemence of the assault on the industrial society had its effect, and the relative weakness of the defense opens weak spots to slow erosion and perhaps renewed assault.

Would it have been better if Peter Drucker had marshalled his magnificent equipment to enter the fray more actively? It is, at the very least, a pertinent question.

12.

Drucker on the Platform

March 18, 1975, 10:00 A.M. Three hundred men, and a scattering of women, sit in the auditorium of the New York University Graduate School of Business Administration, waiting for the program to start.

Every day a hundred thousand business people sit through meetings, in conference rooms, motels, elaborate resorts. They meet at lunch, dinner, even breakfast. They attend everything from far-out "T-group" experiences to sprawling "pony shows." Sometimes they discuss, sometimes they role play, sometimes they look at pictures. But mostly they listen to speeches.

Chautauqua never died for the businessman. It never even declined. For a hundred years there has been a growing market for speakers to man the podia in business sessions. Some gifted orators do nothing but commute from one roast beef meal to the next, presenting the same act night after night. There are the "star turns," whose content is shopworn and whose jokes are familiar, but who never fail to fill a room. There are the specialists, who may possess only dubious platform potency but who supposedly offer insights not to be gotten elsewhere. There are the big names, captains of industry, who read fabulous speeches confected by public relations hacks, but whose very presence adds luster to the program. And there are the hordes of lesser lights, polishing their acts, perhaps trying for the big time, mostly filling out the program.

Peter Drucker is something special as a speaker. He is in constant, almost frantic, demand. Nowadays, in his study at Claremont, he may turn down as many as a dozen requests for appearances. Drucker has a courteous but decisive routine for the turndown. He does not ask the fee, nor does he wait to hear it. He hears the auspices and the location and then almost invariably explains that he has no open dates, and that, besides, he does not ordinarily accept dates that will take him away from home overnight.

The demand for Drucker's name on a meeting program has, for many years, far exceeded the supply. Nevertheless, the frequency of the requests has, if anything, increased. Peter Drucker's name on the bill is something special. It gives legitimacy, depth, and importance to the program. It confers prestige on the auspices and the sponsors of the meeting. And it brings people in.

What kind of speaker is Drucker? He is certainly an entertaining conversationalist, seemingly able to discourse on any topic. Once, at lunch, I happened to mention that I sometimes ride the New Haven branch of the Penn Central. This remark triggered a dazzling half-hour discourse that was, in effect, an economic and social history of New England, built around the New York, New Haven & Hartford Railroad.

Auren Uris, author of many books on management and an old friend of Drucker, recalls the days when Drucker would occasionally visit Research Institute of America to talk with the editorial staff. Challenged by Drucker's amazing conversational flexibility, they resolved to try to introduce a topic about which the universal expert would have nothing to say. The subject they decided to stump Drucker with was that of mountain climbing.

189

When the day came, however, the introduction of mountain climbing touched off an even more coruscating verbal display than they had ever seen before. Peter Drucker seemed to know everything about mountain climbing. The editors decided that it would be pointless to seek an area in which he would be left speechless. They were probably right; but it may be noted that, in that instance, they happened to have led into a particular strength. Drucker is an enthusiastic walker and climber. A visitor to Claremont is apt to find himself breathlessly trying to keep up with his host as Drucker takes one of his beloved tramps through the foothills of the San Gabriel Mountains.

But on the platform it is another matter. No one credits Drucker with a polished delivery. Some say that, when making a speech, he is at his worst with regard to content as well. Robert Townsend observes, "He becomes a big ham in a room full of people. The bigger the audience the more he hams it up and the less useful he is, because he goes for the 'boffo' rather than the real answer." Leo Cherne, himself a gifted speaker, comments, "Drucker shapes himself to the audience. His aim is to stimulate; he measures an audience in terms of possibilities for stimulation. The trouble with this is that the speaker can become so concerned with stimulation that he seduces himself."

Some of Drucker's greatest admirers feel that as a speaker, especially to executive audiences, Drucker is not always at his best. He often appears to speak down to them.

None of this seems to make much difference. People still want to hear Drucker speak.

Drucker is no longer very active as a member of the NYU graduate school faculty. But he is the school's star turn. His annual appearance is an event. NYU business school is not ordinarily classed as one of the "status" institutions. When the big companies recruit for prestigious additions to the corps of young managers, they still go to Harvard, Tuck, Wharton, Chicago, Stanford, Columbia, and the like. But, once a year, NYU is able to produce Peter Drucker. He maintains his loyalty to NYU in much the same way—though less actively—that the great soprano Beverly Sills returns every season in the New York City Opera to sing for their regular fee, when she could command much more anywhere in the world, including across the Lincoln Center plaza at the Met. Peter Drucker is NYU's Beverly Sills.

Drucker's name has filled the Hall. Those in attendance represent a wide diversity of interests. There is the man from the Soviet Trading Mission, and there is the husband and wife team from the Huk-a-Poo Sportswear Company.

The auditorium has the dim, somnolent air of any large room at 10:00 A.M. It is not the optimum time for a speech. But the participants are awake and alert. There is a muted buzz of anticipation. Some businessmen, deeply infected with the meeting virus, will go almost any place at almost any time to listen to a talk. But today is something special.

The topic is listed as "Growth, Diversity and Liquidity: Old Goals and New Needs." Nothing exceptionally provocative about it; most speech titles feature either something "new" or a "challenge." In this case it probably does not make much difference. Drucker would draw if he announced his topic as the residual traces of Sanskrit in the average business memorandum. This is the first of two morning sessions, each running through lunch.

Drucker mounts the podium along with the professor who will introduce him and the two panelists who will comment on his remarks. The format is that of a symposium.

The introduction is fairly typical, that of the speaker who needs no introduction but who is going to get one anyway ("an international authority who, I am sure, is well known to all of us"). The moderator's words reflect his pride in the act he is about to lead in, along with a studied effort to eschew the fulsome.

And then Drucker is at the microphone. With some speakers, the "throat-clearing" minutes are the best part. They rattle off some good jokes, pause for the laughs, and then proceed to forty minutes of boilerplate that justifies the comedy. With Drucker, there are no jokes. There are no preliminaries. Without a warm-up he is into his content: "For the past two hundred and fifty years there have been go-go decades every forty or fifty years. . . ."

The voice is deep, the pace is slow and measured; and the accent seems marked. One member of the audience cranes forward, trying to penetrate the Viennese-flavored intonation. He whispers to a neighbor, "I thought this guy had been in this country for forty years." The neighbor laughs. Everyone is quiet and alert, straining to get the gist.

The thread running through the first few passages of monotone represents one of the staples of Druckerism. Here is Peter Drucker, the student of history, for the first time reiterating his point that nothing happens. "There have always been periods of innovation and boom; in the sixteenth century . . ."

The thrust of this brief hour of European business history soon emerges. Every "go-go" decade has been followed by agitated talk about "zero growth." Furthermore, every forty or fifty years there is a period during which all the emphasis is on the P & L and every such decade is followed by another—or two—in which liquidity and cash are more important than profit.

As he moves along, Drucker keeps pointing out that even such broadly held assumptions about a particular economic period are misleading ("While the Germans were taking their money to the market in wheelbarrows their neighbors experienced mild deflation . . ."). Earnings-per-share, he is saying, is a thoroughly misleading yardstick. He speaks of the current fashions in evaluating company strength with weary disdain. Among his listeners, of whom the majority are very likely avid followers of the earnings-per-share yardstick, heads nod in earnest agreement.

Now Drucker is supporting his point by recourse to a tactic that has become identified with his method over the years. He is talking about population curves ("The sharp drop in the birth rate after 1960 . . ."). Occasionally a well-aimed shot is fired off the side at a target of oppportunity: "By the way, social security *is a fantasy. It doesn't fund anything." The observation is left there, but it has registered on the approving sensibility of the audience.*

Drucker's asides are fascinating tidbits. He delivers them without much emphasis. The listener, startled, must either make a quick note or remember the remark for later emphasis, because the speaker is moving right along in pursuit of his main point. As he talks briefly of the population picture, Drucker flicks off some of his side observations as a pinpoint deflator of established presumptions: "It is not that the birth rate is rising in underdeveloped countries. The birth rate is falling everywhere. In developed countries the mortality rate is falling faster." Some puzzled, intent looks; quick flickering of pencils; but the point is swiftly passed. It never comes up again.

Now Drucker is saying, in summation of one block of his presentation, "Capital formation is shifting from the entrepreneur who invests in the future to the pension trustee who invests in the past." There are appreciative nods. These people have heard economists, and they know that it is not called the "dismal science" for nothing. This kind of neat formulation of an economic point is much more arresting than half an hour of tortuous statsitics.

But, wait a minute; the speaker is now disavowing any particular distinction as an economist. Drucker-watchers are used to the tactic. It consists of sweeping and captivating statements that often shed a startling new light on a familiar situation, coupled with modest disavowal of expertise. The finishing punch of the combination is often a dart shot at the pretensions of professionals or pedagogues; and, sure enough, there comes now a passing gibe at the "conceits" of academic economists.

The accented voice continues without a great deal of inflection, but there is a Jamesian, or perhaps Conradian, roll to the sentences, and the use of language is supple and precise. There is no diminution of attention. The audience is caught up in the performance. The words "I am not prophesying" are like the drumroll before the acrobat does a particularly spectacular

193

trick. *The disclaimer is followed immediately by a prophecy that may be a little hard to pin down later, but one that is nevertheless an authoritative stab at reading the future.*

For those familiar with the high points of Drucker's consulting career there are echoes of past triumphs, usually reflected in loyal disdain toward competitors of the landmark clients of the past. He is saying that every business must know itself, and run itself. But, he asks, what do we see? We see a Westinghouse run by GE, a Montgomery Ward run by Sears.

The point comes at which an observer begins to sense a slight change in the audience. All this is great stuff, they seem to be saying, highly stimulating and enriching, but when do we get down to the nitty-gritty? It is flattering and entertaining to be dazzled as Peter Drucker plucks concepts and events from today and yesterday, links them together in unlikely seeming connections, and then triumphantly demonstrates the connections to be sound and firm. But how does this apply to doing business today?

As if sensing the audience impulse—there has been no apparent trailing off of interest—Drucker shifts into more "practical" matters. Business needs proper goals. "One must grow with a growing market." There are words about cutting inventory. Audience attention heightens by a notch or two. The speaker is telling them that it is all-important to plan for "minimum growth" in desirable directions: "Growth that adds volume without improving productivity is fat; growth that diminishes productivity is cancer." Once again, very neat. But now they are waiting for the "how-to." How do you decide on the proper minimum growth for your business? The question is never going to be answered in any detail.

For we have proceeded to some items of "how-to," but they seem a little elusive. We are talking about structure, and we hear questions that the businessman must ask himself. What is the structure that best minimizes my cost of capital? Which structure will optimize total earnings? The eager listeners want to be told the answers. Instead they are treated to a brief jeremiad

*against the false idol of "leverage" and then given
another question: How much capital do we need to
survive 120 days of financial panic?*

*The "120 days" is a specific, and everybody writes
it down, as Drucker observes that most financial panics
are hurricanes that blow themselves out in 90 days or
less. But still the nuts-and-bolts answers are not forth-
coming. Instead, the speaker is commenting that very
few managements know the answers to these questions,
and thus the field is constantly fertile for some new
economic theory. After a diversionary reminder of historical medical theories under which doctors treated
illness with bleeding, arsenic, and the like, Drucker
entreats his listeners not to place the fate of their businesses in the delusions of economists.*

*He pauses for a moment, eyeing the house, as if con-
sidering whether to apply some further stimulants or
end the treatment now. Drucker opts for a surefire
stimulant, an attack on the corporate income tax as
the "most asinine of taxes . . . governmental and congressional policy is insane."*

*A brief observation on the "macro-economy," which
seems to come as a mild surprise to the audience, and
then a reiteration of the point that go-go decades always
produce new economic theories . . . and then, abruptly,
it's over. Drucker sits, and half the audience is unsure
whether or not to applaud. He has talked for a little
less than half an hour.*

*One businessman takes a quizzical look at the topic
sheet distributed before the session. Here's how it reads:*

TOPIC: Growth, Diversity and Liquidity:
Old Goals and New Needs

*Every forty or fifty years since the early eighteenth
century there has been a decade of "growth mania,"
in which rapid growth has been the sine qua non
in the economy and viewed as potentially limitless.
Each time such a decade has been followed by a
period in which there is talk of "zero growth,"
occasionally with some substance to the talk, as in
the 1920s and 1930s. Every forty or fifty years there*

*is also a decade in which all the emphasis is on
the P & L, a period in which assets seem to be
meaningless, debts desirable and credit obtainable
in infinite amounts at apparently low cost. And every
such decade is then followed by another—or two—
in which liquidity and cash are more important
than profit, or at least more critical to a company's
survival.*

*Professor Drucker maintains that top management
has to be able to manage a business regardless of
fashion changes. It has to be able to balance goals.
That balance becomes crucial in a period of
change from overemphasis on one goal to overemphasis on another. What are the proper goals? What
kind of growth is desirable, what kind only adds
fat? What kind of diversity strengthens a business,
what kind splinters it? The stock market has already
made the transition in goals from values based
on earnings potential to valuations-based liquidity
and cash flow. What can company management
do, both to balance goals and to take advantage of
shifting preferences and conditions with respect
to profitability, growth, diversity and liquidity?*

The businessman slashes large question marks across
the questions included in the second paragraph and
shakes his head slightly. Drucker, this member of the
audience seems to feel, has not really given *answers*
to any of these questions. He has, with elaboration,
delivered the summary sheet as his talk.

The other two panelists give brief talks, by and large
agreeing respectfully with what Drucker has said. Then
it is time for questions from the audience.

The first few questions, as is often the case, are really
minispeeches. A banker delivers an outraged complaint
about Senator Proxmire. ("He wants to manage *my*
money!") Drucker murmurs benevolent agreement and
invites the next question. The questions seem to be
slow in coming, and Drucker appears to pace himself
to fill the vacuum. He will answer and then digress into
historical anecdotes, interesting recollections, and more

surefire darts at the economists and their endless search for the philosopher's stone of financial policy.

Then a questioner rises to dispute Drucker's contemptuous remarks on leverage. Look at Germany and Japan, he says, and the highly leveraged operations in those economies. This is treading on Drucker's home turf. Like a sleepy lion momentarily roused, he leans into the mike and delivers—more rapidly than heretofore—a concise overview of foreign business practice, with particular emphasis on Japan. Satisfied that he has destroyed the underpinning of the question, he lounges back again. There are a few more queries, evoking little interest.

Then somebody asks about executive compensation. An eye on the audience, Drucker looses off a cynical salvo. "There are only bad and worse executive compensation plans." Most encourage the top management to milk the company. Stock options? They reward the executive for doing the wrong thing, rather than encouraging right behavior. Instead of asking, "Did we make the right decisions?" the manager is asking, "How did we close today?" He commingles business and personal interests. And so on. Drucker has stung his listeners, and he knows it. He expands on the follies of executive compensation and the prevalance of high pay for incompetent behavior with relish and satisfaction. Drucker seems to be hoping that there will be more give-and-take, that other listeners will pick up the gauntlet. But his answer may have amounted to overkill; there are no more questions or comments on executive compensation.

One intrepid soul raises the matter of social responsibility alluding to 40 percent unemployment among black youths, doubting a choice of priorities that does not address itself to this problem. Drucker answers dispassionately and somewhat indirectly. There are some homely remarks about the difference between a "green apple" recession and the beginning of a real depression. "When a boy has eaten green apples the only thing to do is let him alone and get it all out." The audience chuckles comfortably, both at the familiar analogy and the point that it makes.

What, a man wants to know, is going to happen to the economy? Drucker repeats his charming caveat that he never makes predictions, and then proceeds to make a prediction: there will be an upturn around the end of summer. Then he shrugs and says, "But don't ask me where."

Throughout the question period there have been muted notes of frustration at the paucity of specific answers to everyday problems. In an aggrieved tone a questioner outlines a highly specific question about cash flow and dividends, and what criteria the businessman can use to control his operations better in these uncertain times. Which measurements does Professor Drucker use in making his judgments, and which measurements does he recommend to his clients?

Drucker seems, for the first time, actually bored. He stirs and intones, "Measurements are cheap; so I use all of them." Click goes the microphone. The session is abruptly over.

But at lunch there is to be another question-and-answer session. Over cocktails the participants talk hopefully of how this period may evoke more precise answers to the problems they have brought with them to this symposium, for which they have paid sixty dollars. One executive, new to a Drucker meeting, says he didn't hear much that was immediately applicable in the morning but that he got a lot out of the session. This man notes two curious things. At a couple of points Drucker had cited statistics pertaining to the packaging industry—this man's field. "Those statistics were way out of line," he notes. He recalls something else. Peter Drucker had said some things about the man's company in one of his books. "It was very interesting," says the newcomer, "but, you know, what Drucker said happened was exactly the opposite of what actually did happen."

Drucker is essentially a creative writer and speaker, and it takes a while to get used to this. As Drucker cheerfully acknowledges, he will pluck statistics out of the air to support a point. He is a *stimulator*. Nevertheless, as you watch a Drucker audience, you will see that, while notes are taken assiduously throughout the talk, the items most enthusiastically noted are the statistics.

At lunch the questions are scattered, without much bite. Drucker is not always willing to engage in lengthy dissertations. One businessman describes, in some considerable detail, the situation confronting his organization at this moment and winds up by asking, "What can I do?" Drucker snaps, "Nothing. You're in trouble."

But there is one question that enables him to respond expansively: "How can we cope with the increasing and seemingly insatiable demands of labor?"

The answer is not tactical, rather, philosophical. Drucker notes with a certain amount of satisfaction that a story in the papers this very morning tells how the workers at Lordstown have forgotten about sabotage and rebellion—as he predicted—and have settled down to work to keep their jobs. But the pressure of hard times is not the answer to the disaffection of workers. Drucker reverts to a theme that has troubled him for many years, a problem to which he confesses he has never found a satisfactory answer. It's not a matter of money. The blue-collar worker feels he is losing status. The damage done by the talk of automation goes beyond fear of unemployment; it is a depersonalizing experience. Drucker quotes what he calls a typical production-line worker: "I got a girl pregnant and left school. My brother stayed in school and learned zero. He's now the training director. [Appreciative laughter.] My cousin also got a broad pregnant—but he paid for an abortion, and now he's teaching economics." [Louder appreciative laughter.]

The worker, says Drucker, feels he is a loser. His economic well-being is eroded by his social insecurity. And even his economic situation becomes more perilous as he grows older, as his union leaders create conflict between the worker who is working and the worker who is on a pension. Drucker recalls ruefully the landmark GM pension agreement of 1949 ("I helped to negotiate it"). The basic idea was to socialize industry without nationalizing it, give workers a stake in the company. But now we find workers negotiating with themselves, bartering present income for future income.

The participants are getting insight into the problem; but, once again, those who wanted hard answers do not receive them. After a few more questions, the first day's symposium is over. Drucker comments to an acquaintance that he is disappointed in himself, that he did not make it very interesting. There was not much passion in the give-and-take. He resolves that, tomorrow, he will see to it that the session is more lively.

March 19, 10:00 A.M. A full auditorium, most of them the same faces as yesterday. Today's area is profits.

TOPIC: Challenge to Management: Maintaining Profitability in a Time of Change

The concept of profit and profitability is under growing attack—and yet at no time in American economic history have pressures on profit and profitability been greater. Professor Drucker examines the function of profit and questions whether talk of "the free enterprise system" confuses rather than helps people to understand. He discusses what is needed to know about the function of profit as the foundation for jobs, as the base for economic stability, and as the risk premium of economic activity.

Do you know how well your business maintains its profitability in a time of inflation, currency disorders, rapid economic changes and wildly fluctuating government policies? What traditional yardsticks can still be trusted? What new yardsticks does top management need to measure both current profits and the basic profitability of its business, its products and its markets?

Professor Drucker discusses what new information is needed in respect to financial structures and for measuring productivity of capital, physical key resources and human resources. He enumerates what top management can do to maintain profitability in a cost and liquidity squeeze, at a time of rising inventory prices and looming inventory losses, and in a climate of growing consumer resistance.

Finally, he asks if there is really such a thing as

*"profit," or are there only "costs of the past," the
province of the accountant, and "costs of the future,"
which are genuine costs notwithstanding? Does the
businessman fool himself when he talks of "profit
maximization"? Professor Drucker discusses how top
management can appraise the minimum profitability a
company needs and how employees, customers and
the public at large might be made to understand
that to earn the minimum of profit needed for the
risks, the survival and the growth of a company is
management's first social responsibility.*

Drucker opens provocatively: "In an inflation, profit
figures are worse than useless. They are misleading."

Then, following the now-familiar, "I am not an
economist," the talk settles down to a rather dry exploration of the origins of the concepts of relationships
between productivity and capital. Drucker notes, in
passing, that Karl Marx did not invent the term "capitalism"—"That's a twentieth-century word." When he
says that Frederick Turner was anticipated by Marx,
there are a few puzzled looks; who is Frederick Turner?
But a somnolence has settled over the assemblage.
Drucker brings them out of it with another peppery
aphorism. Branching onto the topic of another of his
bêtes noires, he observes, "Most sales training is totally
unjustified. At best it makes an incompetent salesman
out of a moron." This wakes the audience up; everyone enjoys it except for a few sales trainers.

What is the answer to more sales? Drucker puts forward as an indisputable fact that there is an almost
unchangeable ratio between sales and calls. The way to
get more sales is to give your salesmen more time to
sell. But, says Drucker, the salesman spends *80 percent*
of his time filling out papers; and salesmen are notori-
ously poor clerks. Only the hospital clerk is worse. Nor
has he ever seen a good salesman whose handwriting
can be read; and so on.

People scribble vigorously these outrageously contrived
statistics and "facts," and a slight smile seems to move
across Drucker's impassive face. He is getting to them.

But now he again indulges in a little side excursion,

into the health-care field. ("Medicare and Medicaid are the greatest measures yet taken to make the world safe for clerks."). The fact is that Peter Drucker is fascinated by *institutions,* not just businesses; and in recent years the problems of the hospital appear to get a greater rise out of him than do those of industry. However, realizing that this is a business audience, he gets back on track once again, this time with some observations on "Human Resources."

The next few minutes are unusually dead. The language and the thoughts seem tired: "We face a major challenge," etc. But once the human area is out of the way, things perk up.

Drucker has sometimes been assailed as being cold and mechanical, unresponsive to human factors. In private conversation it becomes obvious that this is far from true. But when he talks he seems more at ease with abstractions.

Soon we are on the question of profit, and speaker and audience perk up. If you do not have control of profit, he tells us, your business is unmanaged. A provocative statement; is he going to just leave it hanging there, as before, or will he follow it up? This time he follows it up. "Most businesses are constantly involved in establishing beachheads. There may be twenty beachheads, but no beaches." In considering new ventures, it is vital to ask: Is there a beach to that beachhead?

And now Drucker is hammering at his familiar point that success lies in capitalizing on strength, not underpinning weakness. He scornfully dismisses the well-worn rationale for so many activities—"absorption of overhead" ("an obscene term").

Then there is a curious interjection. Drucker pauses, looks out over the audience, and says, "You've heard me say this for so many years, you're tired, I'm tired. *Why haven't we done something about it?*"

Businessmen are afraid of profit. They think there is widespread hostility to business and profit. No, says Drucker, there is not hostility, there is just *ignorance,* promulgated by such people as sociologists ("Sociology is like hives. It is not a disease from which civilization will die—but it itches.").

It's a pep-talk now. "We talk to each other of profit as if it were a *reward!* It is *not* a reward. It is a *cost.* There are no rewards . . . only costs, of yesterday and tomorrow." No more droning now. Drucker speaks with fervor. His audience is caught up. We must determine the minimum profitability that will pay for the *risks* of tomorrow . . . a profit is a social responsibility . . . the communists work at twice the profit margin we do . . . there are no profits, only costs, and so we must stop thinking and talking of profit as a reward.

On this ringing note of the legitimacy of profit, Drucker concludes and sits. Today there is loud and unhesitating applause.

Drucker has awakened them. He has not detailed answers to nitty-gritty problems. But he has let his passion show.

The first of the follow-up panelists is lively and assured. The second presents a few surprises. His commentary is sprinkled with humor. He displays the temerity to disagree with Drucker: "Peter is wrong about accounting models. . . . Peter is mistaken; there is hostility to the free market. . . ." Drucker greets this rebuttal with delight and animation; but some of the audience consider it less majesty. One says of the rebutter, "He couldn't wait to grab the microphone. At another meeting he would have been the main attraction, but here he was just the second banana, and he should realize that."

The questions from the audience are sharper than yesterday, and so are the answers. People are responding to some of the more extreme statements Drucker has thrown into his talk; "Were you serious when you said we should *forget* about profit planning?" Affably, without a trace of embarrassment, Drucker qualifies, coming back in off some of the limbs onto which he has crept for effect: "I didn't mean quite that. . . ."

And now Drucker seems more willing to be specific. Asked how a manager can spot good people, he responds, not with the humorous dismissal that some might have expected, but with a carefully reasoned defense of the merits of peer appraisal over a period of time. Of course, there are still businessmen in the audience who are somewhat grumpy about lack of fulfillment on some of the points forecast in the topic summary. One asks, "Why is your prescription—better use of resources —unique to *this* time of change? Isn't it always a good idea? And what are the new information needs of management?" Drucker says, "I thought I had stressed new informational needs—but here they are." He talks patiently of the need for information on productivity resources, minimum profitability requirements, the costs of capital, risks, and so on.

The session breaks for cocktails and lunch. Those present seem much more stimulated than yesterday.

Near the bar Drucker is surrounded by congratulators, commentators, and questioners. One says, "I agreed with almost everything you said—except, what you said about stock options. . . ." Drucker asks the bartender for another Campari and soda.

Following lunch, they go to questions. Two queries are brisk; the argument is lively. Challenged on his educational stand, Drucker asserts that "our educational system disqualifies people for honest work." Engaged in debate by a banker, he gets off the observation that when a bank says eternity it means ninety days. Queried on the necessity to raise capital in a period of mass unemployment, he asks the questioner to consider the consequences of not raising capital—he doesn't mean *printing* it, but he is resigned to it. "I don't think it's very creative, but that's what we're going to do."

Drucker is willing to get tougher and more precise. A businessman prefaces a question: "Since the last few years have forced everyone to unload inventories . . ." Drucker stops him: "*Everyone?* Everyone is very few. People are *not* unloading inventories." At least, it turns out, not at the rate at which he thinks they should. "I am telling my clients to cut inventories, get liquid." At the magic words "I am telling my clients . . ." the audience leans forward a millimeter or so. This is the real stuff. These are more precise recommendations. It is as if the audience, having passed the test, is now entitled to the secrets of the inner sanctum.

But it is possible to go too far. A beleaguered executive, pushing hard for an answer that bears even more sharply on his particular problem, says, "I don't think that will work for me." With infinite weariness Drucker replies, "Then you had better go out of business. There is no law that says a company must last forever." This evokes a momentary pause—it's not the kind of thing usually said to a member of the audience at a business meeting.

Now the end is in sight. Drucker diverges from the nitty-gritty back to the area of comfortable generality. He offers quirky reassurance: "Don't worry about the banks. If there is a run on the banks they will print money and hand it out. In ten days it's over; the cost is a printing bill."

He is fed a question about the structural changes in the world that will affect business, and he is off once again: "Maybe we are at the end of our 100-year belief in free lunch . . . perhaps we are over the idea that if you define a problem you don't have to do any work. . . . No country today has an effective government. . . . Some of the new states in the UN have fewer people than are in this room; but all of them have an air force, a 370 IBM computer, a cryogenic chamber, and nuclear capacity."

He cannot quit without a few more looks at institutions, educational and otherwise. "Public institutions need a systematic, organized process for abandonment. . . . Hospitals must learn that having a baby is not an illness. . . . When a subject becomes totally obsolete we make it a required course." These are crammed in, without too much reference to the questions that have preceded them.

And then the end is in sight. Incredibly—he can't be entirely serious, his tongue must be in his cheek—Peter Drucker pronounces the ultimate reassurance: "The system is basically sound." He looks around; is that the note to end on? He decides not. And so, with great sincerity and weight, he implores his audience to do everything possible to *"enable your people to work."*

There is a momentary pause, as if Drucker were evaluating this as a concluding note. Deciding in the affirmative, he thanks the audience and sits down. Drucker's shrewd sense of the fitting final curtain is sound. The audience sits pondering this last one. Reporters finish off their notes by underscoring the sentence. Business writer Jane Shoemaker of the *Philadelphia Inquirer* is to write: "If his message can be summarized . . . it boils down to one simple note of caution: make it as easy as possible for your employees to work."

At the end, Drucker is not entirely well satisfied; but he is fairly well pleased that the second day went better than the first.

A Peter Drucker talk, or symposium, is an enormously rewarding experience—if you know what you can look for.

It is not a coruscating exercise in oratory. Drucker chooses words superbly and puts them together masterfully, but his speaking style is straightforward and relatively uninflected. When he is bored by his subject matter, which can happen, his delivery becomes monotonous.

It is not a stand-up comedy act. Drucker is very funny, but he rarely tells jokes. His humorous effects are those of a subtle and wry commentator on the follies of mankind as it bands together in organization. What you see is not Bob Hope, but rather a Viennese Will Rogers with vast erudition and an organizational orientation.

It is not a fact-filled scrutiny of business operations. As noted, Drucker is relaxed—not to say cavalier—about statistics. He will cite the facts that appeal to him and support the point he's making. If there is no appropriate figure handy, he may make one up.

And it is not a group consultation. Drucker does not come to solve the individual problems of each member of the audience—or, indeed, any member of it.

What a Drucker program *is* is a unique experience, both for the business meeting veteran and the newcomer. Drucker offers an urbane tour through business history, recent and remote, with fascinating side trips into previously unknown areas.

It is a verbal voyage of discovery. Even when Drucker talks of familiar things he adduces odd undreamed-of connections with other familiar things that, taken as a whole, shed a startlingly brilliant light on mundane matters.

It is a period of nourishing exposure to a fine mind at work; a mind, now, for which there are few surprises, but which works with awesome effectiveness. True intellect is rare. Drucker would insist that it is far less rare in the boardroom than in the classroom, but nowhere is it plentiful. The member of a Drucker audience comes away, like it or not, drenched in intellect.

Above all, it is a massive dose of stimulation. As Drucker maintains, he does not want his audiences to go away saying, "I never knew that before." Rather he wants them to say, "I always knew that; why haven't I done anything about it?" Peter Drucker plucks from our minds the things we have "always known," gives them new luster and shape, and hands them back to us in usable form.

13.

Drucker as Teacher: Humanity in the Case Method

It is impossible to convey in print the true quality of a good teacher.

Drucker's students and former students say he is a great teacher. When pressed for their recollections, they offer a variety of tributes to his eloquence, his ability to ask penetrating questions, his instinct for stripping away trivia to probe to the heart of a problem. Mostly their reminiscences center around the breadth of worldly-wise *humanity* that Drucker brings to the task of teaching.

But to report what students say is not to convey the essence of a teacher. The writer is better advised to try in some way to present the teacher through his own words and techniques. The bulk of this chapter consists of a number of examples of Peter Drucker's own distinctive approach to teaching by means of the case method.

Drucker does not like much of what happens in the traditionally "prestigious" graduate schools of business administration. He feels that the teaching of management should be a clinical discipline, like the training of doctors. Management can be taught best to experienced mid-career people who are actually managing while they are learning: "That's why I stayed at NYU in the MBA program instead of going to Harvard. It's one of the reasons. My fellows at NYU may not have been as bright as the kids at Harvard, and they may not have driven themselves as hard. But they had the experience, and they were in positions where they could do something with the tools of management that they picked up."

Drucker looks at Harvard graduate students and says that he feels like telling them, "Get out, do something for a few years, get fired at least once, get your ass kicked, fall down on an assignment, succeed on another one—*and learn to respect work*. The great weakness of a Harvard-type program is that it breeds arrogance; students do not learn how hard it is to accomplish anything."

He would like to see some changes in the training of future managers. For one thing, the faculties at business schools should participate much more actively in consulting work. "It's frowned upon in most places because we want pure academicians to be unsoiled by sordid reality. But that's wrong. A pediatrician who has never seen a child on the toilet suffering from diarrhea isn't going to learn to do much about it."

And Drucker is firm in his dedication to the concept of "night school"; teaching business to those engaged in business; "My students for the last twenty-five years have been that kind." When Drucker taught the other kind of business student—the student without business experience—he felt that he was a poor teacher. "They did not learn anything from me; and that's because I could not learn anything from them." The craft of management is difficult to develop when one works on fictitious models.

Drucker uses the case method; Harvard, of course, originated the case method in management education. But Drucker's use of the method is radically different: "I wouldn't use a Harvard-type case." Harvard cases are notably long and detailed. They concentrate on giving the student heavy volumes of data on which to base his analysis. Analysis of a case is a laborious and exceptionally difficult task. Harvard Business School graduate Peter Cohen, in his book *The Gospel According to the Harvard Business School,* writes: "Of all the instruments of fear and terror at the disposal of the Business School, none can match a WAC's (*W*ritten *A*nalysis of *C*ases) effectiveness in reducing a healthy first-class body to a mess of gastric disorders, fluttering eyelids, and recurring nightmares. . . ."

Drucker's cases are short. More important, they are about people, not things and numbers. One can get a full appreciation of this only by reading the cases. So here, with Peter Drucker's permission, is a number of cases that he uses currently at Claremont Graduate School, prefaced by the introductory material given to incoming students.

They are short. They are perceptive. They are well written. They entertain while they teach.

And above all, they are human.

CLAREMONT GRADUATE SCHOOL*

BA 342 BUSINESS POLICY: Peter F. Drucker

This is an advanced course focusing on the fundamental decisions in the life of a business: What is our business and what should it be? What are the objectives? How to set priorities. Strategic long-range decisions; to grow or not to grow—and what is the *right* size? Basic decisions on market, technology, structure and finance.

The course will use cases with students expected to prepare for, and lead, case discussions. Students will also be expected to select one major area (e.g., setting objectives) and prepare a bibliography for the use of the entire class.

NO prerequisites, though *Management Process* and/or *Organization and Administration* will normally be taken earlier. Advanced undergraduate students will be admitted if their undergraduate advisor approves.

The course will be run by alternating lectures and

---

* The remainder of the material in this chapter is © 1975 by Peter F. Drucker and appears with his permission.

case discussions. The lectures will be in the following areas:

- What is a business?
- What is *our* business?
- Objectives, goals, and priorities.
- Strategic planning.
- Managing change and innovation.
- Structures and strategies.

A selection from the following cases will be discussed in class:

#2 Western States Electrical Supply Company
#3 The Crispin Shoe Company
#4 Research Strategy and Business Objectives
#5 Montgomery Ward's Dilemma
#6 What Is a Growth Company?
#7 What Are "Results"?
#8 Celanese and Courtaulds

Written Work

There will be two assignments, due respectively on March 10 and April 21. One assignment will be a written discussion of the attached Case #1, *What Is Our Business, What Is Our Market?* The other assignment will be a bibliography of one area in the field of business policy, which the student is expected to work out for himself. The assignments can be done in any order.

The presentation of the case should be short—a maximum of 15 typewritten pages, double-spaced. It should *not* attempt to try to give an "answer"—the case does not provide enough information for this. It should try to ask the questions: What are the alternatives? What are the things to consider? What are the basic questions altogether? Reading is not necessary to handle the case; some thinking is.

In respect to the bibliography, the student will be expected to decide what field interests him. It might be basic marketing policy. It might be financial structure and financial policy. It might be diversification strategy, and so on. Work on non-business—that is, service institutions, whether the hospital, the university, or the government agency, or the armed services—will be welcome. The student is expected to discuss the area of his choice with the instructor. Then he is expected to make a rapid literature survey in the library. He is then expected to sample the books and to pick from them the ones from which he thinks he can learn the most. After having read these books, he is then expected to make a short bibliography which presents a short list of books in the area—no more than 5 or 6 titles—and discuss very briefly, in a paragraph or two, what each book is trying to do; what its main areas of concern are; what "meat" it contains; and what the student, himself, got out of it. Finally, the student is expected to think through for what purposes he would recommend the book.

It is intended to put all these bibliographies together and to distribute them at the end of the course to all the participants, including the instructor, as a bibliography and reference for future work and reading in the field.

There is no required text. However, students might want to have a look at three books written by the instructor, *Practice of Management* (1954), *Managing for Results* (1966), and *Management: Tasks, Responsibilities, Practices* (1974).

CASE 1: What Is Our Business? What Is Our Market?

The Worldwide Youth Exchange Federation grew out of talks a group of young returning GIs had during the long ride back home from occupied Germany on a troop ship in the spring of 1946. These young men were all veterans of the American Ambulance Corps who had enlisted for non-combat duty with the British well before the U.S. entered the war. After Pearl Harbor they were then transferred to the American forces. Bedell Smith, General Eisenhower's Chief of Staff, heard of them and attached them to his own office, where they served as advance scouts for the relief needs of liberated territory, first in Italy and then in France, and finally in Germany and Austria. These young men—most of whom had been university students who enlisted in 1940 or so—began to talk among themselves of their experiences and then, inevitably, raised the question: "What can we do to prevent a recurrence? What can we do to make peace more secure?" They decided that what was needed was understanding among the peoples, and that such understanding would have to begin with the young. Accordingly, after they got home they began to organize—at first completely at random—exchanges of high school students, under which Americans of high school age would go to Europe, stay with a European family and go to school in Europe for a year; while a European high school youngster would come to this country, stay with an American family and attend an American high school for one year. The idea was an almost immediate success as other GIs picked it up and began to work on it in their own communities. And soon there was need for an organization. In 1950, by which time the annual volume of student exchange between the United States and Europe and between Europe and the United States already exceeded two hundred students each way, the Worldwide Youth Exchange Federation was started with a small grant from a major foundation and with one full-time employee. Since then the organization has grown steadily, year by year, until it now sends something like three thousand American high school youngsters abroad, mostly still to Europe but also to South America, Japan, and Indonesia, and brings roughly the identical number of high school students from overseas to the United States for a stay in an American home and for attendance for one year at an American high school. The staff has grown steadily and now numbers almost 140 professionals, of whom about 80 are stationed in the United States.

Several years ago a young man took over as the new Chief Executive—the first to succeed the original administrator who had started in 1950. Hugh Williamson was barely 30 when he took over. In his junior year in high school he had himself been one of the students under the Worldwide Youth Exchange Federation program—he had spent a happy year in France with a French family and in a French school. He had then gone on to the State University in his native Wisconsin, obtained a Ph.D. in Psychology, and then joined the State Department as an educational specialist, in which capacity he had worked in several South American countries. He then returned, took a job with a big company, but found himself rather bored and was therefore delighted when offered the job as President of Worldwide Youth Exchange Federation.

However, he was appalled by what he found. The staff seemed to be large beyond any need and totally disorganized. The finances were chaotic, to say the least. No one really knew how much it cost to bring a student to this country or to send one abroad. No one seemed to know who was responsible for budgets, for raising money or for authorizing expenditures. There was also total confusion regarding the relationship between the paid staff and the volunteers. In the United States most of the work was done by local chapters run by volunteers, in most cases still the former GIs who, in the late Forties, had given birth to the idea. Overseas there were paid country representatives. There were, however, no local chapters. Oveaseas students returning from the United States—eighteen year olds—were expected to do what legwork was needed in their communities, both to recruit applicants for student exchange and, more important, to find families willing to receive an American student for one year.

Williamson spent almost two years straightening up administration, slimming the staff in New York, where little work was actually being done—though tremendous records were being kept. Actually, he found the organization to be fundamentally very healthy—or so it seemed by the yardsticks which Worldwide Youth Exchange Federation had always applied to its own results, that is by the number of people who were applying for participation in this program. In 1973 25,000 Americans applied to go abroad and 25,000 students in foreign countries applied for a year in the U.S.—about 18,000 of them Europeans and 5,000 Latin Americans. And better than one out of every ten applicants—3,000 Americans and 3,000 foreigners—could actually be placed. Equally satisfactory, at least at first glance, was the performance record, again as measured by the traditional yardstick, that is the number of students who completed their exchange year—the drop-out rate remained well below 5 percent. Both the great majority of the students, something like 93 percent, and the great majority of the hosts, both in the United States and abroad, expressed themselves as very satisfied with their experiences and happy with their year as guest or host respectively.

Yet the more Williamson dug, the more uneasy did he become. He saw financial trouble ahead. For the first time, the true costs of a student were known and they turned out to be very high indeed. The host family, of course, contributed the support of their guest—so there was no need to raise that money. The schools that participated, mostly public high schools or their equivalent abroad, contributed a free place. But even so, each student cost almost $2,000, including his transportation, his counselling and so on. Particularly disturbing to Williamson was the fact that the entire financial burden was being borne by the American chapters; and as he traveled through the United States and visited the chapters he heard more and more complaints about the inequity of the whole burden of the program's being borne by the Americans while the Europeans and Japanese, though equally able to pay their share of the costs, did not contribute a penny. Even more disturbing, as he reflected on his frequent trips about the country, was the fact that the chapters, practically without exception, depended on people who were getting old rapidly, namely the original founders. More and more of the former beneficiaries of the program—that is former exchange students—were reaching the age at which they should take over the responsibility for the organization. But by and large they were being kept out of the organization's affairs, or at least not actively recruited. In Europe, he found that the returning students, who were very enthusiastic at first and willing to work hard, soon went off to the university and disappeared from the organization's ken—whereas no adults in the respective communities, and especially very few of the host families, had been organized to support the Federation activities and to do the work. Finally, he became disturbed by hearing from chapter after chapter and in foreign country after foreign country that host families no longer were standing in line to get high school students from abroad. On the contrary, they had to be convinced that they would not be saddled with a young "hippie" with long and filthy hair, dirty and torn bluejeans, smoking pot and sleeping around. And while the students, of whom Williamson saw a great deal, were almost the opposite of that type —and somewhat shocked him by being utterly "square" and ultra-serious—he realized that teenagers from abroad were no longer automatically welcome everywhere.

Williamson formulated in his own mind what he considered the key questions: the sources of finance; the organization of the chapters and their staffing; and the building of a permanent, self-perpetuating volunteer organization abroad. He also felt that he needed to recruit a board of nationally known names—if only to help him raise money. When he had formulated these questions, he went to an old friend of his family, a highly successful corporation lawyer in his native Wisconsin, whose advice and counsel he had repeatedly sought in the past. The old friend received him most cordially and listened attentively a whole day, asking all kinds of questions. Then he said, "I have been listening to you for an entire day. I am totally confused as to what you think the business of the Worldwide Youth Exchange Federation is and where you see its market. Who are your customers? And what do they 'buy' from you? What is your 'product'? Before you have answered these questions, all the rest are meaningless."

How would you go about answering these questions? Do you think, by the way, that they need to be answered first or that Williamson, with his focus on specifics, is more likely to succeed?

CASE 2: Western States Electrical Supply Company

Tony Martinelli came to the United States from his native Italy around 1890 or so. He had worked as a carpenter and bricklayer at home. But the only work he could find in the United States was as a section hand on the Northern Pacific. However, he rose quickly to section foreman and then to head of a construction crew. After a few years of this life, he found himself in Wenatchee, Washington, and fell in love, both with the rich valley and with a local girl, the daughter of Italian immigrants. He left the railroad and took a job as a carpenter. Within a few years he had made himself independent as a small local building contractor. Tony had two sons, Jim and Joe, who joined him in the business in the early Twenties. During the Depression, when there was no construction work to be done, these two young men realized that rural electrification, just coming in at that time, would mean a substantial business in electrical supplies. Accordingly, they shifted from being building contractors to being electrical wholesalers. And within a few years, despite the Depression, they had a flourishing local electrical wholesale house, which, by the time of World War II, had become the leading electrical supply wholesaler in the Wenatchee Valley.

Jim and Joe ran the business completely by themselves, with the help of a warehouse man and a woman bookkeeper, until the 1950s or so. Then they brought in a distant relative, Frank Mortola, who had received an accounting degree at Gonzola University in Spokane, to take over the office while they concentrated on selling.

Joe's children—he had six—all chose not to go into the business. But Jim's only son, also called Tony, had loved the business from boyhood days—in fact, from age 10 on, he had worked in it every day after school and every weekend. He then went off to the State University, where he got a combined degree in electrical engineering and business. And then, age 22, in 1962, he came back to Wenatchee and went to work for his father and his uncle. He very quickly realized that there were much greater opportunities than his father and uncle had ever availed themselves of. He saw that they had developed a business concept that would easily be transferrable to almost any other small community. But when he broached to them the idea of expansion, he found them both quite unwilling to go beyond Wenatchee. "Why be greedy?" said his father. And so young Tony borrowed money from the bank and bought out both his father and his uncle. His father retired to the fruit farm, which for many years had been his main interest. The uncle stayed on, but as an employee of the company—although with the title of Chairman of the Board.

Tony rapidly brought in two college friends, Hank Krueger and Herb Rosenblum, the former an industrial engineer, the latter a marketing major in college. Hank took on purchasing, procurement and inventory control; Herb became the marketing and especially the market development manager; with Uncle Joe staying on, concerned primarily with credit control which had always been his special interest. And young Tony began to expand. He opened electrical supply houses in every small town in the state of Washington, and then rapidly expanded beyond the boundaries of the state. By 1974 the company, renamed Western States Electrical Supply Company, had become the leading electrical wholesaler in the small towns and rural areas of the entire Northwest and even of British Columbia. It had branches from Vancouver to Cheyenne, Wyoming, and from Fargo, North Dakota, to Reno and to California's Napa Valley. It had stayed out of the big cities, except for Spokane, where the owners of a small but old-established electrical supply house had wanted to sell out to Western States Electrical Supply—and within two years that branch, under new management, was doing three times the volume it had ever done before. But otherwise Western States stayed out of Vancouver and Victoria, out of Seattle and Tacoma, out of Portland, Oregon, out of San Francisco and Salt Lake City.

However, outside the cities it covered the Northwest and did approximately 70 percent of the business in electrical supplies within its market area. When Tony bought out his father and his uncle in 1964, Wenatchee Electrical Supply had done $6 million business and had earned enough to support two families in comfort. By 1974, Tony's new Western States Electrical Supply sold $60 million worth of merchandise and cleared $3 million pre-tax. At that, it paid the local manager in each of its branches more in commission and salary than the owner of a small independent wholesaler in such a community could have normally been able to clear.

The secret, if it can be called this, was that Tony and his management group of Hank Krueger and Herb Rosenblum, supported by Frank Mortola, systematized buying. They systematized inventory keeping and inventory controls so that each local customer could be sure of getting what he needed when he needed it. They introduced a rather sophisticated and fully computerized system of inventory control, order control and credit control. And they systematically explored—it was mostly Herb Rosenblum's job—every area to find the right way to start an electrical wholesale business. Rosenblum also had the job of opening a new branch, running it for the first three months with his own two or three young men, and stepping in whenever a branch got into trouble. Branch managers usually started as warehouse men, very often working after high school or during weekends. By the time they graduated from high school, they knew enough about the business to take on a small local outlet, where they acted as salesmen with a small inventory, backstopped and supervised by the manager of the larger branch nearby. And within three or four years most of them were capable of taking on a fairly substantial branch themselves, thanks largely to the centralized buying and the centralized control system available to them.

By 1974 Western States had become as large and as successful as Tony Martinelli, Jr. had hoped it would be when he bought out his father and his uncle. And then Tony asked: "Where do we go from here?" As he had expected, every one of his associates gave a different answer.

Uncle Joe spoke first: "There is no reason why we should stay out of the big cities forever. We have proven in Spokane that we can be as successful in a big city as in the small towns. Vancouver, Victoria, Seattle, and Tacoma, Portland, Oregon, and Salt Lake City have together as much business as we have in our present market. Add Denver and perhaps eventually San Francisco, and we could triple our volume without having to go beyond our present territory. Maybe it will take a little longer to become profitable in the big cities with their fierce competition, but we have shown that we can do it. This, I think, is the logical line of expansion and will keep us busy for five to ten years."

Next came Hank Krueger. "You know," he said, "that we started to manufacture the most common standard components—plastic covers for switches and plugs. We do it on leased equipment, so that we didn't have to invest any capital. And we get these standard components at almost half or so of what we had to pay for them. I have carefully studied our line. Another 30 or 40 percent of our volume we can easily make ourselves on leased equipment without any capital investment and at a minimum of demand on management. Armored cables would be my first item. We could be in production in six months and double the profit, perhaps triple it; and after that we could easily extend further into manufacturing and not only make more money, but assure ourselves of much better quality. I think manufacturing is essential once we have the volume we now have, and we have proven that we can do it."

Herb Rosenblum cut in at this moment and said: "This is the worst thing we could do. Our great strength is that we can pick the best supplies on the market and bring them to our customers at the best price. We do not want to become the captives of a manufacturing operation. As I see it, we have two major opportunities. You know that I organized a special branch two years ago to supply the mobile home manufacturers in Boise, Idaho. Their requirements are quite similar to those of our small customers. They pay for immediate delivery and for dependable quality supply, and they pay well. That market is going to expand nationally. No one is organized to supply the mobile home manufacturers in the other clusters, and they are in clusters. They are in Southern California around San Diego; they are around Huntsville, Alabama, and around Dallas, Texas; they are in Harrisburg, Indiana. With six or seven mobile home branches, we could cover the entire mobile home industry and be the leading supplier in a major market. The second area of expansion I see is the one largest single market in the nation, which is Texas. It is almost entirely similar to the market we know. Let's stay out of the big cities, like Dallas, and concentrate on the smaller ones and we can build a $50 million business there in five years."

Tony, Jr. had not said a word until then. But he felt he had to join in, so he said: "You know, I have been studying the market for some time. We have been handling electrical supplies exclusively. But in the small towns and rural areas, most of the customers are contractors who do the entire construction job themselves. Next to electrical supplies, their biggest purchases are plumbing supplies. There is essentially no great difference between the two, though we will have to study the technology and the market. And we know how to do this. If we start plumbing supply houses parallel to our electrical supply houses, under independent management but in locations we know and where we are known, we will double our business in five years with a minimum of risk and with the same people we now train to be electrical supply wholesalers."

And then he turned to Frank Mortola and said: "Frank, how many of these things can we do together, given our capital and our manpower?" Mortola grinned —he obviously had been preparing himself for that question—and said: "At most, we can do two, though I would prefer to do only one at a time. Our greatest restraint is not capital. It is branch managers. Capital, I can get you, Tony. But you know managers take three to five years to develop. Pick one of those businesses and we can do it well. Pick two and we have a chance.

If you go beyond two, we will fall flat on our faces. So let's make a choice and stick with it."

You do not know enough about the electrical supply business, the plumbing business, mobile homes, or any other of those businesses, let alone about the market, so please do not try to answer the question, what strategy or strategies Western Supply should adopt. But how should it go about deciding on its strategy? What questions should be asked? What are the critical factors in each of the strategies?

By the way, do you feel competent to answer the question, what top management the company would need to expand at the rate it projects, even if it only picks one of these strategies?

CASE 3: The Crispin Shoe Company

Having been started as a neighborhood shoe store around the turn of the century, the Crispin Shoe Company began to grow rapidly after World War I when Paul Crispin took over from his ailing father. From one small store in a working-class district of Cincinnati, Crispin grew in the Twenties into a forty-store chain in Ohio and Indiana, carrying low-cost but good quality shoes for the entire family, mostly in working-class neighborhoods. The period of truly rapid expansion was, however, the Depression; then Crispin's policy of low costs, low mark-ups, good quality and no credit really paid off. By 1937 Crispin has 450 stores—mostly, of course, very small and staffed by a manager and one salesperson only. During that period Crispin also succeeded in acquiring its own manufacturing plants—efficient and well-run New England shoe manufacturers of both women's and men's shoes which had gone down during the Depression and were for sale at very low prices. And during World War II Crispin boomed. But then it began to stagnate. It stuck to its old policies and methods: cheap, serviceable shoes where the customers more and more wanted fashion; small stores in residential or downtown neighborhoods where buyers more and more moved to shopping centers; above all, the "one best buy" in each major category, that is one low-priced but well-made shoe where customers increasingly wanted selection and the opportunity to "trade up." Paul Crispin tried to counteract the steady decline by heavy advertising, by special promotions, and by becoming even lower priced. But he was unwilling to change basic policies, and did not even permit any discussion of them in his presence. As a result, the entire chain lost increasingly its standing in the market place; indeed it acquired—largely unjustifiably—the reputation of being "low-quality." Even old customers drifted off.

Then, in 1952, Crispin, by now thoroughly discouraged, retired and withdrew completely. He was succeeded by a trio of young men—the oldest barely forty, the youngest not even thirty—who had joined Crispin right after World War II, had worked their way up through store management, buying and store control, and knew the company thoroughly—and also had long itched to change it. The three—Jack, the oldest, and a shoe-store manager by background; Jim, the middle one in age, a buyer by background; and Bob, the youngest and an accountant (and the only one with a college degree) —agreed to work as a group. Jack became Chairman; Jim President, and Bob Financial VP. The surviving members of the founding family—Paul Crispin's three married sisters and one old aunt—supported them enthusiastically; they had long been tired of the slow but steady decay of the company of which they were all substantial owners (though the company had gone public in the 1920s and was listed on the New York Stock Exchange, with the majority of the stock held by a large number of mostly small investors, mainly in the Midwest) .

Jack, Jim and Bob were convinced that the company was fundamentally sound but needed complete overhaul. In one big "bloodbath" they shut down 225 of the company's then existing 640 stores—old downtown stores, old small stores in decaying neighborhoods, old dingy and dirty stores that would have required massive investment to spruce up, and so on. The money this released they poured into renovating a small number of stores that were in the "right" locations, but above all into a massive offensive into shopping centers—with a brand new kind of store, bigger, with open shelves, colorful, and with merchandise designed for a new type of "affluent"—and above all—*young* buyer. The three men were in full agreement on strategy. First, they said, the buyer today (i.e., in the 1950s) is young, affluent, fashion conscious and wants to spend money; he or she needs "young" merchandise, and wants to trade up—and that meant that instead of the "one best buy," Crispin began to offer each style in three selections (brazenly stolen from Sears, of course): Good, BETTER AND BEST! Secondly, the three agreed that the place where the customer buys is the shopping center or the discount store—and so they pushed aggressively into the new shopping centers with stores of their own, and developed a particularly successful "leased shoe department" which they installed and ran in discount stores. Above all where Crispin had promoted wear and utility—its slogan had been for many years, "The shoe you will still want to wear at your daughter's wedding" —the emphasis was now on style, fashion, and design.

In another seven years, Crispin doubled and more than doubled volume and profits, and it continued flowing through the Sixties. Crispin had been turned around, had become one of the leading shoe store chains in volume and in number of stores, and the number one shoe company in the United States in terms of profit margins and profits.

In February, 1967—fifteen years after they had taken over—the three top management members of Crispin went off together on a combined victory celebration and skiing holiday. The second evening out Bob—who usually took the lead in discussions regarding objectives and strategy—said: "We three knew that this decade in the United States was going to be the teenagers' era—we have always paid attention to the demographics. As a result, we are sitting pretty—of course, that's what we planned all along. I figure that by 1971 we'll again double our present volume and our present profits— just by doing what we have learned to do. BUT then the party will be over. Consumption of shoes per person is, as we know (and our competitors apparently don't) a function of age rather than of income. Wealthier people spend more per pair of shoes; but they don't buy more pairs. The one difference is between the teenager, male or female, and the adult—the teenager buys three to four times as many pairs a year. This, we know, has been the basic reality of our business since the Thirties—and there is no reason to believe that it will change. And, after this coming decade the proportion of teenagers in the United States population will stop going up, and will soon thereafter begin to go down. We have to think NOW what we'll do—and start working for it pretty soon."

Both Jack and Jim agreed—indeed Bob had only voiced their own thoughts. And both Jack and Jim immediately KNEW what to do. "We have learned," said Jack, "how to run retail businesses with high volume, low overhead and in a great many locations —especially if it's fashion or wearing apparel or things people buy often but not so often that it's a routine. We should expand into young men's and young women's wear, into greeting cards, into all kinds of retail operations where our knowledge of the customer, our ability to develop merchandise and to buy, and our ability to find the right locations where people shop, are crucial. I think we can triple the business we are doing without having to learn very much beyond what we have learned designing, buying and selling footwear."

"I don't disagree with that," said Jack; "but that's not where I'd take the company. There is too much competition; there isn't exactly a glaring shortage of boutiques in the shopping centers. And any damn fool can sell greeting cards. But the same kind of buying public for SHOES we have seen come into being in this country since Paul Crispin opened his first branch store in 1919, is now surging ahead every place in the world. You know that I go to Europe and to the Far East regularly to buy shoes and sneakers. In Europe they still have yesterday's shoe store—smack downtown, occupying expensive real estate with fabulous rentals and overheads, or in slums, dingy, dirty, without stock and selection. In most of Asia or South America they don't even have that. And yet they have the same buying public we have—and soon they'll have as much purchasing power in many of these places. Indeed," said Jack, "sometimes I wonder whether we shouldn't even proposition the governments of the Communist countries in Europe—the Hungarians or the Czechs—and offer to build and manage shoe chains for them. We know the shoe retail business as no one else does; and for twenty-five years to come it will offer even greater opportunities outside the US than it ever did in our lifetime within the US."

The two wrangled on the rest of their skiing vacation —and well beyond it, each agreeing with the other but still preferring his favorite direction. It was the first major disagreement within the group since it had taken over. And rather than fight it out, the three silently agreed to let each—Jack and Jim—"experiment" with the policy he favored and advocated. In the next few years, i.e., in the late Sixties, Crispin therefore bought up a few small domestic chains outside of the shoe field, mainly in "young fashions." And it bought up a few small shoe chains in a few countries outside the US—one in Spain, one in Belgium, one in Colombia, and one in Singapore. None of these acquisitions was large—after all they were meant to be "experiments." Yet each, after the manner of acquisitions, pretty soon got into trouble and required management and money —and above all, direction and purpose. The domestic shoe business did indeed continue to rise on the tide of the "youth explosion" of the Sixties. Performance and results of the company soared—and so did the stock price. But the three top executives knew perfectly well that the wonderful showing was, in effect, cashing in on yesterday, and that their new ventures were in deep trouble—and with them the company.

It was Bob who again, in the fall of 1971, forced the issue. He called a weekend meeting of the three at his home and said, "Look, all three of us know that we are not making progress. I think all three of us are in agreement on fundamentals. We need to redefine what our business should be. But we also know that we have to decide on *one* direction. We have neither the resources nor the energy to run in more than one direction at once—and if the right options for us are non-shoe fashion retail in the US and shoe retail outside (and I think they are, and so do you) then we better decide on one and forget the other. And we are in agreement, I know, that we need to push ahead with all we've got once we have decided on the direction. Teasing a big market won't get us anywhere except into trouble. We have to think through our program, set objectives, work out strategy (whether we acquire, for instance, or start our own, and what we should be trying to acquire), have people who can do the work, in short take it seriously. You two fellows agree?"

Jack and Jim nodded assent.

"All right," said Bob, "then let's not start again arguing the merits of the two directions; all three of us know these arguments forward, backward and sideways—and they don't convince anyone any more. Let's rather ask: what *questions* do we need to ask to identify our strengths and to size up the opportunity? What do we need to *know*—about ourselves as well as about markets and business opportunities, money and people—to be able to decide under what conditions one or the other of these two options is the right course for *us?* And," he said, "let's put down ONE GROUND RULE: All right, Crispin is a big company by now; but let's not act like big shots; let's not say 'call a management consultant or appoint a staff to make a study.' The three of us know all there is to be known—and it's our decision anyhow."

Needless to say, Jack and Jim did appoint a staff man —it's *YOU.*

CASE 4:   Research Strategy and Business Objectives

Three pharmaceutical companies—to be original, let us call them "Able," "Baker," and "Charlie"—are among the most successful pharmaceutical businesses in the world. Two, "Able," and "Baker," are very large. "Charlie" is medium-sized, but growing fast.

All three companies spend about the same percentage

of their revenues on research. But then the similarity ends. Each of them approaches research quite differently.

"Able"—the oldest company and the leader in the industry since the end of World War I (also, the most international of the companies) —spends a great deal of research money on one carefully selected area. It picks this area—an exceedingly risky decision—when pure research results indicate a genuine "breakthrough." Then, long before commercial products are available, it hires the very best people in the field, usually the people who have made the original breakthroughs in theory, and puts them to work. Its aim is to gain early leadership in a major area, acquire dominance in it, then maintain this leadership position for many, many years— if not for many decades. Outside of these areas, however, the company spends no research money and is perfectly willing not to be a factor at all. In the 1920s, the strategy was originated when the original work on vitamins was first published. The company thereupon hired the Nobel Prize–winning chemists who had done the work, brought in the biochemists and pharmacologists and medical people who developed vitamins, and became—within a few years—the world's largest supplier of vitamins and remains so to this day. It did not go into another research area, but stayed within the development and exploitation of vitamins until the mid-Thirties. Then the sulfa drugs were picked up, again when they were not much more than a "scientific curiosity," and by 1940 the company had acquired world leadership in the sulfas. It did not go into the microbial antibiotics, e.g., penicillin. However, to this day it has world leadership in the sulfa drugs which are still, despite the rise of antibiotics, something like one-third the market for drugs against infectious disease (especially in Europe). The next major move did not take place until 1950 or so, when the central nervous system drugs —the first tranquillizers—came up. Then the company again went massively into research and emerged with a near-monopoly position in the tranquillizer field. And ten years later, in the late 1960s, it went heavily into microbiology and cell structure—again, on the basis of very early results in theoretical research. It paid no attention to fields which it decided not to concentrate upon. It not only totally neglected the antibiotics, it equally neglected, and quite deliberately so, the whole field of fertility control and so on. It takes big positions in big fields at a very early stage, at great risk, but also—in case of success—at great reward.

The strategy of company "Baker" is completely different. Its research lab, perhaps the most famous research lab in the pharmaceutical industry, works in an enormous number of fields. It does not, however, start work in a field until the basic scientific theoretical work has been done. Then it goes to work. The aim is to come up with a small number of drugs in each field which are clearly superior and offer significant advances to medical practice. Of every ten products that come out of the laboratory, the company markets no more than two or three. When it becomes reasonably clear that an effective drug will result from a line of research, the company carefully scrutinizes the product, and indeed, the entire field. First, is the new product likely to be medically so superior as to become the new "standard"? Secondly, is it likely to have major impact throughout the field of health care and medical practice rather than be confined to one specialty area, even a large one? And finally, is it likely to remain the "standard" for a good many years, rather than be overtaken by competitive products? If the answer to any of these three questions is "No," the company will license or sell the development, rather than convert it into a product of its own. This has been highly profitable in two ways. In the first place, it has generated licensing incomes almost equal to the profits the company makes on the drugs it makes and sells under its own name. Second, it has assured that each of the company's products is considered the "leader" by the medical profession (though occasionally the company has licensed or sold a product that then became the "leader" in another company's—including competitors —product line).

"Charlie" company does no "research." All it does is "develop." It will not tackle any of the products "Able" or "Baker" companies consider attractive. It looks for areas where a fairly simple, but patentable, development can give it a near-monopoly position in a small but important area. It looks for areas in medical and surgical practice where existing products are not effective, and where a fairly simple change can greatly improve the doctors' or surgeons' performance. And it looks for fields that are so small that once there is a truly superior product, there is no incentive for anyone else to try to go in and compete. Its first product was a simple enzyme—actually known for forty years—to make cataract operations virtually bloodless and greatly ease the eye surgeon's job. All the work that had to be done was to find a way to extend the shelf-life of the enzyme, which up till then could only be kept for a few hours under very heavy refrigeration, and even then tended to fall apart. The next product was a very simple ointment to put on the umbilical cord of mothers and infants to prevent infection and speed up healing. It has become standard in every maternity hospital throughout the world. The company has just now brought out a product to replace the toxic solution with which newborn babies used to be washed to prevent infection. Again, primarily a matter of compounding rather than discovering. In each area, the world market is so limited—maybe to $20 million—that a single supplier, provided he offers a truly superior product, can occupy a near-monopoly position with a minimum of competition and practically no pressure on price.

What do these three different strategies assume in respect to business objectives, in respect to the structure and behavior of the market, in respect to the basic mission and objectives of the company?

CASE 5: Montgomery Ward's Dilemma

Prior to World War I, Montgomery Ward was ahead of Sears. Then, in the Twenties, Sears realized before Montgomery Ward did that the American customer had acquired wheels, and Sears began to build stores. By 1930, Sears was already well ahead. Yet until World

War II, Montgomery Ward was a strong contender. Then it fell drastically behind, in large part because the company's autocratic Chief Executive, Sewell Avery, decided that America would experience a catastrophic depression after World War II, and refused to modernize stores or to invest in merchandising. He clung to his mistake long after events had disproven it.

When Avery left in the early Fifties, Montgomery Ward was a shambles. A new management was hastily brought in, largely from Sears Roebuck. It tried to rebuild the company by imitating Sears Roebuck. It succeeded in preventing the collapse of Montgomery Ward. But Montgomery Ward has not regained its momentum, even though it has regained modest profitability. The gap between Sears and Montgomery Ward is steadily widening. During the Sixties, Montgomery Ward merged with another "number 2" company, the Container Corporation of America, to form "Marcor." It is, therefore, no longer quite as easy to compare Montgomery Ward to Sears. But on the basis of available figures, Sears now does a retail business of well over $10 billion and Montgomery Ward does a little more than $2 billion, that is, only one-fifth. Montgomery Ward makes less than one-tenth of Sears' income—$50 million, against $500 million. Its return on sales is under 2 percent, as against 5 percent for Sears.

Worse still, Montgomery Ward has been outflanked in its strategy. Two companies which did not imitate Sears, but developed strategies of their own, Penney and Kresge, have raced ahead of Montgomery Ward to become, respectively, "number 3" and "number 4" among non-food retailers. Penney, twenty years ago, was as stagnant as Montgomery Ward. But the policy which it adopted was radically different. Instead of trying to compete with Sears as the buyer for the American family, Penney deliberately set out to concentrate on fast-moving lines, carry only a small but carefully chosen selection and, above all, go after the lower income group. Kresge, in its K-Marts, went into large shopping center discount operations, again focusing on selected areas—such as fashion footwear for teenagers—high turnover, and especially on the youth market. As a result, Montgomery

Ward has been successful neither in catching up with Sears nor in developing an alternative to Sears. But at least the company is no longer bleeding to death, as it was twenty years ago.

However, it also has not been a success.

Assume that you are the new top management of Montgomery Ward, such as might be put in if Mobile Oil succeeds in its take-over bid for the Marcor Corporation, the holding company for Montgomery Ward. The big programs of the Fifties and Sixties—closing old stores, building new stores, and, above all, building an organization—have been accomplished. Financial means are available. The one thing that is lacking is a winning strategy. How would you go about thinking through what the alternatives might be?

CASE 6: What Is a Growth Company?

An old established baker of bread and cakes—distributed widely in one of the country's major metropolitan areas —was bought, during the "conglomerate" craze of the late Sixties by one of the glamor "go-go" companies of that time—the bakery's stock was selling at 8 times earnings on the stock market, the conglomerate had offered 14 times earnings, that is, had made an irresistible offer, and had paid with its own stock that then sold at 37 times earnings—so everybody was happy, or should have been. The president, a middle-aged but very vigorous member of the founding family—in fact the grandson of the Swedish baker who had started the business around 1890—agreed to stay on with a five-year contract.

Six months after the acquisition had been consummated the bakery's president was called to New York headquarters for a meeting with the president of the conglomerate. "You know, John," the conglomerate president said, "that it is our policy that every one of our divisions shows 10 percent growth a year and makes a return of at least 10 percent pre-tax on investment. Your division is growing only at 1 or 2 percent a year and shows only 7 percent pretax—no more than we can get in a savings-bank account. Our staff people are ready to sit down with you and turn your business around so that it can meet our growth and profit objectives."

"I am afraid," answered the bakery's president, "that they would be wasting their time and mine. A bakery is not a growth business, and nothing you do can make it into one in a developed country. People don't eat more bread or even more cakes as their incomes go up: they eat less. A bakery has built-in protection against a downturn; in fact, we'd probably do best in a really serious depression. But our growth isn't going to be faster than that of population overall. And as for profits, we get paid for being efficient—I know we need to be far more efficient but that would require fairly massive investment in building new automated bakeries—and with our price-earnings ratio we have never felt able to raise the kind of money we need—and even after we've spent it, our rate of return isn't going to be more than 1 percent pre-tax at best."

"*This is unacceptable,*" snapped the conglomerate's president. "I agree," said the bakery man. "Indeed this is precisely the reason we gladly accepted your offer to buy us out—we had to free our family's own money for more attractive investments; and all our money was in grandpa's bakery. That's however also the reason why all of us immediately sold your company's stock. And, finally," said the bakery man, "that's the reason why I am quite willing for you to buy up my employment contract—and if you want to run a bread bakery as a 'go-go' company you had better buy me out—I wouldn't know how to try."

Can one be satisfied with a business that earns less than the minimum cost of capital and cannot, for instance, raise the capital it needs to become efficient, i.e., to be able to survive and to contribute? If not, what (if anything) can be done? And who is right: the man who says that this kind of business cannot be run as a business or the man who says that if the market is there —and the company makes BREAD, not buggy whips, and has the market and the market demand—it is management's job to earn a return adequate to the needs of the company, i.e., a return that can attract the needed capital? Or are both wrong?

CASE 7:   What Are "Results"?

Robert Armstrong had joined the struggling family company as soon as he came out of the Navy after World War II. A few years later his father suddenly died and Armstrong had to take over what was then a very small, and indeed, practically marginal business. For fifteen to twenty years the business took all his time —or almost all of it. For Armstrong had always had a strong interest in health care—as a youngster he seriously thought of going to medical school and might have done so had he not been drafted while in college during World War II. He began to work for one of the major community hospitals in his metropolitan area almost immediately, was elected to the board in the early 1950s and chairman of the Board in 1964. And he took these duties seriously and gave unstintingly of his time and energy.

By the late Sixties the Armstrong Company had become a fairly substantial business—sales around $100 million or so; and where Robert Armstrong had been "the management" twenty years earlier, he had built what he considered an unusually competent management team. Though not yet fifty, business began to bore him—and he also began to resent the heavy traveling schedule which the business imposed on him.

At this juncture the Administrator of the hospital suddenly suffered a stroke and had to retire. The Board appointed a Selection Committee—Robert Armstrong, Chairman. Before the first meeting of the Committee, Armstrong got together privately with the hospital's Chief of Medical Services—a highly respected internist who had also for many years been Armstrong's personal physician—to think through with him what kind of a man the Committee should be looking for. To Armstrong's total surprise, the doctor said: "Look Bob, cut out the nonsense. You don't have to 'look' for the man to head up St. Luke's. YOU are the man—no one knows more about the place than you do. No one is better accepted. And I know—you told me so last October at your annual physical—that your present job bores you, that they don't need you in the company any more, and that you and Libby are tired of your eternal traveling. All right, so you are making a great deal more dough as president of Armstrong than we pay a hospital administrator. But you have enough money and don't need a big income—and hospital administrators aren't that badly paid anyhow and make as much as you pay your vice-presidents—at least that's what you told us when we last raised the administrator's salary in the board meeting six months ago."

The more Armstrong thought about this, the more sense it made to him—and Libby was enthusiastic. But also, the more Armstrong thought about this, the more uneasy he became about his ability to do the job. He went back to the doctor and said: "If I take this job, how do I measure my performance? What results should I be after? What is performance in a hosptial, and what are results?" The doctor grinned broadly and said: "I knew you'd ask these questions—and that's why I'd love to see you take the job. I know what 'results' are in my work and in my practice. But neither I nor anyone else knows what they are in and for the hospital—and maybe it's time some disagreeable type like you asks these questions."

Armstrong did take the job—and five to ten years later, that is now, he still isn't sure how to ask the questions, let alone what the answers are—could you help him?

CASE 8: Celanese and Courtaulds

For some twenty years or so, the manufacturers of "artificial silk," as rayon and acetate were originally known, occupied a special ecological niche in the economy. Their raw material was wood pulp. But the large wood processors, that is the paper companies, did not have the chemical expertise to go into rayon making. At the same time, none of the chemical companies knew anything about wood pulp. So, while their field was limited, they also enjoyed it with little disturbance from big and powerful competitors.

All this changed dramatically with the arrival of nylon, and then with the development of the other chemical petrol fibers—the polyesters and so on. This meant, on the one hand, that the powerful chemical companies, a DuPont or a Union Carbide in this country, or an Imperial Chemical Industries in Great Britain and so on—suddenly became powerful competitors in the field of artificial fibers. Equally important: the big oil companies began to look upon synthetic fibers as a field to put their main product, that is crude oil, to market. And the big oil companies had financial means available which were totally beyond the reach of such medium-size businesses as were then engaged in the "artificial silk" industry.

Faced with this dilemma, the two leading companies in the United States and Great Britain, respectively, adopted different strategies. Celanese Corporation of America, one of the largest independent "artificial silk" manufacturers in the United States, decided to become the preferred channel through which foreign chemical companies would market their research in the United States. It argued that such foreign chemical companies as Imperial Chemical Industries in Great Britain or Bayer in Germany, while "giants" in their own rights, still lacked the means, and, above all, the market knowledge to invade the American market—an assumption that proved correct for twenty years, that is until the Seventies. Therefore, they concluded that these companies would be willing to license a company with a strong position in the American market and with adequate chemical competence, to develop and market their research developments in the US. And this assumption —at least for twenty years, when Celanese first licensed the English Orlon and Dacron patents from Imperial Chemical Industries—has paid off handsomely.

Courtaulds of England, in a position very similar to that of Celanese, followed a totally different strategy. It bought major users of fibers, that is major textile manufacturers. It became, in effect, one of the largest manufacturers of textile fabrics in the United Kingdom. And this strategy also proved successful.

Under what conditions would each of these strategies be likely to work? What was the thinking behind them? What are the risks of each? Would the English strategy have worked in the United States? And would the American strategy have worked in the United Kingdom?

14.

Worldwide Cultural Variations
in Management Style

Within three decades of the end of World War II the concepts of management as a discipline had been accepted throughout the world. Developed countries acknowledged the need for management skills and the overhaul of their organizational frameworks as a prerequisite for participation in the global corporate society. Yet-to-be-developed countries sought management expertise so that they might build the organizations they would require to function as participants in the new world order.

These newly perceived needs have made Peter Drucker a counselor with an international clientele. He works with governments, businesses, and institutions throughout the noncommunist world, and his concepts are digested and adopted—though with minimal acknowledgment—behind what used to be called the iron curtain. Drucker is in a position like that of the conductor Herbert Von Karajan, of whom the following apocryphal anecdote is told. Von Karajan hurries out of a train station in a European capital and jumps into a cab. The taxi driver asks, "Where to?" With a sweep of the hand the eminent conductor replies, "It doesn't matter. I am in demand everywhere!"

The fact that Drucker is "in demand everywhere" gives him a unique opportunity to observe the ways in which management and organizational styles vary in different locations and cultures. Drucker is keenly attuned to these variations; he must bear them in mind constantly as he talks with managers from diverse national backgrounds. He finds certain basic similarities, imposed by the nature of management and organizations no matter where they operate. But he finds interesting differences as well.

In at least one important sense, Drucker observes that there are greater differences within cultures than between cultures. For example, big business everywhere is different from small business: "It is much more difficult for a manager to move from, say, GE to a small company in the United States than it is for him to manage within a big business in Japan. Big businesses have certain things in common. The manager gets used to the support of an ample staff; to formal reporting and decision processes; to the formal assignment of responsibilities. He grows accustomed to the atmosphere of a big business in which the system carries him to a heavy extent."

Standards are usually lower in a small business, says Drucker; or at least they are less well defined. He adds emphatically that he does not urge that small businessmen adopt the standards of big business. They are not necessary and may be needlessly restrictive: "It would be like putting a strapless bra on a nine-year-old."

Similarily, in many cases the small business that is attempting to increase in size goes through a much greater identity crisis than would be encountered were the same business to operate in its size class in a different culture.

Type of industry may impose similarities throughout the world, which override cultural differences. For example, says Drucker, "In every place the textile industry is still very much a nineteenth-century industry. So the one or two textile companies that are modern companies stick out like sore thumbs. And they are unpopular. A few textile companies are run like modern businesses, with the emphasis on technology rather than on whom you know. Competitors simply do not understand this. They ask each other, 'What are those people up to? This isn't the way to run a shirting business!' The textile industry, of course, is very old; only within the last thirty years has it begun to break out of deeply embedded family tradition."

There are, however, important cultural differences in the way business is done around the world. In part, Drucker points out, these have to do with capital market structure: "In Germany, for instance, you either stay out of the public capital market altogether or you become a captive of the banks. There's no in-between. Since there is no really active capital market, and no capital gain in our sense, the emphasis rests very heavily on maintaining a stable dividend. This is much more important than showing an earnings gain."

In Japan, says Drucker, "Eighty to 90 percent of capital comes from the banks, so the emphasis is on earning enough to pay the interest with a good margin. There are no stock options or profit-sharing bonuses, and management cannot be fired except in a real catastrophe. So there is no motivation for profitability. The motivation is to cover the costs of capital."

There are differences in other areas, too. "In the United States," Drucker remarks, "we tend to look upon top management as the people who work the hardest in the business. In Japan top management doesn't do any work. *Work* is done by juniors. Top management takes care of relations and personnel decisions. The juniors—meaning forty-five-year-old department heads—do the work and make, collectively, the business decisions. Not that the role of top management is superfluous or merely ceremonial; far from it. Top management has a vital task in concerning itself with the incredibly important relations with government, with industry associations, and the innumerable other relationships that dominate Japanese life. And they make personnel decisions. It is not a ceremonial task, but it is very much a protocol task."

In Germany, to take another example, top management goes to the opposite extreme. "There," says Drucker, "they overwork. Typically, you have an overconcentration of decision-making at the top. In Germany there is also a sharp line—although it is diminishing—between the owner-entrepreneur and the professional manager. The owner-entrepreneur still considers himself—and is considered—as the possessor of 'divine right.' "

Continuing to comment on cultural influences on how business is conducted in Germany, Drucker remarks that there it is unheard of for anybody to move from sales into finance, or even finance into production, or from production into marketing. The crossing of lines happens only at the very top. Below the top, career lines are strictly functional.

In Germany there is also the "mystique of the engineer." People who have never done anything but engineering are accepted, without the slightest question, as heads of businesses.

Drucker contrasts the German mystique of the engineer with what he sees in France as the "mystique of the *polytechnicien*." A graduate of *l'école polytechnique* who has spent some time working in government is considered by the French "to be clearly qualified to do anything." Graduates of the prestige schools go into government, where, according to Drucker, they become *inspecteurs de finance*—department heads—and then move into top positions in industry, each accompanied by a retinue of young *polytechniciens*. These functionaries have no specific tasks. They are, says Drucker, the top manager's spies, his "eyes and ears."

Between Germany and France, then, the greatest differences are in approved career ladders. In Japan, on the other hand, a manager's specialty is unimportant, but says Drucker, "the university you come from is everything."

The routes to the summit vary. Says Drucker: "In Germany it is unheard of for a manufacturing or a marketing fellow to get to the top. One must be an engineer or a financial man with a law degree . . . and it helps if he has worked for the government." Unlike

Japan, it is functional area, not university, that makes all the difference.

And then there are differences in style. Drucker points out that it is difficult for a German company to form a task force to study a problem. To take junior managers from the line and assign them to a problem makes German management uncomfortable . . . "They are, after all, *juniors.* You are violating the lines of authority."

Drucker goes further in illustrating cultural influence on management style: "There are, for example, many companies in Germany today where the managers speak English with each other because this means they can use first names and no titles. They have abolished titles in Germany. You make a point of not using Director or Doctor or Professor; just Mister so-and-so; but you do it very self-consciously. When German managers speak English they can call each other Hans and Berthold and Karl; the moment they speak German they become formal."

In Drucker's view the French are more rank conscious than the Germans: "At a management meeting in France they do not invite people of different ranks. At a seminar I conducted in France not long ago my host told me that everybody there was at least a director-general and most were presidents. And this was a public meeting."

Such formal rank consciousness is no longer the rule in Germany. However, Drucker comments, you may have a meeting in Germany at which the audience comprises people from different levels, "but the only ones who ask questions are the 'four-star generals.' One man got up and said, 'Well, I do not run a very big company, but at least I *own* it.' "

One of the major reasons for England's current troubles, as Drucker sees it, is that good people do not go into the manufacturing industry. They go into civil service or into banking. Even "trade" is more acceptable than manufacturing.

"In Germany," he says, "it's the other way around. There the civil service has a fairly low standing—as it does in Japan, by the way. But in England bright young people go into banking, into insurance—into the 'City,' not into basic industries, which are really understaffed. A gentleman can be a banker, but he cannot be a manufacturing manager."

Drucker sees historic and cultural reasons for this. In the middle of the nineteenth century the manufacturer was usually a Dissenter—not a member of the Church of England establishment. The days of heavy emphasis on the importance of formal religion are past, but the cultural residue remains. "While management is imbedded in the English culture," says Drucker, "of all the countries I know, money is still most revered in England. It is most important. The English are incredibly money conscious."

The discipline of management has achieved universality, but its practice takes divergent paths as it flows through the cultural terrain. Drucker sees the divergences, and he savors them.

15.

Some Predictions
of Prophet Peter

Peter Drucker is an inveterate prophesier.

When he talks he is careful to say that he "never makes predictions." But, to Drucker, the future has the lure of the bottle to the dipsomaniac. He cannot stay away from the future. He knows forecasting is risky. He has described emphatically what he sees as the folly of a man who dares to say what lies ahead.

And yet he does it.

Drucker makes two kinds of predictions. One kind is better described as a projection. He studies trends, projects them ahead, and then tells what he sees. Drucker does not call this "predicting" at all. He maintains that anyone who looks at population curves, for example, will be able to state with assurance that certain things will happen. Nevertheless, he began to do this before others did, before "futurism" became a highly paid profession.

But there are moments when Drucker will flash forth with an off-the-cuff forecast. At these moments emotion, not logic, is apt to control the process. Depressed at what he sees as increasing irresponsibility and license in print and on the air he will declare somberly that a terrible reaction is coming, one that may mean the end of free expression in the United States.

The studies and projections tell us a lot about the future. The off-the-cuff outbursts may tell us more about Drucker. Both are worth attention.

Here is Peter Drucker in his role of "projector," talking about how the United States is in the process of becoming a "have-not" nation: ". . . the painful truth is that our basic long-range position in the international economy is not one of strength, but of great potential weakness. The overriding need of the American economy will be to find a supply of raw materials to keep our industrial machine going. And a rapidly increasing amount of these raw materials will have to come from abroad . . . . Crude oil, which we used to export in floods, now has to be imported in increasing amounts."

Thus Drucker, in 1957, in *America's Next Twenty Years*. I do not mean, by the selection of this quotation, to go overboard in attributing to Drucker awesome powers of precognition. He was not predicting the *political* events in the Middle East, notably the formation and activities of OPEC, which have strangulated the industrial nations. But he was describing a developing situation in which America would be increasingly at the mercy of other countries. Although never one to overlook the irrational factors of human behavior, Drucker did not go on record as foreseeing an oil boycott mounted primarily as a weapon against Israel. (Who did?)

Drucker pointed out that America was rapidly using up, not only oil, but a wide variety of raw materials: iron, wood pulp, chrome, and so on. Observing that the United States with 10 percent of the world's population was using about 50 percent of the world's raw materials, he estimated that the cupboard would soon run bare. Moreover, he took note of the fact that other industrial nations were even more dependent on imports of raw materials than was the United States.

Drucker was not making this prediction up out of his head. The Paley Commission, appointed by President Truman in 1951, had made the study that provided the underpinning for his views. But Drucker's interpretation led him to believe that the Paley Commission had seriously understated the danger. For example, it had foreseen America's power needs as doubling within twenty-five years. He saw the rise in power usage as being much more steep. Furthermore, noting that the commission was talking about the United States alone, Drucker remarked that raw material usage was increasing even faster in other countries.

Drucker did not talk about cutting back on energy usage. He has never agreed with those who say the world can be saved that way. Instead, he proposed a *management* solution, through which a new American economic policy would assure its power needs for the future. He stressed that something would have to be done fast, that this was a critical problem that would soon become a dangerous situation if ignored.

His first suggested goal was the increase of American export capacity fast enough to solve what he saw as a soon-to-be-critical balance of payments problem. Unless the United States became competitive in the world market, it could no longer pay its international bills.

Then, the United States would somehow have to see to it that the production of raw materials would be expanded heavily throughout the world. We could not expect to expand our share of a static supply; we would have no allies left in the world. Furthermore, supplier countries would be developing their own industries, and they would use their resources to supply themselves first, rather than to help the United States out of a hole.

The third tenet of this policy was political. The United States would have to identify and recognize the needs and aspirations of people all over the "free world" so that they would continue to be willing to cooperate with us. We could not buy such cooperation, nor coerce it.

The "free world" would have to be made strong socially and politically. U.S. policy would have to symbolize the beliefs and values of the non-Communist, "and must express the reality of responsible American leadership."

Here there is no hint that America should withdraw from its position as leader of the non-Communist world. America should take an even more vigorous position out in front. Was this imperialism? Drucker posed the question himself, but did not give a direct answer. In effect he said that it was not imperialism in the bad old sense, but rather a new and positive form of economic imperialism, conducted with the assent and for the benefit of the colonized, and led, not by soldiers, but by businessmen. The real strength of America in this struggle was the *manager* who was enlightened enough to see that machinery was not the answer; who rather possessed "intellectual discipline and an ethical attitude toward the job to be done." These managers were strong because of their "respect for human beings as the basic resource—rather than the concept of labor as a cost—and the use of people as a social, intellectual, moral, and spiritual resource, rather than as a purely economic one."

We may note several things about this position. As an aside, one might point out that here Drucker is prefiguring the concept of "Human Resource Accounting" which was to come into vogue among industrial psychologists some ten years later. More to the point, it is essential Drucker of the time, both in what it says and what it leaves out. The possibility of détente does not enter into the equation; Drucker was accepting the continuation of the cold war. His answers were aimed at the "free world"; overshadowing all calculations is the continuing struggle with the "Reds."

Even more notable is Drucker's overarching faith in the archetypal manager as the solver of the world's problems.

At this time, in 1957, it seemed that he was talking particularly about the American manager. Drucker had previously disavowed any belief in an American "monopoly" on managers or management. He had, indeed, been accused—especially by Henry Luce and his publications—of not sufficiently accepting the idea of an "American Century" but of always stressing the universality of management as a function. Nevertheless, his message at this point was widely interpreted as being that the American manager—supported by the government—would spread the gospel of entrepreneurship and management techniques. It would be hard work and a great challenge, but the manager—with his combination of expertise, moral fiber and humanity—would be worthy of it.

This evangelical view of American management does not look so good from the vantage point of twenty years later. American management has not solved the world's problems. As we note elsewhere, Drucker maintains that, through the development of the much-abused multinational corporations, American management may yet fulfill this role. But certainly the exporting of United States executive know-how to Iran and Kuwait did not head off the oil shortage.

However, Drucker did see the problem as it was developing, and described, in general but accurate terms, the situation we find ourselves in today. He spoke of raw materials over a broad range, not just oil; and we now see the ominous possibilities of OPEC-like cartels assailing us on other fronts.

At this time Drucker was concerned about another source problem. He was developing his concept of the importance of "knowledge" to the society—and he looked ahead from the mid-1950s to see what was going to happen to the colleges. What he saw was alarming.

There would be a tremendous explosion in college enrollments. By 1975 there might be as many as 12 million Americans going to college—a wild figure at the time, but pretty accurate as it turned out. How would the colleges and universities handle the explosion? It would take money. Families would, he foresaw, flounder under the immense burden of increasing tuition costs. Even so, institutions of higher education, no matter how steeply they jacked up their fees, would still be getting deeper and deeper into the hole.

And who would do the teaching? Drucker felt that there would be a shortage of capable people to instruct all these eager high-school graduates arriving on campus: "Our real problem is not to get more youngsters into the colleges; it is not even to get more able youngsters there. The real problem is to get more able under-

248

graduates to go into teaching." (Time has modified Drucker's view—so sunny at that time—of the value of graduate schools.)

But the big problem was money. The cost of education would go to $50 billion by 1975. (He was underestimating the inroads of inflation.) One possibility was to have the federal government foot the bill. This possibility Drucker acknowledged as something that might come about—but he deplored it. He pointed out that government financing of education invariably meant government control of education. He saw the country "rushing into the worst kind of Ministry of Education—something on the French or Italian model perhaps, uncontrolled and uncontrollable, rigid, pedantic, timid, and yet all-powerful."

Somehow there had to be a better solution; a private solution, a *managed* solution. He pointed to what he saw as the analogy with health care, saying that these services were being handled adequately through voluntary organizations. (His opinion of voluntary health-care organizations was to change, and not for the better. He is certainly not alone in that.)

Drucker advanced tentative ideas about spreading the cost of education over longer periods of time, perhaps through a scheme of guaranteed government loans. Here he had his finger fairly accurately on the development that was, in fact, to come to pass.

However it had to be done, Drucker was insistent that higher education on a wide front would have to be made possible—permanently. He took note of the arguments of those who said that it would be better if the number of students going to college was cut down. Drucker saw it differently. He pointed out that financial problems, while great, grew out of a noble ideal—that of *classless* education. College could not revert to being the province only of those rich enough to pay for it themselves.

Drucker's answer was different. He went all-out in advocacy of the idea that "higher" education should become *general* education. In the long run, the country could remain great only through such broadest dissemination of knowledge. The financial problems could and would be solved by *management*.

The key to Drucker's approach to planning and forecasting lies in this line from *America's Next Twenty Years: "The major events that determine the future have already happened—irrevocably."*

The approach is typified by Drucker's study of population curves and the conclusions he draws from them. In the mid-1950s he announced that the momentous economic event of the decade had gone virtually unnoticed: the record high births during the period 1948 to 1956. The development, Drucker said, ran counter to what might have been expected. The young women who were bearing these babies were the generation born in the deep-Depression years of 1932 to 1934, when the birth rate was very low. Obviously there were fewer young people getting married, but they were having more babies.

From that point (1957) on, the number of young people reaching marriageable age would increase. So the birth-rate would increase, since "romance is reliably constant." "Romance" may be reliably constant, but there were a couple of developments in the offing that Drucker left out of his calculations. For one thing, within a decade the concept of marriage as the inevitable culmination of romance was to be considerably downgraded. For another—and it is surprising that Drucker, the great connector of disparate phenomena, did not crank this in—the pill and other birth-control devices would become controlling factors on the usufructs of romance, to the joy and profit of the drug industry on which Drucker had been keeping a benevolent and approving eye.

And then there was soon to be the women's liberation movement itself. For this, Peter Drucker has never had any feel. His world is an old-fashioned man's world, for all that he will now discuss, with lucidity if not with passion, the problems and the roles of women in society. However, since he did not see this coming, or discounted its consequences, he did not add it to the mix from which emerged his population projections.

In any event, Drucker disputed the prophets, including the census bureau, who were saying that America would reach a point of zero population growth in a few years and then start to decline. Here, since he was leaving certain factors out of his computations, he was not on as sure ground as he thought. Nevertheless, some of the inferences he drew at that time, particularly on the employment situation, are interesting.

He projected a paradox: there would be more people, and thus more jobs, but not enough people to fill the jobs. While the total population would grow rapidly through the 1960s and into the 1970s, the working population would grow slowly, if at all. So jobs would go begging: *"The supply of people to do the work, and of long hours to do it in, will in fact be so short as to make any prolonged period of large-scale national unemployment highly improbable."*

A wrong prediction, obviously, in the light of the distressing unemployment rate of the 1970s. But, when we examine the situation more closely, we can see some possible indications of where Drucker went wrong. In considerable part he may have been misled because he did not include in his considerations certain phenomena that at other times he has been highly conscious of, and to which he attributes great importance. These phenomena are the *knowledge explosion* and the need of the worker for *status* and *function*.

Unemployment was running at 9.2 percent in the middle of 1975. Surely Drucker's "highly improbable" situation was a grim reality. But, within that period, we were beginning to see oddities. The *New York Times* reported that jobs were going unfilled in many places —skilled and unskilled jobs alike. Employers were looking for toolmakers in Peoria, security guards in Detroit, machinists in Houston, short-order cooks in Pittsburgh, and so on. In southern California the jobless rate was above 10 percent; yet, at one unemployment office, officials were trying unsuccessfully to fill thirty-two jobs for secretaries, forty jobs for cooks, thirty-seven openings for security guards, seventy for machinists, and numerous others for clerks, waitresses, domestics and beauticians. Many were saying that anybody who wants a job can get one; and they had the evidence to prove it. So the paradox continued; an army of unemployed, with jobs going begging. Certainly this was not the picture remembered from the 1930s, when men would just about do anything to make a dollar, but found nothing to do.

What was the matter? In some cases job-seekers were simply not qualified for the jobs being offered. Work that had once required just muscle now takes training and skill. Drucker had foreseen this. In commenting on the impact of automation he remarked that the concept would not eliminate jobs, but that it would create different kinds of jobs: ". . . incredibly large numbers of men will be required behind the scenes in new, highly skilled jobs as machine builders, machine installers, repair men, controllers of the machinery and of its performance and as 'programmers' to prepare and feed information into the machine." He added that there would be great need for workers in design and engineering roles and for managerial tasks.

The jobs were there, but there were not enough people who were qualified to fill them. Drucker had called for a massive national effort to equip citizens with the knowledge necessary to fill roles in the new industrial order, but this had not happened to a great enough extent.

But what about the unskilled jobs? Why weren't the unemployed going to work as waiters or janitors? Part of the reason is that people can often make just about as much in unemployment benefits or on welfare as they can at these jobs. But this is by no means the whole story. Unskilled work is widely regarded as menial and subservient—*and people do not want to do it anymore.* Drucker had proclaimed that the industrial society must give all of its members *status* and *function.* The man who refuses to work behind a lunch counter does so to a considerable degree because he feels that, in our society, what you do is what you are. Slinging hash bestows no status on the slinger; and the function— when seen in the great scheme of things—is minuscule. People have come to demand more of life than their parents and grandparents did, and below a certain level they will not go.

So it is true that Peter Drucker's prediction of no

unemployment has emphatically not panned out. However, when we go back and restudy other concepts he has articulated we form a better understanding of the nature of the unemployment situation; and we see why it is apt to remain with us for a depressingly long time.

Drucker was shaky in his clouded view of the employment situation. But he was a lot surer as he looked at the possibilities of inflation. Commenting in the middle of the 1950s, he saw that sharply rising inflation might well have an enormously destructive effect. He stated flatly that inflation could be brought under control in only one way. Increased productivity was the paramount need of the American economy. If wages were allowed to rise without concomitant rises in productivity, inflation would grow into a cause of severe economic and social disruption.

At the time he was writing, Drucker pointed out that every working American had to support one-and-a-half people besides himself. By 1976 he would have to support three-and-a-half other people. And he would be working fewer hours. In the face of these coming realities, inflation was a distinct threat. And so it came to pass.

The very word *automation* struck fear into the hearts of many Americans. Drucker welcomed it—but he was at pains to point out what it consisted of. Automation is not mechanical or electronic gimmicks. It is a concept resting on several principles. One is that economic activity is an integrated process. The second is that there is form and order behind the seemingly random flux of economic phenomena. Finally, automation is self-regulating.

Working from these principles, Drucker describes automation as being simply a projection of twentieth-century philosophy into the economic sphere. The businessman did not have to be a philosopher to use a computer, but he would have to understand that it was more than a box of tricks.

This calm view of automation never "took" with labor leaders, or with a great many businessmen either. Workers continued to think of it as machines that would replace them. Managers approached it as a set of magical gadgets that would do things easier, faster, and cheaper.

Drucker also forecast that automation would bestow what he called a "new stability" on the economy. Piecemeal capital investment was simply not possible under automation. There would be a high premium on planning. But the new stability would bring calm and order into the business and employment picture.

Drucker recognized the risks. But he may have overrated the ability of managers to adjust to the new reality, while he underrated the "straitjacket" effect that automation works on many industrial processes. His confidence in managerial acumen was probably in this case overly generous. The "new stability" has become, for many unhappy companies and industries, the "new rigidity," with enormous capital costs and vastly decreased flexibility to respond to changes in the marketplace.

When he essayed to speculate on the coming issues in American politics, Drucker was overly logical. He cited matters that he thought, optimistically, to be those that *should* emerge as issues among rational candidates coming before rational voters. He spoke of the "new migration" that was concentrating population in the cities. He called attention to the alarming fact that we were "living off our water capital," and said that action on water conservation "should therefore be the hottest of political potatoes nearly everywhere in the country from now on."

Although Drucker did not, at that time, foresee that air pollution would also become an issue, the "clean water" forecast has held up well.

Drucker did add that conservation of all kinds would gain prominence in politics, and there his prediction is unassailable, if less than a blockbuster.

Power, transportation, and housing would push forward as issues, he said. The schools would become a focus of political strife. He meant the values and objectives of education, and the adequacy of teachers and facilities. He did not forewarn of the brouhaha over busing.

He did predict with general but reasonable accuracy

that the fight for black equality would shift from a demand for equal employment to a demand for equal opportunities for advancement. And he commented with accuracy that race relations would become a problem of the northern cities, with diminishing emphasis on what was happening in the South.

The trade unions, he felt, would diminish in political importance as jobs shifted from unskilled to skilled and as the work population began to be dominated by white-collar people. The acceptance or rejection of unionization by white-collar workers would determine whether big labor would continue as a powerful force or dwindle to an aging pressure group.

Somehow a way would have to be found to provide health care for everybody. And somehow the tax structure would have to be made to encourage continued business growth. As for inflation, Drucker saw this as an incipiently destructive issue, one that could tear the country apart. Monetary stability, therefore, should and would be prominent in political campaigns.

All these are domestic issues. This was the province that Drucker chose to focus on in *America's Next Twenty Years*—with a last-page caveat recognizing that foreign affairs might, in the end, play a decisive role in determining what was ahead for the United States.

Altogether, this brief book is a stimulating excursion backward in time, providing a view of today from twenty years ago. The point is not to keep score on Drucker's hits, misses, and near-misses—he scores them all—but to note his choices of the really important developments in American life. By and large he saw the way the complex of currents was moving—although he did not always gauge the speed of individual streams or fully consider how these currents would interact with one another.

It's one thing to make long-range predictions in writing. The prophet sits in a quiet study. He focuses the inward eye on the future. He roughs out what he sees. Then he has second thoughts. He modifies. He adapts. He eliminates. The result is even-tempered, coherent speculation.

This is the calm Drucker, the Buddha of so many

dust jacket photographs. There is another Drucker who, like the rest of us, gets upset about things and utters predictions in the heat of current emotion. When the ordinary individual does this, we can and do forget about it. When Peter Drucker does it, it may be interesting to examine what he says. (The following observations were made by Drucker during an interview in February 1975.)

Take, for example, the idea of "freedom of the press." In conversation with an interviewer, Drucker touched on the thoroughgoing scrutiny and criticism that the American intelligence apparatus has been undergoing in the mid-1970s. He feels that the CIA, FBI, and other branches of government are being judged harshly now for things they did ten or fifteen years ago, when the climate was very different. "In the atmosphere of the Sixties, the position was a little frightening. Many people like me took a rather optimistic view. We felt that what seemed like revolution was just the over-zealousness of the *New York Times* in blowing up panty-raids to immense proportions. To old cynics like us, the students seemed to be saying that we won't burn the university until a television crew arrives. But if you had been on the receiving end I think you might have been a little worried. I think you might have done some stupid things that now, years later, when a great quiet has descended on us, seem unjustifiable. But if you say to the *New York Times* today, aren't you acting irresponsibly, the answer is likely to be, well, the other side can hire its own press agents. Reporting is no longer enough. We have partisans. We have press agents."

Drucker, disturbed by what he sees, expands and extrapolates: "A pluralist system has always felt that the common good will come out of the clash of conflicting partisan interests. But today you have something different. There is a public entertainment quality to these constant attacks on institutions. It's very frightening because these are the traditional preludes to tyranny. *Five years from now somebody who proposes the suppression of freedom of the press will have very strong public support."*

Here is Drucker the conservative; "conservative" in a different and more narrow sense than that in which he usually applies the term himself. He is disgusted: "A great mass of the public are tired of pornography, of violence, and of irresponsibility. A great many people in responsible positions feel the same way—although they don't dare say so in public today. Let me put it this way. We don't have an Official Secrets Act the way the British have. *We will.* The press is going to fight it. But we will have one. And we will have other measures, tougher measures." (Since Drucker predicted this in the spring of 1975 what he feared has come very close. Later in the year, Congress took up a bill which is an American version of the "official secrets" act. Many observers give it an excellent chance of becoming law.)

Now a Druckerian digression: "Nobody ever accuses the Swiss police of police brutality. Do you know what the rules and regulations of the Swiss police are? A Swiss policeman who sees anybody whom he deems suspicious has the duty to order that person to court. If the person does not obey, the policeman has a duty to shoot him, and if he shoots him, he has the duty to kill him. If he does not shoot and shoot to kill, he faces a departmental trial. And it happens quite often. If you are stopped and you are innocent, you have nothing to fear."

Drucker emphasizes that these are the views of the Swiss officials; they are not his views.

He continues: "Now you know that, in this country, our 'police problem' is the result of our bad conscience about the blacks. That's all. But you'd be surprised how many citizens, including blacks, are awfully tired of vandalism and how fast you can get to the opposite."

Drucker says things that other prominent people will not say. He engages topics about which others tiptoe. Moving to another aspect he says, "It makes for a very dangerous situation. The 'New York liberal'—who is by no means confined to New York—is very dangerous. The parallel between Berlin in the 1920s and 1930s and New York is not entirely farfetched. The resistance to 'liberalism' is growing fast. We see it in various ways. We see it in education. The one great shift in elementary schools is that after twenty-five years, when all the emphasis was on the educationally deprived child, there is now growing concern about what used to be called the gifted child. And next door in Pasadena, there has been a revolt against progressive education. Four or five of the public schools have been converted into what they call fundamental schools, which are just old-fashioned schools with great emphasis on discipline and the three Rs. And much to the consternation of the liberal establishment the kids do better, partly because the parents insist they do better."

Back to "decency" (remember this is Drucker talking in February 1975): "Communities are going to continue to pass ordinances forbidding pornographic literature on newsstands and in stores. And I'm not so sure that the next time it comes up before the Supreme Court of California or the United States that it won't be upheld. What could happen is very dangerous. There are sharp shifts toward the right. If George Wallace had not been shot, what would the odds be against his being a Democratic presidential candidate? Even now the most likely winning ticket for the Democrats would be Wallace-Kennedy. A ticket for the real bigots."

And we are at the stage of political prognostication (said in February 1975): "Ford is doing better than I expected, much better. Even if he mismanages himself badly, I cannot see any other Democratic ticket winning. Can you?"

The interviewer murmurs no, but he can see a Republican ticket losing.

"Yes," says Drucker, "but it would have to work awfully hard. With a slight break in the economic situation. This is not a depression; it is a green-apple recession. A little boy has eaten a lot of green apples and he's terribly sick. The worst thing you can do is try to keep it down. He has to get it up. If he stops vomiting, put your finger in his throat and start him up again. All you can do is hold his hand, give him enough liquid and stroke his fevered brow. But when it's out, it's out, and if he has survived without damage, two years later he can eat green apples again."

But, can politicians survive an unemployment rate

of 10 percent? "They will have to live with it for six months. The worst thing is that they legislate about it, and the legislation then becomes effective when it's no longer needed. Let's assume the rate of inflation goes down to 5, 6, 7 percent. In ordinary times this would be considered raging inflation, but these are not ordinary times. And let's assume unemployment goes down to 6 percent."

The cold political pragmatist speaks: "A 6 percent unemployment rate means that practically no adult male white heads of households are unemployed. Even among mature working women, the rate will be very low. True, we will still have higher rates among blacks, 12 percent among black teenagers. But many blacks do not vote, black teenagers don't vote, and we do not expect teenagers to have jobs. We expect them to be in school. We do not consider a 15 percent teenager unemployed rate to be a big problem. It is a horrible problem for the mayor of Newark; but nobody else gives a damn. They can't get working papers. To be a truck driver you have to be twenty-five to get insurance. So the teenager shouldn't have a job; he's too young. That this makes no sense is immaterial."

And Drucker feels that foreign developments are likely to strengthen Ford's chances: "There will be no war in the Middle East. The Arabs will use Dr. Kissinger to give them what they really want. They don't want higher oil prices. They wanted $5 to $8 a barrel."

And President Ford has something else going for him: "On top of this, he has a totally incompetent Congress; an enormous number of freshman Democratic representatives who are already running for reelection. They're in by a fluke. Watergate put them in. Watergate is not going to be forgotten, but it won't be the controlling factor any more. And any Democratic ticket besides Wallace-Kennedy is faceless. Mr. Jackson and Mr. Udall may be good people but nobody knows what they look like. But—can Kennedy stand exposure?"

On the whole, Drucker felt in the spring of 1975 that things look pretty good for a Republican victory in 1976.

Yet he is by no means happy: "I have been a registered Democrat for thirty years. And each of the two times that I did not vote for a Democrat—in 1948 when I abstained rather than vote for Truman, and in 1972 when I voted for Nixon rather than abstain—I've been wrong!"

This—within a few minutes—has been Drucker the white-hot predictor and Drucker the sayer of things that people usually don't say, or say obliquely. We see his contempt for "doctrinaire liberalism"; his cynicism about politicians and voters; his disdain for much of the accepted wisdom of the past fifty years; and his ambivalence toward what he sees as a climate of pornography, violence, and irresponsibility. On the one hand these things disgust him, and he would like to see something done about them. On the other hand he deeply fears the consequences of the actions that might be taken against them.

And so Drucker the dualist goes on, dualist in many aspects. He seeks the ways in which man can live in time and eternity. He espouses freedom, but calls for discipline. He upholds the Western political tradition, but is contemptuous of many of its workings. He abhors repression in the abstract, but does not look on it with utter disfavor when he confronts what to him are ugly realities of modern life.

A dualist—split, searching, hoping that life can be made manageable. And in this he speaks for a great many of us.

16.

Drucker on Government, the World, Education, and Society

A talk with Peter Drucker is a wide-ranging excursion through the world of yesterday, today and tomorrow. He is an enthusiastic and unpredictable conversationalist.

Print cannot convey the flavor of talk. But it can suggest it. The reader may be interested in "hearing" Peter Drucker, transcribed from a taped conversation.

On Government

We maintain the belief that government is an operating agency. This idea was understandable in a time when agencies did not exist, and whenever someone proposed to do something, an agency had to be created. Today, however, there are all kinds of institutions that government does not use. There are many areas in which the execution of policy could be turned over to a nongovernmental institution and be handled better for less money. This is particularly true of Health, Education and Welfare, which is probably the most grotesquely obscene of the Washington bureaucracies, in part because those three services don't belong in one department. There are 380,000 employees in HEW.

In 1900 governments were probably too lean and undernourished. Then we began to act on the horrible axiom that anything a government does is forever. Programs are never abolished. They just get fatter, based on the notion that the man who weighs five hundred pounds can run the fastest.

Now, it is perfectly true that there are permanent tasks best performed by government; administration of justice is better left to the government than to the private vendetta. But much of what the government does it should stop doing.

It was not constitutional or political theory that limited governments. It was the fact that everyone knew that no government could raise, through taxation, more than a very small part of the gross national product.

Charlemagne tried to do this. He attempted to build a big government on the basis of natural produce. This meant the court stayed at one imperial castle for four to six weeks until it had eaten up all the corn, beets, and salt beef. Then it traveled to another castle. After Charlemagne's death his empire fell to pieces almost immediately. You cannot run a government by ox cart —any more than you can run it by jet plane.

Napoleon's greatest strength was not as a military strategist but as a fiscal strategist. He got twice as large a proportion of the national income out of France as anyone had ever gotten before. Nevertheless, he overextended. He took much out of the countries supposedly on his side, and in the end he was defeated—not by the Russians or the Austrians but by the defection of his allies. He set a record, however. He managed to take 6 or 7 percent of personal income and that was unheard of. The great bloodsuckers who preceded him— and the French were always very good at this—did not come close to that mark. We read about how the wars of Louis XIV left France drained and the crown bankrupt. But the best that Louis XIV was able to get was, maybe, 2 percent.

Prior to World War I there was no legislature that did not start with the question, "How much revenue can we get?" and then they had to decide how to allocate it. They had to think through to objectives. They had to make priority decisions. They had to face the fact that they had to tell people, "Well, you can have this, but only if you give up something else."

In World War I governments found that the economy can be "mobilized." And this was bad. We have heard the legend of how Russia collapsed because of corruption among the ruling class and the military officers. The worst corruption was fiscal corruption.

Since then, every legislature and every bureaucracy has acted on the assumption that there are no limits, and the sickness has spread from government to other institutions. In a hospital it should be possible to say, "It's nice to have fresh flowers in every vase every morning," but this would mean that we have to stop treating epileptics. Which do you prefer? You can't say this any more; you can't come out against fresh flowers in every vase. You have to argue ideology—or give in.

The first function of a governing board is to allocate big priority decisions. You can make the right decisions if you have the priorities. When I was on the board of the State University of New Jersey we voted to abolish the old demonstration high school. It had been an unspeakably expensive institution for two hundred gold-plated kids—not even gold-plated, solid gold. The decision took two years, and it released a storm in northern New Jersey. The legislature brought six suits against us. My phone did not stop ringing for three weeks. At the other end there would always be a tax-payer asking, "Didn't you think when you made the decision?" I would say that we had thought about it for two and a half years. And I would say, "Look, you make the decision. Do you want to keep the high school, or do you want to keep the speech clinic, which is the only one in the New York metropolitan area and which treats three thousand kids for the same money? Which are you going to keep?" And that would be the end of it. The taxpayer would say, "Well, why didn't you tell me so in the first place?"

When the governing body, or the legislature, lays out priorities, people will accept them. That's why the last budget reform act, poor though it is, is a step in the right direction. It tries to start with available revenues rather than with programs. If the legislature is to become effective again, it must regain control of the budget. The modern government budget is a British invention. We don't have it here yet. Congress passes acts requiring spending without providing for the revenues. This is one major reason that we are in our present condition.

Governments and institutions keep losing programs going far longer than business can. Business can't afford it. Industry has no bottomless reservoir. Ford announced that they were abolishing the Edsel, which was an absurd statement. You and I abolished the Edsel; it took Ford two years to accept it. That's all they could afford.

But it took me twenty years to get a hospital to accept the fact that maternity doesn't belong in a hospital. The maternity wing in a hospital is doing a very simple job at maximum expense and often great danger. A hospital is not a good place to have a baby. Ninety-nine percent of deliveries do not need a physician. There aren't any surprises in delivery any more; basically you need a facility with delivery rooms, transfusion equipment, and the capability for minor surgery. This need not be part of a full-scale hospital.

Our poverty programs do not benefit the black poor. They benefit the black middle class by providing cushy jobs. I sat on the board of Montclair State College. The college ran forty-two minority student programs. In 1970 there were no more minority students in the place than there were in 1950. Furthermore, in 1950 the students were taking academic courses and doing well. Twenty years later they were all in special programs and not doing well.

I asked, why forty-two programs? The answer was that you can get money for new programs up to a certain point, but you can't maintain a successful program, because when it succeeds it's no longer needed. But the real answer was, who the hell cares about the black students? With forty-two programs we have 180 black administrators who get at least $15,000 each. In a sense the programs were doing something for blacks because they provided jobs for these people. But every one was capable of getting another job.

One of the things that government must learn is the process of systematic, methodical abandonment. Have everything that is decreed expire in five years unless there is positive action to continue.

The best hope in instituting that is through taxpayers who vote. But politicians have found a way around taxpayers who vote. It's called inflation. Inflation is a way of taxation without representation. Have we reached the point at which the citizenry will not put up with inflation any more? I hear talk about it but I don't see any real signs.

Government runs on the idea that the more things you do, the more effective you are. And the moment you establish something it becomes a vested interest. I was consultant to the Royal Commission examining the Canadian government. In the course of our examination we found the Halifax Commission. The Halifax disaster took place in 1917 when a munitions ship blew up in Halifax harbor. People in Canada, the United States, and Great Britain gave money for the survivors, and a commission was set up. By 1925 the last survivor's survivor had been paid off. But in 1963 the Halifax Commission was flourishing with 2,800 people on the payroll.

There was an answer, of course. The Canadian government had been boasting for years about the number of French-Canadians in federal employment. The government was employing these people and placing them into two areas, the Halifax Disaster Commission and the Department of Northern Affairs, which had more employees than there were Indians and Eskimos in Canada. This made it possible for the Minister of Finance, for example, to avoid having a single French-speaking administrator or professional in his department.

There is nothing unique about this. Every government has its Halifax Disaster Commissions. If we had had a Minister of Transportation in 1900, you would by now have a billion-dollar project for reeducation of horses and a big genetics program to breed horses with wheels. As a result we would have the first horse who could operate his knee joint in both directions. The only trouble would be that he would not be able to stand up.

This is the congenital disease of government, partly because civil servants have tenure. Some of the reasons for that tenure are good, but many of the results are bad because you have a built-in vested interest in continuation of programs.

The first inflation resulted from American silver streaming into Spain and then inundating all of Europe. This in turn had tremendous impact on the Orient. To a large extent, the downfall of the Ming dynasty in China came about because of the impact of European inflation in an economy that was based partly on money and partly on wisely fixed exchange relationships. The Westerners who for a thousand years had had absolutely no bullion now had bullion to spare. This drove up prices and, in the process, destroyed the stability of a very wicked bureaucratic system.

For many years inflation was localized. In 1923 Germans needed wheelbarrows to carry money to the store; neighboring France experienced a deflation. Great Britain had inflation. The United States had deflation but now you have worldwide inflation, which no individual government can handle. This is very frightening if you are a finance minister, whether French, American, Finnish, or Japanese. You are up against something that seems brand new and over which you have no control. You cannot devise a national economic policy that has any effect.

So you look for scapegoats. The multinational corporation, which has come into being as a result of the reality of world economy, is attacked as a cause of it.

On the World

There are many causes for the formation of what is truly becoming one world. One important cause is the universality of information, which was first seen clearly by Marshall McLuhan in his Cambridge Ph.D. thesis before there really were any electronic media. McLuhan wrote his thesis on the impact of the printed book on the medieval university. It was the technology of printing that destroyed the medieval university and led to the growth of the modern one, he said. The book, which appeared to be a container for information, actually determined the information to be conveyed and led to the creation of modern disciplines. The medium is the message.

Books, of course, with few exceptions, are totally linear. The alphabet—which incidentally is one of the best examples of industrial engineering ever devised—is an extreme device of scientific management in which all possible words and thoughts can be represented by repetition of a few simple symbols. But the alphabet has its limitations. The Chinese had some good reasons for rejecting it. The Chinese ideogram is incompatible with the alphabet. My grandsons, four and six, know their letters but can't put them together. If these were ideograms of houses and animals and children, they could read them.

There is certainly no doubt that for the first time in history we have a situation in which there is universal recognition and understanding of experience, even if the experience is not personally felt. Even in the remotest villages of the Andes or Nepal, there is no need to explain an airplane, or an automobile, or the mushroom cloud. In that sense we have a universality of experience of the material civilization. The same is not true of ideas: you could probably not explain the PTA to an Australian aborigine. But there is universal recognition of what is possible in the material sphere, and a consequent raising and universalization of aspirations and expectations. People have come to want a standard of life that they can define quite specifically because they have heard about it or seen it through the media.

Take the Indian film industry. It is the largest in the world (the second is Egyptian, the third Japanese). The film is all-powerful in countries that are still pre-television. When one looks at Indian films he abandons any idea that Hollywood is the capital of bad taste. But that is not the point. For the Indian public, the

Indian environment is grotesquely idealized. All women are beautiful; the poor are dressed in theatrical costume. And so on.

This is just one example of how the new media are creating what is almost a uniformity of perceived experience and expectations and appetites.

On Education

I was one of the first to see the educational explosion. I was also one of the first to see that it was over in the early 1960s. I reached the conclusion, and I'm only half-joking, that by 1990 we would reach a state where you would need a Ph.D. to be admitted to first grade.

To say "no" to a Ph.D. candidate is to close off his access to many careers, both academic and industrial. The power to say "no" in a question of this magnitude is too much power for one man. An unfavorable decision must be concurred in by at least one more member of the faculty. I insist on it. Moreover, the reasons for the decision should be available to the candidate. This is merely due process. The candidate should be able to be reasonably sure that, if the university errs, it will err on the side of the student.

With the Buckley amendment (allowing students access to their own files) on the books, these deliberations will be a matter of public record, no matter how much some faculty members may kick and scream about it. There is little chance that the move toward openness will enforce a bias in favor of the student.

The mentality of the educator is partly to blame. The schoolmaster from time immemorial has believed that the ass is an organ of learning: the longer you sit, the more you learn. There is no evidence that this is true, but it has always been accepted because sitting is something you can measure.

The educator's partner in insanity is the employment manager who keeps looking for degrees as prerequisites for hiring.

On Society

The universal middle class takes its values from the dominant example of middle-class society. This happens to be the American one at the moment. Tomorrow it may be Japan.

We do not live in a bourgeois country; we live in a proletarian country. But it is clearly middle-class, even though there are no bourgeois values at all. It is a middle-class proletariat.

There was a time when there was a clearly visible group of upperclass people whose style of life in values, education, health care, and material expenditures was looked up to as a standard of aspiration. At the same time you had people who clearly identified themselves as working class. Neither group is around any longer.

Workers on the assembly line see themselves as rejects. It has nothing to do with money. They do not consider that they are respectable members of the working class; in terms of universal expectations there is no working class, only middle class. They have no self-respect.

They are most unlike the Detroit mechanics of the 1930s. If Walter Reuther had been born two years earlier he, rather than Charlie Wilson, might have been president of General Motors. They had very similar backgrounds. But the 1929 depression came before Reuther was able to become a supervisor. He would have been a plant manager by 1933, and he could have made it to the top of the heap. Reuther was ambitious, ruthless, tough, and very able. He was tougher than Charlie Wilson, perhaps not as nice a person, but a more interesting one. He fitted the GM values like a glove.

17.

Drucker's Defense of the Multinationals

Cassandra did not make a lot of friends by foretelling all those things that were going to happen to Troy. Even when her predictions turned out to be true, her popularity curve did not move upward. Quite the contrary.

Prophesying makes enemies. The prophet is assailed for heralding changes that some people will not welcome. When the changes come about, he is held responsible for them, even when he was simply saying what was going to happen, not claiming that it would be an unalloyed blessing.

Early in the game, Peter Drucker foresaw the coming of the multinational corporations. He continued to study their rise, regarding them as an inevitable development within the age of industrial man. However, Drucker has never depicted himself as merely a predictor of the phenomenon who makes no value judgments on what he predicts. He does not try to get off the hook by saying, "I am the singer, not the song." He has been, and continues to be, a strong advocate of the global giants; not in all their manifestations, but as a general proposition.

As one of the early commentators on the onset of the worldwide giants, and as the progenitor of the concept of the "Global Shopping Center," Drucker has received his share of the flak aimed at the multinationals. The case against corporate internationalism has been made with considerable vehemence and impact in *Global Reach* by Richard J. Barnet and Ronald E. Müller. Since Peter Drucker is so closely identified with the movement that comes under attack in *Global Reach,* let's examine the charges and Drucker's response to them.

Richard Barnet is a founder and codirector of the Institute for Policy Studies in Washington. He has taught in universities, and at the time of the publication of *Global Reach* he was helping to develop the Transnational Institute, "an organization devoted to the problems of world economy and politics." Ronald E. Müller is an economics professor and writer. Barnet and Müller disagree thoroughly with Drucker over the usefulness and role of the multinationals. Considered from Drucker's point of view, the controversy takes place on two levels. Conceptually and ideologically, Drucker takes sharp intellectual issue with the critics of the global giants (although he himself is by no means a wholehearted proponent of bigness or of anything done by multinational companies) . However, there is another level upon which Drucker responds to the school of thought exemplified by Barnet and Müller. Drucker's gut reaction of revulsion to behavioral scientists in general and economists in particular is part of it, as is his disdain for what he considers the meddling and the muddled thinking of liberal idealogues. So—when confronted with the ideas of such critics—Drucker is able to mount a reasoned rebuttal, but he goes beyond this into the warmer regions of emotion.

We may first examine the argument against the multinationals as it is put by Barnet and Müller; then take a look at Drucker's intellectual case for the development; and finally, observe Drucker's gut impulse to lash back at those for whose thinking he has little regard.

271

To begin with, Barnet and Müller point to the undeniable fact that the multinationals are very big. They estimate that international corporations control more than $200 billion in physical assets. In terms of sales and production figures, General Motors is bigger than Switzerland, Pakistan, and South Africa all rolled into one. Royal Dutch Shell is bigger than Iran, Venezuela, and Turkey.

But size is not the primary problem. The really striking aspect of the multinational is not its gigantic stature but the "worldview" that invests its strategy and tactics. Put simply, this worldview is a selfish one. The globals are stateless. The book quotes a spokesman for Union Carbide: "It is not proper for any international corporation to put the welfare of any country in which it does business above that of any other." Another authority is cited: "The international corporation has no country to which it owes more loyalty than any other, nor any country where it feels completely at home."

So these looming entities ignore sovereign boundaries. They are beholden to no government or political movement. Yet they exert immense economic and political power. And so the authors raise the inevitable and highly pertinent question, "Who elected them?" Barnet and Müller say of the global managers: "And in the end they must answer the 1970's version of the same question that has confronted every new elite aspiring to political leadership and social management: by what right do a self-selected group of druggists, biscuit makers and computer designers become the architects of the new world? To establish their political legitimacy, the aspiring World Managers must be able to demonstrate that the maximization of global profits is compatible with human survival."

A couple of remarks may be made about this statement. The problem of the legitimacy of the corporate manager as a wielder of social and political power is one that has, as we see elsewhere in this book, troubled Drucker for many years. He acknowledges that he has never come to an entirely satisfactory answer. But Drucker is inclined to face up to the reality of the manager's increasing power, and try to find some way around the difficulty. He does not give the impression of feeling that, if you confront the world managers with trumpeted accusations of lack of legitimacy, they will fold their tents and depart.

But there is something else in the quoted remark; a tone of looking-down-the-nose snobbishness that is exactly the kind of thing that enrages Drucker. The reference to "druggists, biscuit makers and computer designers" is in equal parts inaccurate and offensive. It is, to say the least, imprecise to call the head of Nabisco a "biscuit maker" or the president of Pfizer a "druggist." So why should the characterizations be included? The only answer is that the authors are expressing a fathomless depth of contempt for those who deal in such mundane commodities, and conveying their disdainful derision for the pretensions of "unqualified" people who dare to try to run the world. The unspoken corollary is that the only people who are really qualified to exert power are those who are acceptable to the authors. No doubt professors of economics would be deemed acceptable.

This attitude of superiority is one that invariably impels Drucker to some of his most barbed observations.

Barnet and Müller make other points about the multinationals. They say that the subsidiaries in various countries follow policies that are designed by the headquarters of the companies, which are mostly based in the United States. They state that these companies are primarily interested in profit rather than in altruism. Neither of these insights is likely to come as much of a bombshell to any but the most sheltered of readers.

Global Reach goes beyond these observations. On the matter of profit, the authors do not merely say that this is what the world managers are most interested in. They maintain that the heads of the giant corporations are asking for "loyalty" and unbridled sway on the basis that the successful quest for profits brings prosperity and harmony to the world. And they declare that this request is meretricious, because the globals, by means of their freedom from responsibility to any sovereign power, are able to play planetary games to maximize their profits at the expense of great masses of the world's people. For example, the big corporations undervalue exports and overvalue imports to give themselves the best possible tax breaks in all of the countries of their operation. The technology they export to the impoverished nations does not help those nations because it does not really create jobs. The ministrations of the giants widen, rather than narrow, the gap between rich and poor. And so on.

All this is possible because, while the multinationals are getting bigger, countries are getting smaller. The emerging nations are no match in size, power, or sophistication for the corporations that loot their resources, exploit and mislead their people, and merrily juggle numbers, production facilities, and markets on a worldwide game board to fill their coffers.

But Barnet and Müller claim to have detected an even more insidious and arcane evil in the operations of global corporations. The multinationals are depicted as being so adept at manipulating the minds of ordinary men and women that they cast a kind of spell. They are able to use advertising and public-relations techniques to give people a "spurious feeling of being middle class." (Obviously the authors deplore this as a disservice to the people who are thus hoodwinked, but there seems also to be a tinge of resentment that segments of various populations are encouraged to foster delusions of middle-class-manship when they have no right to that status.)

In the same fashion the globals are able to win mindless support in the United States. The authors of *Global Reach* give an example of how this is done: "The National Association of Manufacturers . . . has set up a computerized system for getting company views to the right people at the right time. A computerized mailing of 14,000 plants of the biggest 100 U.S.-based global corporations (soon to be expanded to the biggest 500), divided according to Congressional districts, has been prepared in the NAM headquarters."

Apart from the breathless tone of this less-than-earth-shaking revelation, the reader may be struck by the repeated use of the word "computerized" in what can only be construed as a pejorative fashion. While the authors—as educated men—would disavow any intention of emulating the Luddites by attaching vaguely sinister implications to the existence of new technology, this is the impression conveyed by the citation and by other passages in the book.

The ordinary citizen and the consumer are seduced by the giant companies—and, worse, they "must, of course, pay the costs" of their own seduction. The reader, weary of a long line of similar attacks on the "system," may pardonably wonder what this has to do with multinational operation. Moreover, along with Peter Drucker, he may find that the writers are imputing far more power to advertising and marketing specialists than they actually possess. Drucker's derisive references to Madison Avenue techniques can be found in abundance, and are sampled in this book. He may go overboard in discounting the effectiveness of advertising; but Barnet and Müller—skeptical of any profession of ethics uttered by a businessman—seem to be uncritical in accepting the claims of the message merchants so long as that acceptance helps them to make their case.

A substantial part of *Global Reach* is devoted to the effect of the multinationals on countries around the world. Then, about halfway through, the focus shifts. The authors turn their attention to the role that the globals are playing in what is called the "Latin-Americanization of the United States." In a way that sometimes comes perilously close to economic jingoism, Barnet and Müller denounce the big companies for taking jobs out of the United States and giving them to workers in other parts of the world. The corporate giants are hit with the responsibility for shortages, inflation, unemployment and what is seen as a broadening disparity between rich and poor in this country.

When the time comes to suggest answers to these vast problems, the writers of *Global Reach* are candid in admitting that they do not have many. Somehow the multinationals must be made accountable. There should be far greater dissemination of information about their operations than is available now. Sovereignty must be restored to public authority at all levels: international, national, state, local, and neighborhood. But "how

275

this is to be done is by no means clear." There must be a more equitable distribution of the wealth of the nation and the world; who is to make the allocation is not specified, but the implication is that a minimum requirement will be an advanced degree in one or more of the social sciences. There should be a major investment program in alternate technologies to make the American people self-sufficient of foreign countries; again it is not clear who will undertake this effort or what happens to the foreign countries. Barnet and Müller speculate, with every evidence of seriousness, on the proposition that presidents of companies such as General Motors should run in general elections for their offices.

And, throughout, Peter Drucker receives ample billing in a villain's role. He is debited with the fatherhood of the concept of the Global Shopping Center. He is quoted as calling for the destruction of the monster, nationalism. His alleged heartlessness is documented by his remark that "within the vast mass of poverty that is India" there is a sizable modern economy, comprising 10 percent or more of the Indian population, or 50 million people. He is hung with the supposed albatross of his "notorious" comment that "the factory girl or the salesgirl in Lima or Bombay [or the Harlem ghetto] wants a lipstick. . . . There is no purchase that gives her as much value for a few cents." We are given a picture of the complacent Peter Drucker nodding in approval while rapacious moguls use the mysterious powers of advertising to hypnotize undernourished citizens of the world's poorer countries into spending their pittances on soft drinks instead of something that would be good for them.

Now it may be useful to see what Drucker says to all this. First we may consider his more formal, reasoned commentary on the multinationals. Then we can get some indication of his more emotional reaction to this sort of attack.

Drucker calls the multinational corporation the "outstanding social innovation" to appear on the scene since World War II. Characteristically, he attempts to put the development in the framework of history. Global business enterprise is nothing new, he assures us. Multinationals, such as the Singer Company, flourished in the nineteenth century. Moreover, the global enterprise is not an American development. The German Siemens company was a multinational in the 1850s. Going back further, he points out that the current rise in global corporations may mean that economy and sovereignty are becoming divorced from each other, but that up until three hundred years ago this was the way the world ran.

This calm historical view infuriates some people when they are in the throes of immense agitation over what they consider to be an urgent, current, and unprecedented problem. Nevertheless, it is Drucker's way. No matter what the situation, he never feels that the vision of protagonists will be impaired by the perspective of the ages.

Drucker remarks that the burgeoning of the "Global Supermarket" for consumer goods has come about in an unexpected way because the demand pattern that has emerged in the economy of the world is not what the economists expected it would be. He says that the customer has "proved again that he knows better than the experts" what he wants. Drucker ascribes great power to the universal demand for a little mobility, a little knowledge, a little luxury. And he sees nothing wrong in responding to these needs and making a profit while doing so.

Drucker spends little time and effort serving as an apologist for the multinational corporation. He accepts it as a development, and undertakes to analyze it, projects its implications, and look for ways that it can be made to work better. He admits the encroachment of the global company on sovereignty, but—fortified by the historical view—he observes that few governments have really "suffered from the delusion that they are truly 'independent' economically."

Without moralizing, Drucker approaches the problems of worldwide economic strategy. He states that the overall strategic responsibility must be centralized, but that this must be translated into specific strategies for individual markets. But, he says, "the multinational strategy which is decentralized, that is, a strategy which considers each unit and each market as an autonomous business," is doomed to fail. This, of course, comes into head-on confrontation with one of the particulars in the indictment rendered by Barnet and Müller and other critics of the globals.

The picture given in *Global Reach* is one of smooth-running monster corporations, calculating every move, that manipulate governments and populations to their own ends. Drucker, on the contrary, is concerned that most multinationals are managed so ineffectually: "Few multinationals have thought through business strategy so far."

Drucker admits that the management of the giants is a problem, and that there is not yet a satisfactory pattern for top-management structure. He says that only one clear conclusion has emerged; the top management must not at the same time be the management of any of the operating companies, particularly the operating company in the country where headquarters are located.

He comments on the human problems of remoteness and fatigue. Decisions have to be made at the scene of action. The manager from headquarters who zooms in on a jet to get things straightened out is ill-equipped physically and informationally to serve the needs of the moment. And then there is the human need for roots. Drucker looks with disfavor on the practice of transferring executives from place to place around the globe in the way that pieces are moved on a game board—"three years in Kansas City, three years in Aruba." He points out that managers have a right to be concerned with aging parents and growing children, and that it is unrealistic to assume that executives can be readily transplanted.

Responding to the now-familiar attacks on the globals, Drucker does not dismiss them out of hand. He says that each attack, by itself, can be refuted, but that nevertheless there is a problem. The critics, he maintains, have not contributed to the situation; they are formulating the problem wrongly.

For example, Drucker claims that "no business, no matter how rich and big it may be, has any power

278

against a national government." No doubt this is true —if the government is responding to a clear, objective conception of the needs of its citizens. But to accept this proposition is to avoid the issue. Government officials can be bought, and it is admitted and documented that multinationals have bought them as a staple of doing business.

The counterarguments of Drucker are perhaps more persuasive when he confronts the accusation that global corporations acquire and misuse political power. He responds that the multinational is a problem not because it gets involved in politics, but because its decisions and actions are divorced (and properly so) from political sovereignty and based on economic rationality. This, he admits, is a real problem, one not susceptible to any easy solution.

The reassertion of national sovereignty is not the answer. De Gaulle tried this, says Drucker, and succeeded only in weakening the position of the French economy in the world. He says that a better answer would be in a new concept of international law to deal with the reality of the planetary ventures. But this sort of generalization is based on Drucker's position that the globals tend to stay out of politics; and in this he may be more sanguine than the facts warrant. For example, in *Management: Tasks—Responsibilities—Practices*, he says that although ITT tried to pressure Nixon to work against the Allende government in Chile, this "only ensured that the Nixon administration—despite its hostility to the new Chilean government —would do nothing and remain scrupulously uninvolved." The disclosures of the Senate Intelligence Committee in November 1975 show that Nixon, through the CIA, was anything but "scrupulously uninvolved" in Chile.

Drucker insists that the developing countries of the world need the multinationals. These countries need capital and technology—and where else will they get them?

However, Drucker admits that there are difficulties. The developing countries suffer from a balance-of-payments problem. The more capital they bring in, the more foreign exchange they must produce. Complicating this, there is the factor of national identity. The citizens of a developing country, who are just beginning to give scope to their aspirations, do not take kindly to the feeling of subordination to giant entities headquartered in distant parts of the world. This is not paranoia; the tensions are real and understandable. But acknowledgement of this does not carry with it the corollary that the multinationals must somehow be willed out of existence.

Perhaps the most significant remark that Drucker makes about the multinational corporation is his observation that it is a prototype. In spite of the tensions engendered by nationalism, the world needs international organizations—to preserve the environment, for example. There are few really functioning international organizations. We need them. So the global corporation "may therefore well become the prototype and forerunner of a truly multinational public-service agency of tomorrow"—just as, domestically, the management of business can be seen to have been the forerunner and prototype of "management" for public service institutions.

The cycle comes round again. Drucker is expressing his optimistic feeling that society *can* be managed; but, to do this takes skillful management. He accepts the multinational as a reality. He admits the tensions and problems created by the phenomenon. He makes some suggestions about how to solve those problems. He reiterates his faith in better management as a force for good. And he suggests that—rather than bemoaning the development of the multinationals and averting our eyes from the sight—we face them as facts, try to make them better, and look for the lessons that will make the world more livable.

Such a view may not be as spectacular as an all-out denunciation of the giant companies, but it is probably more constructive. It is certainly more realistic.

But these are the arguments of the reasoning, moderate, word-weighing Peter Drucker. As mentioned, there is another side of Drucker—with a much more volatile flashpoint—uncovered when tracts such as *Global Reach* achieve prominence.

He gets mad. He gets mad, not because of criticism directed at him—few people handle derogatory comments with such equanimity—but because of his gut feeling that much of what is wrong with society is caused or exacerbated by learned know-nothingness. In the appendix of this book, "The Sayings of Chairman Peter," the reader can find a generous serving of Drucker's acid observations on behavioral scientists, professors and, most particularly, economists. It is not just that they annoy him; he feels that their complacent and self-assured utterances are misleading and harmful. Without personal animosity toward Barnet and Müller as individuals, he can be scathing about them as representatives of a style of thinking.

Faced with a recital of the arguments of the anti-globals, Drucker becomes impatient. "These people can never get the difference between profits and sales straight. When they say revenue they mean either one. They are equally imprecise when they say 'underdeveloped.' For the extractive industries, yes, there are underdeveloped countries. For a pharmaceutical company, there is no such thing. And, even in a poor country, people can pay for the small luxury involved in buying a Coca-Cola."

The multinationals are damned if they do and damned if they don't. They are castigated for going into the "underdeveloped" countries and castigated if they stay out of them. "The cold fact," says Drucker, "is that the poorer nations are not important in the overall strategies of many globals. Dow Chemical has a plant in Peru employing 500 people. This is a hell of a lot of people to the Peruvians, but it means less than one-tenth of one percent of profits to Dow, if that. The Finance Minister of Peru complains to me that he is hurt, he resents the fact that the President of Dow Chemical has not yet come to see him. Well, when the President visits Maccu Picchu he will probably call at the plant. But, no matter how you define it, 95 percent of his employees are in developed countries and 95 percent of his profits come from there. The man

281

would be grossly misusing his time if he were to spend three days visiting officials in Peru."

Then there is the argument that the huge corporations do not provide the poorer countries with the technology and tools that really suit the situation. What is overlooked by this argument, says Drucker, is the intangible matter of personal and national pride. He tells the story of a Latin-American country that needed machinery to run a certain industry. Officials of the nation came to a giant company in the United States. The Americans said, "The machinery we turn out is too big and sophisticated for you. But there is a plant in Canada that makes what you need; you can adapt their equipment most easily." No; this would not do. Stung by the implication that they should take "less than the best," the Latin Americans insisted upon the larger, more expensive, less practical machinery. And this, says Drucker, is typical. No matter how poor the country, they will not settle for a 727. If there is a Concorde to be had, they want a Concorde. The argument that the multinationals fob off inappropriate and overly sophisticated technology on the poor nations overlooks the strong preferences of the customer to go first class.

There is another point. The underdeveloped countries need technology. It must start somewhere. If the technology that a multinational brings in is too sophisticated, then there will be an effort to build the level of skill in the country. The poor nations exhibit a pattern of masses of unskilled people, a very few educated and skilled people, and nothing in between. There is a vast bottom, a thin top, and no middle. The middle must be developed. The importation of "labor-intensive" projects—even if the global giants were willing to bring them in, which they are not—will do nothing to build the middle. Obvious inequities appear when the multinationals go in. It would be fine if everything developed at the same time, according to an orderly schedule devised in some American academic bastion. Unfortunately, in reality, this is not the case.

As to the claim that the giants are milking the less-developed countries, taking vast amounts of money out of them, Drucker replies that this is nonsense. They are not taking it out, he says, they are putting it in. One reason is that it is difficult to get money out, because of various restrictions. Another reason is that the subsidiaries are simply not profitable. This is not to say that the giants place subsidiaries there as an altruistic venture. They hope to make them profitable. When they do, Drucker maintains, it is reasonable to assume that the host country will be assisted rather than harmed.

Drucker gets maddest when he is confronted with the picture of the huge corporation using its vast influence to hoodwink the "shopgirl" into spending her few pennies on a Coke or a lipstick. Economists, he says, have always suffered from one enormous inherent defect: a contempt for human beings. They think that the poor need an economist to tell them they are poor.

Wrong, says Peter Drucker. The poor shopgirl is a very realistic young woman. She knows she is poor. Being poor has made her a discriminating shopper. She wants to get the most for her money. But "the most" means the most in *her* terms, not those of a university economist. Whether she is undernourished or not depends on the point of view. She is undernourished in terms of a Harvard nutritionist; she is quite well-nourished in terms of the Peruvian Indian. To say this is not to be heartless; it is merely to state the truth.

So on occasion she buys a Coca-Cola. This small luxury gives her, for one moment, the feeling that she is in control. For a minute she breaks through the horribly narrow economic restraints that hold her captive. But is that the only benefit she obtains for her expenditure of a few cents? No. The soft drink does contain some nutrition. It is also a slight stimulant. Furthermore, it is pure; you don't get dysentery from a Coke. Now, none of these things is important to a remote expert who observes what he considers the shopgirl's unbalanced diet, but they are important to her.

Her purchase of a lipstick does not nourish her. However, it provides, perhaps, a momentary emotional stimulation that is of more value to her than a use of the money that an economist would find worthy of his approval. She is affirming a kind of independence. True, she may be indulging in the "delusion of middle class" that Barnet and Müller find so objectionable, but it is her money and she can do as she likes with it. Why, asks Drucker, are behavioral scientists so upset when a member of the "poorer classes" seems to act as if he or she were not in that category? Is it entirely because it disorders their careful calculations of how various classifications of human beings should act? Or is there also a measure of snobbery in this? "When I was a boy in England," Drucker recalls, "a shopgirl or factory girl who did not wear black woolen stockings and shoes handed down from her grandmother—with holes out for the bunions—was ostracized by her workmates. It was by no means unusual for the 'respectable' girls to go to the management and ask that the rebel be sacked, because it was obvious that she was no better than she should be. I see this same kind of thing in the strong feeling that a girl who puts on a lipstick that she has seen in a movie or magazine is no better than she should be. Those who criticize seem to be saying that she should 'know her place.' "

Yes, says Drucker, the economist has a certain kind of logic on his side when he says the girl should not spend the money on a lipstick; she should save it up to buy a sewing machine. But it may take a lifetime to save enough for the machine. And, even if she buys it, she is well aware of the chance that it will be stolen. This, says Drucker, is a factor that the experts overlook. They feel that, if people in the barrios of the world are sufficiently poor and live in sufficiently horrible conditions, they become honest. The historic support for this sociological proposition is very scant.

Economists dislike conspicuous waste when it is practiced by certain people. By logic, says Drucker, they should abhor the fiesta that, for a moment, turns a poor section of a Latin American town into a whirl of gaiety and color. However, he says, the economist probably does not dislike the fiesta so much that he will pass up the chance to take home movies when he visits the town on vacation.

Drucker is not "making a case" for the multinationals in the accepted sense. In his view they are a logical and inevitable historical development. There is always a forum for those who take high moralistic positions to denounce the inevitable; King Canute had, no doubt, some sympathetic auditors.

But as a conservative, Drucker dislikes waste, and he deplores the waste of so much energy, let alone paper and print, in what he considers wrong-headed and futile pursuits. The global giants exist, and even the loudest and most concerted exercises in handwriting will not change that fact. Moreover, he feels, the strictures of sociologists and economists are suspect. He does not regard them, by and large, as helpful commentators or constructive thinkers.

Men who take over giant corporations do not automatically becomes great philosophers or philanthropists. This is not their role. The best we can hope for is that they do their jobs well. And the job is management.

The underdeveloped parts of the world have not blossomed overnight. The coming of the multinationals has not ushered in a planetary Golden Age of Pericles. But they do hold promise as the prototypes of possible international entities devoted to social objectives.

In the end, Drucker says of the critics, "For thirty years they have cried for internationalism. Now they have it, but they don't like the form in which it has come."

18.

The Past and
Present Futurist

Every age has had its futurists—people who speculate and fantasize on what may lie ahead. Only the styles change. Down through history, thinkers and dreamers have related their visions of the future for a variety of purposes. Sir Thomas More wrote *Utopia* to draw moral and political lessons. Cyrano de Bergerac related his imaginary visits to the moon and the sun to have some satirical fun with his contemporaries.

It is typical of our day that futurism has become a "discipline." For example, the ruling powers of a suburban community are trying to draw up a new town plan that will assure ordered growth while preserving the character of the place. To assist their deliberations the town fathers call in a consultant who is formally designated as a "futurist." Drawing from an assemblage of sources, the futurist projects trends and offers predictions about what is going to happen in terms of population growth and movement, industrial development, education, social needs, and the like. Since, as has been noted, we live in an age of consultants, it is only natural that the futurist should take his place in the pantheon. Futurism has become a profession, with its own conventions and formalities, its own scale of ethics and standards of admittance, and its own schedule of fees. Without doubt, it will not be long before universities offer a full selection of courses in the "School of Futurism."

There is another brand of futurism that is more familiar to all of us. This variation consists in the exploitation of fear of the future through books and the entertainment media. We have movies such as *Rollerball, Westworld, If . . ., A Clockwork Orange*. We have novels of similar cast. They look at what lies ahead, and they tell us that it is full of horrors.

But of course there is yet another and ostensibly more responsible variation on the futurist movement. This kind of futurism attempts to anticipate what is to come and to help mankind to control its destiny. The work of the futurists of this school has become a lively source of best-selling nonfiction.

When one examines the work of the "constructive" futurists and compares it to current futuristic fiction, he sees more similarities than differences. The dominant theme of both kinds of work is that the future is *hell*. As Arnold A. Rogow of the City University of New York remarked (in *Saturday Review*, December 12, 1970), "The most influential form of non-fiction literature in the Seventies is likely to be a succession of books telling us that because of race, poverty, Vietnam, urban decay, drug addiction, the alienation of youth . . . and other calamities, the condition of America is bleak or even hopeless. The futurists who ride the crest of this wave are not doing anything new when they describe a tomorrow in which the world is an ugly and mechanical place in which existence is routinized into a crowded and unutterably dreary existence. This lode has been mined for hundreds of years. What is different today is the attitude of the audience. Once readers of what has been called the "dung-ho" school of futuristic literature regarded what they read as a kind of perverse diversion. The awful spectacle of what the world *might* be like provided a shuddery thrill; the more skillful the writer at selection and projection of developments, the greater the thrill. But there was no general sense of agreement that the dismal forecasts were to be taken seriously.

Nowadays it is different. We are meant to accept as foreordained fact the calamities that the futurists display before us. And it follows that we are to conclude that most, if not all, change is bad—and that the faster it comes the worse it is. The corollary to this bill of future particulars is that we have to be willing to resort to the most radical of means to cope with change, if only to retain a modicum of peace and sanity while everything is shifting and falling apart around us. Like Lewis Carroll's Red Queen we will have to run as hard as we can just to stay in the same place.

This approach to futurism is based on the primordial fear of change coupled with a masochistic resignation to the notion that malignant change is engulfing us. Once, in what was perhaps a less sophisticated age, new developments were greeted more optimistically. Tennyson expressed the sunny outlook of literate England in the Industrial Revolution when he exhorted, "Let the great world spin forever down the ringing grooves of change." (It might be worthwhile to note, with reference to the eminent poet's innocent optimism, that public response to technology is almost always based on considerable ignorance of the workings of that technology. Tennyson wrote that memorable line in *Locksley Hall* after being mightily impressed with the new marvel of the age, the railroad train. Being nearsighted, he thought the train wheels ran in grooves in the tracks.)

Today, equally ignorant, we look upon change, particularly technological change, much more gloomily. And the futurists feed—and feed on—our fears.

Drucker has always been a futurist—but in a different sense. Throughout his work he is concerned with the "futurity" of present actions and decisions. He extrapolates from current developments to describe what is to come. While he offers predictions, predictions are not his primary mission. His contribution is to identify major trends and to help to shape ways in which mankind cannot just live with them, but live more happily through them. Even before the outbreak of World War

II he was speculating on the nature of the society that might be built on the foundations of the structure that he was certain would come to an end. In subsequent books and essays—notably *The New Society* and *Landmarks of Tomorrow*—he has paid particular attention to technology and its effect on society. But he has never treated machines as being dominant. He concentrates on human beings. He attempts to outline philosophical guidelines and intellectual disciplines that will serve mankind in dealing with the future. But always Drucker accepts change as the way of the world. He rejects the notion that somehow change can be forestalled. And he does not characterize change as destructive or dehumanizing. He does not apotheosize it either. He says, "Change is inevitable. How we live with it and what we do with it is the measure of us as civilized people."

This might be called an older style of futurism. The newer approach is exemplified by Alvin Toffler in his best-selling *Future Shock*. A year before Toffler's gigantic success, Drucker published *The Age of Discontinuity*. The two books offer an interesting contrast in approaches to the future.

Toffler concentrates from the outset, not just on change, but on the velocity of change. It is not merely that bad changes are confronting us every day; they are coming along so fast that we can't cope with them. As a result we are weltering in a miasma of ills—stress, neurosis, alienation, conflict.

Toffler gives details that are designed to be read in a horrific context. The world's population will double in little more than a decade. Economic growth is booming along at an unprecedented rate. The rate of development of technology has risen to breakneck speed. Once the average time span between the introduction of a new invention and its peak production was about thirty-five years; this includes the refrigerator, vacuum cleaner, and so forth. For the group of appliances that were introduced between 1939 and 1959—television, for instance—the span had shrunk to eight years. Now new inventions come into our lives and change them at higher speed.

From one point of view, this last phenomenon might

be considered beneficial, in that we enjoy these new things much faster than we used to. But, no. Change, and particularly the rapidity of change, makes everything *temporary*. Nothing is fixed; we live as transients in the world. And this is making us sick.

Future Shock amasses much interesting detail to make its point. We live in a "throw-away" society. We use paper towels and napkins once and discard them. We buy TV dinners and throw away the trays. We trade in our cars every year or so. And every day there are more things to throw away. The shelves of supermarkets teem with duplicate products. And—backed by the massive machinery of advertising and public relations—fads and styles change with equal rapidity. Our preferences are manipulated; we shift from one enthusiasm to another, and every shift brings with it shoals of new things to be used briefly and then thrown away.

We are not only using things faster, we are moving faster. Within a single year nearly 37 million Americans changed their place of residence. "This is more than the total population of Cambodia, Ghana, Guatemala, Honduras, Iraq, Israel, Mongolia, Nicaragua and Tunisia combined. It is as if the entire population of all these countries had suddenly been relocated." In moving around so fast we lose our roots and add to the burden of transience that we feel.

We meet more people than we did before. We form more relationships, but they are not as deep as they used to be. We become accustomed to making and losing friends quickly, and this breeds "disaffiliation."

And we are constantly bombarded with new knowledge. We consume newspapers, magazines, radio, and television. Every time we form a new idea we are already in the process of discarding it, to replace it with an even newer idea. All this conduces confusion, anxiety, apathy and ultimate breakdown.

What can be done about this? Personally, we can deliberately slow down the rate of change in certain controllable areas. We can refuse to eat at fast-food places; we can refrain from buying throw-away products. We can hang onto our cars and remain out of step with the latest fashions. We can get rid of the stereo set that has been assaulting our eardrums. We can "destimulate" ourselves through deliberate acts of slowdown or rejection.

We must educate our children to cope with and manage change. Everything in the curriculum must be judged on the paramount basis of its future usefulness. No more wasteful concentration on the past. What good are fixed disciplines like English, mathematics, and economics if they do not have a future focus? To ensure this we must create "Councils of the Future" in every school and community. Through the medium of these councils, the fresh winds of the future can be made to blow through the Halls of Academe.

As for technology, Toffler admits that little can be done about turning it off; but we must have responsible technology. Every new development will have to undergo stringent ecological tests before it is "unleashed" on the public. Our political structure must be overhauled to provide, among other things, a technological ombudsman to oversee these things.

Indeed, government and other institutions will have to undergo nothing short of revolution to cope with the onrush of malignant change. For example, technology makes it possible to poll an entire populace about important question, and do it instantaneously. This will cleanse us of the encrustations of an obsolete representative democracy. In each neighborhood of the world, constituent assemblies will meet to take stock and assign priorities for the rest of the century.

Other institutions will have to make equally drastic adjustments. For example, the long-lasting monogamous marriage will not altogether disappear, but it will become a rarity.

And so on. Change is bad. It is happening faster and faster. Our attitude toward change is not to welcome it or accept it, but to fear it. We must safeguard ourselves against the future.

This version of futurism—and its manifestations proliferate—piles up details, emphasizes confusion and negative effect, and underscores the calamitous nature of change. It offers answers, but they tend to be unrealistic or superficial or hortatory. The big impact of the book lies not in the prescriptions, but rather in the delicious thrill of horror that the reader undergoes as he sees the awful future unfolded before him. One might well be justified in adding books such as *Future Shock* to the list of elements causing tension, stress, and apathy in the populace.

In *The Age of Discontinuity*, Drucker works with the same general set of materials. His approach and viewpoint, however, are distinctly different.

Drucker begins by noting a fundamental change affecting futurism. Traditionally, the futurist is one who extrapolates from present trends. But in large degree, says Drucker, this is no longer possible. There have been quantum jumps—in technology and the physical and behavioral sciences alike—of such magnitude as to make accurate projection highly unreliable and perhaps impossible. Before we could observe a current development and project its continuity. But the new developments are so profound and complex that we cannot foresee their consequences. We are no longer dealing with continuities, but with discontinuities. Since prediction is impossible, what is left is to understand the nature of the discontinuities, see them in historical perspective, and develop the disciplines, techniques—and, above all, the philosophical viewpoint—to not merely cope with them but to build upon them a better society for everyone.

The major discontinuities exist in several areas.

New technologies are rendering existing businesses obsolete and creating new industries. The industries of the fifty years leading up to the late 1960s were, by and large, derived from the scientific developments of the middle and late nineteenth century. Cause and effect could be traced in orderly fashion. Now scientific developments are so rapid, and proceed from so many diverse and sometimes unlikely sources, that it is extremely difficult to see what is coming next. Furthermore, these developments are so complex as to be virtually opaque to even the best-informed layman. The closing decades of the twentieth century will see rapid emergence of technological innovation and application in ways that are almost impossible to foresee.

The economy of the world has operated on a set of principles and assumptions that have been in force for hundreds of years. We still think of separate nations as economic units, whose discrete economies are as different from one another as their customs, languages, and laws. We see "international commerce" as a process of bargaining and trading between these distinctly separate entities. But that view is becoming obsolete. The world is becoming a place where "common information generates the same economic appetites, aspirations and demands—cutting across national boundaries and languages and largely disregarding political ideologies as well." It is a "global shopping center." But we have not yet developed—with one exception—economic institutions to deal with this new reality. The one exception is the much-maligned multinational corporation. Furthermore, we do not have economic policies and theories suitable for a world economy. This failure is exacerbating a gulf between rich (and largely white) nations and those that are poor (and largely nonwhite). This is the prime economic problem with which we must deal; otherwise we run an extreme risk of worldwide warfare that will swallow up rich and poor nations alike.

We are no longer a society of individuals. Today's society is pluralistic. As the population grows we tend to work more and more as parts of groups. All of the important economic and social tasks of the world are now entrusted to institutions, public and private; and all of these institutions are run by managers. There is growing disenchantment with these institutions; notably government, but also religious, educational, and business institutions. It is not a matter of a pluralistic society that lies in our future; we are in it now, largely without understanding it or even thinking about it very much. The discontinuity set up by the new society of institutions creates enormous challenges.

The most important of the discontinuities is the emergence of *knowledge* as the crucial resource of economy and society. In the Industrial Revolution skill replaced brawn; now knowledge will become essential to the performance of tasks formerly requiring skill.

293

The elevation of knowledge to this central role calls for profound changes in the way we learn, the way we work, and the way we govern ourselves.

The Age of Discontinuity is structured as a series of examinations of these four discontinuities; their causes, their historical relationships, their interrelationships, and their effects. Drucker's emphasis is on showing us relationships, not disparities. The four developments impinge on each other in various ways, which he delineates. The new technologies contribute to the global shopping center; the development of institutions relates to the increasing importance of knowledge as a resource; people must learn to function within the institutions that are becoming preeminent in the new world.

Drucker uses detail to underpin his points, but he does not pile incident upon incident for effect. His approach neither glorifies change nor characterizes it as an abomination. He accepts the fact of change, and of increasingly rapid change—precisely because the events reported are accomplished facts, they are unlikely to disappear. He does not predict what will happen; the "discontinuities" make it impossible to do that. But he tells us what we will have to be concerned with. He declares that predictions based on the trends of the past sixty years—which are the substance of most futurist work—are likely to be wrong. What we can look forward to is not the extension of trends but the development of entirely new ones.

Drucker is fully aware of the dangers in a time of exceedingly rapid change; but there is a kind of exhilaration in his view as well. Change is not a disaster, but a challenge. And always the focus is on human beings. We are not helpless bits of flotsam, bobbing on the surging wave of a mindless and mechanistic future. We can, with intelligence and will, control our fate.

It might be noted that, in reviewing *The Age of Discontinuity* for *The New Republic* (June 21, 1969), Edward T. Chase acknowledges Drucker's considerable merit, but in the end finds him deficient in heart: "For Drucker treats the market as a kind of eternal verity;

he shows no awareness of its victims, no anger, no compassion."

Readers may judge for themselves the relative degrees of humanity as between Peter Drucker and the writers of the kinds of books of which *Future Shock* is a prime example. Perhaps a more important question is that of a thoughtful and constructive approach to the future. For spine-tingling thrills and chills, Toffler may be a better bet; for understanding, it is Drucker.

19.

Drucker Looks Back— and Ahead

When asked to sum up his career, Drucker responds dutifully and courteously. However, it is contrary to his nature to look back. His eyes tend to swing around to focus on the future.

This chapter is a distillation of Drucker's observations of what he has done or not done, and what he has been trying to do. He is still deeply interested in the problems confronting the manager; and so the conversation tends to move in that direction.

Today, nearly forty years after he wrote *The Future of Industrial Man*, Drucker has modified, to some degree, his view of the corporation as the representative social institution of our time, without, however, changing the basic principles of his philosophical approach.

"It has become clear to me," he says, "that our society has become a society of organizations, of which the corporation was only the prototype." He goes on to point out that the corporation was the first one to become clearly visible and the first one to be studied. Since then we have seen the rapid growth of a whole range of institutions—the university, the hospital, the research laboratory and so on. Every one of the basic tasks of society is now being discharged through a large institution. These organizations have the same characteristics, the same problems, the same basic needs and the same opportunities as the corporation. The large corporation is still the most visible of institutions, but no longer the dominant one. "The others have grown faster, and in many ways they seem more interested in the management of the society. But at the same time they present great problems. They have the interest in managing society, but they are, by-and-large, unmanaged, not mismanaged, but unmanaged."

Within a few decades we have changed the crystalline structure of the domestic society. Our existing political and social theories, almost all of which stem from the seventeenth century, do not fit any more, and the misfit becomes more egregious and critical as time goes on. Our existing approaches to political and social economics have been exploded or undermined. They have been subverted by the breaking down of traditional boundaries —one manifestation of which is the emergence of a general working class.

The world has become very homogenous; largely because of the communications media; but also because "two world wars, especially the second, has brought ordinary people into exposures that were simply unthinkable a few generations ago."

And yet, people have not changed. They want the same things they have always wanted. They want roots. People become more conscious of the need to belong to a community as they are increasingly faced with the need to deal with huge social entities. They tend, if anything, to become more parochial in many ways. It is a mistake to look at what people want in terms of "consumer preferences." Consumer is the wrong word. Individuals the world over have certain wants, some material and some not. They want a little mobility, a little freedom from the constraints of a traditional society, and a little information, enough to link them to the rest of the world.

In addition they want, and need, a home. As society becomes more complex and amorphous, we need, not smaller, but more definable communities. Paradoxically, as the world moves toward greater integration, it should at the same time become more localized.

These needs are, on the whole, not extreme. They are felt and expressed in moderation. Human beings have a general understanding of the necessity to function within large social structures, but at the same time they must maintain a sufficient degree of individuality.

Community need not be the place where we live. It is often the place where we work. For most adults the work scene is the most meaningful community, not because we spend most of our waking hours there but because the relationships to other people are both structured and highly plastic. And the work place gives us instant identification—"I work for GE."

There is nothing particularly new in this, Drucker points out. We have always been known, to a great extent, by what we do. Look at the large number of family names that have their origin in occupations. Indeed, "until a few years ago the Stockholm telephone book did not list people alphabetically by name. Everybody's name is Svenson or Anderson anyway. The phone book listed them by title: 'Master joiner's widow,' etc. This was the case until a few years ago. It was of course predicated on the belief that once you had achieved a simple status you remained in it. But as the society became more mobile they had to change it. If others did not know you had been promoted from departmental director to divisional director of the bank they didn't know where to find you. So they had to switch to the alphabet. Now, if you don't know the first name and the address you can't find anybody, because there are five thousand Sven Larsens in Stockholm." This need for identification leads to the universal tendency to become title-happy.

Has he gotten his message across to the management community? Drucker is satisfied that he has tried; he is not sure of the degree to which he has succeeded.

"In addressing myself to managers," he says, "I want to accomplish two things only. I want to convince managers that they should take the highest view of their craft, realizing what they do is important and has to be done seriously and with a striving for excellence. The second point I am trying to make is that the gap between the leaders and the average is easily closed with a little effort.

"I am not a bit concerned with who is right. That's why I don't belong in academia. If I read a book, I don't ask if the author is 'right,' but rather, what can I get out of it? In addressing myself to an audience, in person or in print, I say, 'Look, you're all busy people. Time can't be stored; if you don't get anything out of today, it's wasted. It will never come back again. There has to be justification for each day you take out of your lives. So please, before we part, jot down two things —no more than two—that you're going to do tomorrow, or stop doing tomorrow. I hope that my impact will lead toward improvement in one little area—not tomorrow, but right now.' And I hope that what I say gives managers a bigger view of their function as intellectually demanding and esthetically satisfying."

Today the manager is confronted with the job of managing technicians who know far more about what they do than he can ever know. The military services are extremely worried about it. The traditional NCO was a supervisor. Today, particularly in the Air Force, the great majority of people with NCO rank are not supervising anybody. They are technicians or professionals, who cannot be managed in the conventional way. Drucker observes, "The master sergeant who runs a communications center in the war room of the Pentagon can say to a general—or to the Secretary of Defense, for that matter—'With due respect, sir, I will not do that, because it makes no sense.' The general may not like it, but they cannot get another man."

The manager in industry nowadays is trying to supervise the work of similar people. The only way you can do it is by thinking through what his role and contribution will be and setting very clear, measurable objectives that both parties understand and accept.

Drucker says, "The model for management in this situation is not Alfred P. Sloan but Rudolf Bing. I respect his approach to what he did while he was running the Metropolitan Opera. Rudy seems to be about six feet, eight inches tall; facially he resembles one of those terribly sad basset hounds and appears to have about as much sense of humor. Once at a party a cuddly little model sidled up to Rudy, flapping her false eyelashes. She cooed, 'Mr. Bing, aren't you afraid of all those temperamental prima donnas with their tantrums?' Rudy looked down at her and said, 'My dear child, I don't know what you are talking about. Temperamental prima donnas, tantrums, that's what I get paid for handling. As long as she brings them in at the box office.' And then, talking more to himself than to the model, whom he had forgotten, he said, 'Under one condition. When the playbill says Tosca, she sings Tosca!'

"That in a nutshell is how you manage a professional. It's your job to enable him to bring them in at the box office. If this involves tantrums, you put up with the tantrums."

What can a manager do to equip himself for his task? "If I were a young manager," Drucker replies, "I would make it my business to learn about economics, particularly international economics. Managers don't know enough about economics. This is largely the fault of the schools, which teach it wretchedly.

"The rising young executive will, more and more, be expected to have at least a smattering of knowledge in all major functional areas. It won't do any more to say 'I'm a marketing man, I don't know any accounting.' You must know at least enough about accounting so that a comptroller cannot make a monkey out of you—and that is not very much.

"You will not need to know how everything works. Being familiar with the mysteries of the computer is not important. I don't know how the telephone works, and why the hell should I?

"But you will have to learn a lot about managing people you cannot supervise. Most people still think that management is supervision; it isn't. You can't supervise professional and technical people in the traditional sense. You have to figure out how to get the maximum contribution, how to integrate their expertise with the organization, how to give them recogni-

300

tion without, say, making a very poor manager out of a first-rate chemist.

"For the manager who wants to learn, the best access to economics in this country is popular journals, not learned ones. The fellow who reads—let's say at random —*Business Week,* the *London Economist, Wall Street Journal* and *Fortune* gets a pretty good grasp of the subject.

"Managers are action-focused. And usually action-focused people are not book-learners. For example, one of the problems of the American medical profession is that there is no correlation between performance in medical school and performance in practice. None. I once made a study of physicians, looking at correlation between education and standing as a diagnostician. Of the two best diagnosticians in New York at the time, one was a German. He had gotten four years of credit at the University of Hamburg for his service as a medical corpsman in World War I, and had gone to medical school for just one year. The other had finished last in his class. Today he would not be admitted to special training."

Industry spends a lot of time thinking about management development. Drucker's approach to the problem emphasizes simplicity and flexibility.

"In developing managers, I would not have a single formula. I would always start out with what a man has done. I always try to find a man or woman's strength, because that's the only thing to build on. Then I would ask what he needs to get full benefit from that strength.

"Skills one can acquire. But the fellow who cannot work with people is in trouble. The tax accountant may not be going to change, but he can at least learn to say 'Good morning.' I had a client in the late Forties; maybe the world's most brilliant consulting engineer, in a small consulting firm which was fabulously proficient. He was, of all the bastards I had ever met in my life, about the worst. He was absolutely impossible. The way he treated people turned my stomach. Finally we got him to take some counseling. The change was remarkable. He came back overflowing with the milk of human kindness. After two or three weeks I ran into his chief engineer and asked him how things were going. He said, 'Unspeakable. I don't think we can stand it another week.'

"I asked, 'What's the matter? Has Charlie gone back to his old habits?'

"He said, 'Hell, no. I wish he would. You know, now he comes into the office, the son of a bitch, and says GOOD MORNING!—and we worry all day whether he means it or not'!"

Drucker comes back continually to the questions of the manager's responsibility in dealing with society at large and with the people who work for him. He says, "Managers must accept the idea that they are involved in activities that affect the public, and that the spotlight can be turned on them at any time. There's a very old rule; don't do anything that you would not want to have to explain to a Senate investigation.

"It is bad practice for one manager to make a personnel decision, simply because one man's judgment is no man's judgment. IBM offers people the right to go all the way to the top with any grievance. It's rarely used —but it's there. This keeps managers from acting with gross bias and arbitrariness, and that is a necessity. The idea of scrupulous fairness and openness will have to spread. This is not because most decisions are unfair; they're not. But simply because the spotlight will be increasingly beamed on management practice, and properly so.

"We will have to learn a great deal more about the placement of people. We have towering selection procedures which accomplish very little because they are so towering. At that stage there is almost nothing of importance that you can know about the applicant or that he can know about the organization. No matter how elaborate a selection procedure you have, you are going to get the random distribution of the human race."

There is not much about advertising in this book. Drucker has never shown high regard for the advertising profession. He says little about it, really, except for an occasional barbed side-comment about the "great intellects of Madison Avenue." At the same time, he is not one to wring his hands about the "awful waste" involved in advertising: "Only unsuccessful advertising makes a product more expensive. The question is whether the product is worth anything or not. Even the most scorned product may have a value to the user. Mouthwash is derided as having no utility. Well, a lot of people have, apparently, a kind of bad taste or tired feeling in the mouth, and mouthwash refreshes them. You might say it has only modest hygiene benefits, and that you can probably get the same effect with salt; but who the hell wants salt in his mouth?"

Drucker looks benevolently upon the kinds of marketing "frills" that social critics attack: "All right, my phone is green instead of black, matching the beat-up file cabinets. A few years ago you could get only black. I don't really care; the green one doesn't work any better; but when they make enough of them the color does not add anything to the cost."

That advertising encourages people to spend money on other than purely pragmatic grounds does not bother Drucker at all: "People in other ages did not act any differently. Human beings have always indulged their vanity and innate desire for a little ornamentation, a little distinction. Arguments against displays of vanity are moralists' arguments. We often see a kind of nineteenth century resentment against the poor for not acting as if they were poor."

Here is Drucker talking about what he has accomplished.

"I've anticipated a great many things that are now staples, not because they are terribly profound but precisely because they are terribly obvious. The only claim I would make is that, in the 1940s, I looked at the modern organization and found it worth studying. This was a time when economists looked upon business and saw General Motors, let's say, or First National City Bank, as the individual isolated trader in the market. And political scientists didn't see any organizations at all. When I published *Concept of the Corporation* a friend wrote a review in a political science journal, concluding with the words, 'It is to be hoped that this gifted author will now dedicate himself to more important subjects.'

"I was at the right spot at the right moment. Interest in the discipline of management would probably have arisen anyway. It was ready; it was ripe. And here the impact of my work has been much greater on the political and social sciences than on economics, where I have had practically no impact at all.

"And the impact of my management principles has been primarily on the practitioner, as it was meant to be, not on the schools of business.

"I would never have considered myself to be any good in the operational area. I'm a very poor manager, and that's putting it mildly. I have been able to see how things work, and this surprised me, because I never considered myself to have any gift in that area. And another thing that surprises me is the satisfaction I'm getting out of making things work.

"I can connect unlikely facts and trends; probably because of the need to make a little information go a long way. I had the benefit of a poor education that no one pretended was any good, so for eight years there was no effort to get me to stop reading under the desk, as long as I didn't make trouble. That's really the only reading I've ever done. But a journalist's flypaper memory for trivia has enabled me to hang onto the facts I pick up; and along with this I suppose I have a journalist's kind of feel for what makes sense and what doesn't.

"I'm better about things than about people. I'm more interested in people than in ideas, but I'm better at ideas.

"I can see how the organization—the corporation, the institution—can be made effective, and I think we are closer to solving the problem of status and function within the organization than we were forty years ago.

"But the industrial society, that's another matter. I'm not sure it can be done. What have I done to bring it into successful being? I'm not sure that I've done very much about the important things. The areas that seemed to me of greatest importance, these are the areas in which I've had the least impact. The self-governing plant community, for example, which at one time I thought to be my most important contribution, has made no impact.

"On the other hand, in an area about which I am not terribly interested—formal organizational structure—I've had a fabulous impact. And here I've had an even greater impact, perhaps, on institutions than on businesses. Hospitals, for example. But these are areas that, although I think they are important; are not central.

"Some of my most important ideas have had no impact because they were premature. In 1949 when I raised questions about private institutions no one paid the slightest attention. Twenty-five years later people have found that the question of who controls private institutions is a very important one, if only because of their impact on capital markets.

"But when I talked about business organization, the timing was right, just five seconds before the general public became receptive. That's the definition of the successful pioneer; one who is just a single subway stop ahead.

"However, looking at what I've done in studying the institution—the corporation being just a prototype—I feel fairly surefooted. My work may not be complete, but it's consistent, and it's operational.

"We have learned a lot about structure. We have learned an enormous amount about personnel management in the middle level, and performance is significantly better.

"We talk about financial controls. A lot of what we do here is not because we want to do it but because Uncle Sam forces us to do it. In 1944 in the Pittsburgh Plate Glass Company, they knew what they paid in wages but they didn't have the foggiest notion of how much it cost to produce plate glass. We've learned a lot in this area; but not enough.

"We know more about top management's job—but very few companies really do much about it. The greatest overall change has been in awareness of the problems, not in performance. Maybe I'm unduly critical of the performance level; the change in awareness, however, is what I think is most significant."

20.

The Bottom Line

You examine Peter Drucker's thinking, writing, teaching, consulting—and you still find no facile means of categorizing him.

The contradictions remain. He is a European who has become a phenomenally best-selling author in English. He is an authority on organizational structure who has never been part of an organization. He is a wildly successful counselor on business matters who has never been a businessman. He is a conservative who delineates the flaws and follies in the most revered of institutions. He is a teacher who insists that he must be able to learn from his students. He is a philosopher whose philosophy falls into no classic mold.

And he is a shaper of a world order from which he stands aloof, sometimes in sardonic detachment, sometimes in melancholy appraisal.

We live in a corporate society. Organizations control our lives. That control will broaden and deepen, rather than diminish. Drucker—himself a confirmed individualist—saw early that the organization, business and nonbusiness, constituted the wave of the future.

Seeing this, he set out to do a number of things. He has tried to define the goals, the structure, and the ethics of organizations in ways that will make the organization a better instrument for achievement—not of money or success, but of the best possible way of life for the most people. Since organizations must be managed, Drucker has identified and defined the principles and practice of effective management. He has anticipated and examined the great questions of our age, and has attempted to relate ideals to the practicalities of existence. And he has sought the answer to the question of how man can live within the structure of the corporate society and still find the individual fulfillment that is the objective—and the right—of all men.

Drucker has not created the world we live in; but he has done as much to shape it as anyone has. He has done this because he has a unique ability to penetrate and influence—not necessarily the intellectual community —but the community of professional managers who do run things, often without much regard for what the intellectual community may think.

Drucker is not a zealot, a "true believer," in Eric Hoffer's phrase. Drucker mistrusts zealotry. He feels the world's business must be done through management and judgment, not exhortation and enthusiasm. He possesses neither the grandeur nor the divine folly of the saint. He is the cool, detached generator and assayer of ideas, impelled always by the search for the "best possible," not the ideal.

But Drucker doesn't dwell in the realm of ideas. He takes his risks. He enters the arena. He puts his ideas to the test in a wide range of real-world situations.

He can be—and has been—overconfident. He can seem cold, insensitive, even brutal; although here, I would maintain, appearances are deceiving. Drucker is always human, always conscious of the needs of human beings. He sees human needs and aspirations as being inextricably entwined with the duty to contribute within the framework of society; and sometimes, in his emphasis on duty, he may seem lacking in heart. But in his efforts to define the ways in which man can live and function with dignity in a complex and difficult world,

Drucker has done more than a multitude who preach fervently about their solicitude for humankind.

Drucker saw the vacuum beginning to gape in a crumbling society, and he has contributed significantly to the structure we have erected to take the place of the values and institutions that are gone. That structure is imperfect. There are great inequities and injustices. Enormous sections of it are not yet complete. But it is working. And there is promise that, given the dedication, the common sense and the faith that we need, we can make it work better.

Drucker works with us, in a way, but he is apart from us. He is always the outsider; observing, thinking, testing his thought, and giving us charts into the future if we want to follow them.

In the end, this very quality of "outsideness," this cool refusal to be pigeonholed or to avoid questions because they are the special province of a particular elite, is Drucker's great strength. He has combined with it great qualities of energy, intelligence and eloquence; and he has made things happen.

We may not like everything about the corporate society, but it is our world. It is a world that Drucker foresaw, defined, and helped to create.

Appendix:
The Sayings of Chairman Peter

Drucker refers to his mind, deprecatingly, as a storehouse of trivia. Trivia it is not; it is an awesome assemblage of disparate facts that Drucker is able to adduce to support his points. Filtered through his verbal acuity, these facts are often compressed into startling observations that shed a new light on some familiar situation. Drucker also uses his gift for aphorism to puncture sacred cows. His keen eye and skill with words make him entertaining—and dangerous. Here is a sampling.

Capital formation is shifting from the entrepreneur who invests in the future to the pension trustee who invests in the past.

Growth that adds volume without improving productivity is fat. Growth that diminishes productivity is cancer.

The corporate income tax is the most asinine of taxes.

Go-go decades always produce new economic theories.

The price of petroleum is the largest deflationary suction factor ever devised.

Most sales training is totally unjustified. At best it makes an incompetent salesman out of a moron.

Many businessmen are always establishing new beachheads. They never ask, "Is there a *beach* to that beachhead?"

"Absorption of overhead" is one of the most obscene terms I have ever heard.

There is no hostility to business. It exists only on the front page of the *New York Times*, with other fabled monsters.

We must stop talking of profit as a reward. It is a cost. There are no rewards; only the costs of yesterday and tomorrow.

When the government talks about "raising capital" it means printing it. That's not very creative, but it's what we're going to do.

If you have too many problems maybe you should go out of business. There is no law that says a company must last forever.

If all the underdeveloped countries were to disappear, the large multinationals wouldn't even notice.

As to the idea that advertising motivates people, remember the Edsel.

For twenty-five years the bona fide liberal has been screaming for true internationalism. He got it—the multinational corporation—in a form he didn't like.

We are dedicated to the preservation and strengthening of small business and our tax policy is designated to destroy small business. Small businesses are selling out because of tax laws designed for ITT.

Capitalism has been proved a false god because it leads inevitably to class war among rigidly defined classes. Socialism has been proved false because it has been demonstrated that it cannot abolish these classes.

There is, strictly speaking, but one kind of economically profitable investment: in goods which produce other, more valuable, goods.

The modern corporation is a political institution; its purpose is the creation of legitimate power in the industrial sphere.

If we eliminate the profit motive, the result will not be the equal and peaceful society of the millennium but the emergence of some other outlet for man's basic lust for power.

Profitability is the sovereign criterion of the enterprise.

Profitability is not the purpose of business enterprise but a limiting factor on it. . . . The problem is not the maximization of profit but the achievement of sufficient profit to cover the risks of economic activity and thus to avoid loss.

What the business thinks it produces is not of first importance.

Business has only two basic functions—marketing and innovation.

The only things that evolve by themselves in an organization are disorder, friction and malperformance.

Far too much reorganization goes on all the time. Organizitis is like a spastic colon.

Reorganization is surgery. One doesn't just cut.

There are no good executive compensation plans. There are only bad and worse.

Stock option plans reward the executive for doing the wrong thing. Instead of asking, "Are we making the right decisions?" he asks, "How did we close today?" It is encouragement to loot the corporation.

We know nothing about motivation. All we can do is write books about it.

So much of what we call management consists in making it difficult for people to work.

Job enrichment has been around for sixty years. It's been successful every time it has been tried, but industry is not interested.

Management says the first job of the supervisor is human relations. But when promotion time comes they promote the fellow who puts in his paperwork.

Supervisors resist most new programs because the programs all say that their subordinates know as much about the job as they do.

Management by objectives works if you know the objectives. Ninety percent of the time you don't.

The great trouble with a Harvard-type program is the arrogance it breeds. Students do not learn how difficult it is to accomplish anything.

Graduate school faculties are made up of people who have never been out working in organizations, who have never found out about the brilliant marketing strategy that doesn't work because the consumer does not behave the way you think he ought to.

In business school classrooms they construct wonderful models of a non-world.

Working with people is difficult, but not impossible.

The tax accountant isn't going to change. But at least he can learn to say "good morning."

Promotion should not be more important than accomplishment, or avoiding instability more important than taking the right risk.

Ignorance of the function of management is one of the most serious weaknesses of an industrial society—and it is almost universal.

Success in running a business carries by itself no promise of success outside business.

Any serious attempt to make management "scientific" or a "profession" is deleterious.

Production is not the application of tools to materials, but logic to work.

Whenever a man's failure can clearly be traced to management's mistakes, he has to be kept on the payroll.

The new financial managers run heavily to Ph.D. degrees and Phi Beta Kappa keys.

Marketing is a fashionable term. The sales manager becames a marketing vice-president. But a gravedigger is still a gravedigger even when he is called a mortician—only the price of burial goes up.

Fast personnel decisions are likely to be wrong.

If a manager spends more than 10 percent of his time on "human relations" the group is probably too large.

A crisis that recurs must not recur again.

The most common cause of executive failure is unwillingness or inability to change with the demands of a new position.

A "generalist" is a specialist who can relate his own small area to the universe of knowledge.

Strong people always have strong weaknesses.

The question is not "how will he get along?" but "what will he contribute?"

Priorities are easy. "Posteriorities"—what jobs not to tackle—are tough.

Decision making is the *specific* executive task.

The effective executive does not make many decisions. He solves generic problems through policy.

Start with what is right rather than what is acceptable.

In making decisions you don't start with facts; you start with opinions.

The traditional measurement is not the right measurement; if it were there would be no need for decisions.

Finding the appropriate measurement is not a mathematical exercise; it is a risk-taking judgment.

We always remember best the irrelevant.

To improve communications, work not on the utterer but the recipient.

Every task of developed society requires management.

Entrepreneurial innovation will be as important to management as the management function.

Management is a bridge between civilization and culture.

Management is the one institution that can transcend the boundaries of the national state.

Long-range planning does not deal with future decisions, but with the futurity of present decisions.

Instead of a management science, which provides knowledge, concepts and discipline, we may be developing a gadget bag of techniques for the efficiency expert. [From an address to the fiftieth anniversary conference of the Harvard Graduate School of Business Administration, 1958]

"Scientific" is not synonymous with quantification—if it were, astrology would be the queen of sciences.

Ethics stays in the preface of the average business science book.

Emphasis on "minimizing risk" is futile.

What's going to happen to the executive's job in the next ten years? Nothing. It is amazing how many jobs are exactly the same as they were in 1900.

It is bad practice for one manager to make a personal decision, simply because one man's judgment is no man's judgment.

Managers will have to learn that they are public personnel and institute due process, particularly in people decisions.

There is an enormous number of managers who have retired on the job.

We must learn not to discriminate against the man who has a genuine, true, major outside interest. It did not do General Wavell any harm to be known as a fairly good minor English poet. At Sears Roebuck it would kill you.

If you make the organization your life, you are defenseless against the inevitable disappointments.

To depend on the personnel department to do management development is basically a misunderstanding. A marriage counselor can help with a marriage, but it's your job.

Before World War II most managers did not know that they were managing.

Don't put the fate of your business in the delusions of economists.

Sociology is like acne. Civilization does not die from the disease, but it itches.

In all recorded history there has not been one economist who had to worry about where the next meal would come from.

Economists have always suffered from one big inherent defect. They love humanity but they hate human beings.

Behavioral scientists complain about the "undernourished" shopgirl in Lima who buys a Coke or a lipstick. She may be undernourished in terms of a Harvard economist, but she's probably quite well nourished in terms of the Peruvian Indian.

Economists think the poor need them to tell them that they are poor.

Moralists really talk out of class consciousness. They

complain that the shopgirl buys a lipstick. They are really saying she should know her place.

We always look for somebody below us. A friend of mine, a great Jewish scholar, said the Pharisees are with us always. Only now they are economists.

[On sensitivity training] I'm one of those very simple people who believe that one is not entitled to inflict damage on the living body. For the weak, the lame, the defenseless, the shy, the vulnerable, this is a very dangerous thing. The real sadists, the wolves, tear the little lambs to pieces. The casualty rate is unacceptable.

If we applied the FDA rules of safety to psychotherapy there would not be one panacea on the market.

Our educational system disqualifies people for honest work.

When a subject becomes totally obsolete we make it a required course.

The schoolmaster since time immemorial has believed that the ass is an organ of learning. The longer you sit, the more you learn.

Now they are converting "progressive" schools into what they call fundamental schools, which are just old-fashioned schools with great emphasis on discipline and the three Rs. And much to the consternation of the liberal establishment the kids do better, partly because the parents insist they do better.

Harvard, to me, combines the worst of German academic arrogance with bad American theological seminary habits.

Medicare and Medicaid are the greatest measures yet devised to make the world safe for clerks.

Physicians are delayed adolescents. Their training does not permit them to become adults.

One of the problems of the American medical profession is that there is no correlation between performance in medical school and performance in practice. None.

Social security is a fantasy. It doesn't fund anything.

The communists work at twice the profit margin we do.

The growth of pension plans makes unions negotiate with themselves. They bargain present income against future income.

We may now be nearing the end of our hundred-year belief in Free Lunch.

Our love affair with government is over, although we keep the old mistress around.

No country today has an effective government.

Some new states have fewer people than are sitting in this room. But all have four things: an air force, a 370 IBM computer, a cryogenic chamber, and nuclear capability.

What people want most is a little mobility, a little freedom from the constraints of a traditional society . . . and a little information that links them to the world.

For my sins I worked with the Nigerians when they became independent. I told them that what they needed was a late eighteenth-century English mechanic who could design a better hoe. They asked me, "Is that what they do at MIT?" I said no, of course not. They said, "We are going to do what they do at MIT." Anything else is second-class.

In Latin America we have far exceeded the goals of the "decade of progress." But the idea that everything develops at the same time, and that it can be developed from outside, is nonsense.

You hear that Brazil has no race problem. We had no race problem either as long as the "niggers" were down in Dixie. Race is Brazil's biggest problem.

The poor, because they are poor, are very much concerned with value. They don't buy bargains because they know they can't afford them.

Nobody has ever gotten dysentery from Coke. There is a point in its popularity in places where the water is bad.

Many believe that if people are sufficiently poor and live in sufficiently horrible conditions, they become honest.

American congressmen have always suffered from the belief that the rest of the world does not exist.

The national state has become nonfunctional. No country in the world has an effective domestic policy.

When you look at Indian films you give up any idea that Hollywood is the capital of bad taste.

We do not live in a bourgeois country. It is a proletarian country, with no bourgeois values at all.

Look at governmental programs for the past fifty years. Every single one—except for warfare— achieved the exact opposite of its announced goal.

We have an agricultural policy that is supposed to strengthen and preserve the family farmer. It has made the farm very productive but it has destroyed the family farmer in the process.

If a government commission had worked on the horse, you would have had the first horse who could operate his knee joint in both directions. The only trouble would have been that he couldn't stand up.

Today we are indulging in a binge of adversary proceedings in the belief that somehow the common good will come out of vastly oversimplified polemics.

Today there is a public entertainment quality to investigative journalism and it's very frightening, because these are the traditional preludes to tyranny. Five years from now anyone who advocates suppression of the press will receive very strong support.

We don't believe in progress . . . we practice innovation.

Totalitarianism is the final result of science without morality.

[In 1957] Within fifteen or twenty years we may well be the major "have not" country in the world.

Beyond relieving starvation, food relief should be given sparingly; it destroys incentive.

The task is not to make the poor wealthy, but productive.

The burden of decision frightens the young; they want to drop out to avoid it.

The political ecologist assumes that his subject matter is far too complex ever to be fully understood—just as his counterpart, the natural ecologist, assumes this in respect to the natural environment.

Few great presidents are original thinkers.

We subordinate economics to politics—but we express moral and political issues in economic terms.

I hope we are over our belief that if you define a problem you don't have to do any work.

Years ago working people saw themselves as part of a group—the working class. Today the worker on the assembly line sees himself as a reject.

Persistent unemployment is not just an economic catastrophe; it is a social disenfranchisement.

A considerable amount of [monotony] is necessary and certainly good for the great majority of men.

Public institutions need a systematic, organized process for *abandonment*.

The large corporation is still the most visible organization but no longer the dominant one. The others have grown faster. They are, by and large, unmanaged.

Institutions mistake good intentions for objectives. They say "health care"; that's an intention, not an objective.

The wonder of modern institutions is not that they work so badly, but that anything works at all.

Very few EDP people perform; in part because they are arrogant, in part because they are ignorant, and in part because they are too enamored of their goddamned tool.

As to the EDP function being placed on a higher level in the organization, that's a lot of bullshit. I decide whether I want a washing machine. It's the mechanic's job to keep it running.

Automation properly does not start with production at all, but with an analysis of the business and its re-design on automation principles.

The computer is a moron.

The main impact of the computer has been the provision of unlimited jobs for clerks.

Like any good journalist, I have a retentive memory for trivia, like flypaper . . . plus the journalist's feel for what makes sense and what doesn't.

I'm better about things than about people. I'm more interested in people, but I'm better at ideas.

Like any journalist, I'm a frustrated novelist.

I was lucky. When God rained manna from heaven, I had a spoon.

My greatest strength as a consultant is to be ignorant and ask a few questions.

When you have 186 objectives nothing gets done. I always ask, "What's the one thing you want to do?" In Mexico they call me Señor Una Cosa.

If a client leaves this room feeling he has learned a lot he hadn't known before, he is either a stupid client or I've done a poor job. He should leave saying, I know all this—why haven't I done anything about it?

I'm not a bit concerned with who is right. That's why I don't belong in academia.

Management Library

The first section of this bibliography is a list of Peter Drucker's books and major articles.

The second section is a representative list of books concentrating on the management areas in which Peter Drucker has been most involved.

Books by Peter F. Drucker

Friedrich Julius Stahl, Konservative Staatslehre und Geschichtliche Entwicklung. Tuebingen: Mohr, 1933.
An essay on the political writings of Stahl, an important, early nineteenth-century philosophy professor. Drucker wrote this book as an anti-Nazi manifesto.

The End of Economic Man. New York: John Day Co., 1939. (Reprint by Harper & Row, 1969.)
This is Drucker's first full-length book. He presents the reasons for the rise of fascism and analyzes the

failure of established institutions. Drucker makes a strong case for the need for a new social and economic order.

The Future of Industrial Man. New York: John Day Co., 1942.
The author explores the question, Can individual freedom be preserved in an industrial society? Corporate dominance, managerial power, automation, and the dangers of monopoly and totalitarianism are major topics considered in this book.

Concept of the Corporation. New York: John Day Co., 1946. (Reprint by John Day Co., 1972.)
Classic study of the methods used by General Motors as it grew from a small company to an industrial giant. This important study of a large-scale organization provides in-depth, factual information regarding management, automation, decentralization, labor unions, prices, and profits.

The New Society. New York: Harper & Row, 1950.
In this important book, Drucker pulls together the threads that run through his first two books, The End of Economic Man *and* The Future of Industrial Man. *He refines his view of the new world order. He expands on the idea of the corporation as the representative social institution. He offers a picture of the way the world will work in the latter decades of the twentieth century, a picture that has held up remarkably.*

The Practice of Management. New York: Harper & Row, 1954.
Analyzing the nature of management, this is a helpful guide to corporate managers who want to examine their own performance, diagnose their own faults and improve their own productivity as well as the productivity of their own company. Illustrations come from such companies as Sears, Roebuck & Co., GM, Ford, IBM, Chrysler, and AT & T.

324

America's Next Twenty Years. New York: Harper & Row, 1957.

This is a collection of essays in which Drucker analyzes historic developments and projects trends into the future. He covers, among other topics, education, politics, and economics.

The Landmarks for Tomorrow. New York: Harper & Row, 1959.

In the first few chapters, Drucker describes new world patterns which have developed in recent years. He then discusses the challenges we must meet in education, government and economics. The book concludes with Drucker's observations of the spiritual reality of human existence.

Managing for Results. New York: Harper & Row, 1964.

This practical work asserts that economic performance is the specific function and contribution of business and the reason for its existence.

The Effective Executive. New York: Harper & Row, 1967.

A systematic study of those practices which are essential for executive success. The author discusses five practices: (1) time management, (2) personal contribution to the organization, (3) making strength productive, (4) establishment of priorities, (5) effective decision making.

The Age of Discontinuity: Guidelines to Our Changing Society. New York: Harper & Row, 1969.

Deals with four major areas of discontinuity: (1) the explosion of the new technology that results in major new industries, (2) the change from an international economy to a world economy, (3) a new, socio-political reality of pluralistic institutions, (4) the new universe of knowledge based on mass education in this important manifesto. For action, Peter Drucker asks "What must we do today to shape tomorrow?"

Preparing Tomorrow's Business Leaders Today. Edited by Peter F. Drucker. Englewood Cliffs, N.J.: Prentice-Hall, 1969.

Developed from a symposium on the occasion of the fifth anniversary of the Graduate School of Business Administration, New York University. The book discusses changes in business and business schools over a fifty-year period, new developments within the business society, emergence of multinational corporations and business school education. Contributors include Peter Drucker, John Diebold, Howard W. Johnson, Franklin A. Lindsay and H. M. Boettinger.

Technology, Management and Society (Selected Essays). New York: Harper & Row, 1970.

Collection of essays covering technological trends in the twentieth century such as: long-range planning, relationship of technology, science and culture, and the once and future manager.

Men, Ideas, and Politics. New York: Harper & Row, 1971.

These essays cover a broad spectrum of subject matter: Henry Ford, Japanese management, effective presidents, and campus rebellion. Two articles in particular show aspects of Drucker's thinking that are not often seen. One is a deeply felt commentary on Kierkegaard; the other is a fascinating analysis of the political philosophy of John C. Calhoun.

Management: Tasks—Responsibilities—Practices. New York: Harper & Row, 1974.

Management *is a compendium of Drucker on management. It touches on many of the themes that have run through his previous work; and it breaks new ground as well. Here Drucker discusses the tasks of management, the work of the manager, and the nature of organization. He reviews the development of management as a discipline, and projects its role into the future. This book is, in many ways, the essential reference work for the executive.*

Major Articles by Peter F. Drucker

"What Became of the Prussian Army." *Virginia Quarterly Review* (January 1941).

"Meaning and Function of Economic Policy Today." *Review of Politics* (April 1943).

"Keynes, White, and Postwar Currency." *Harper's* (July 1943).

"Exit King Cotton." *Harper's* (May 1946).

"Keynes: Economics as a Magical System." *Virginia Quarterly Review* (October 1946).

"Way to Industrial Peace." *Harper's* (January 1946).

"Who Should Get a Raise and When?" *Harper's* (March 1946).

"Henry Ford: Success and Failure." *Harper's* (July 1947).

"Key to American Politics: Calhoun's Pluralism." *Review of Politics* (October 1948).

"Function of Profits." *Fortune* (March 1949).

"The Unfashionable Kierkegaard." *Sewanee Review* (October 1949).

"Are We Having Too Many Babies?" *Saturday Evening Post* (May 6, 1950).

"Mirage of Pensions." *Harper's* (February 1950).

"Labor in Industrial Society." *Annals of the American Academy of Political and Social Science* (March 1951).

"Frontier for This Century." *Harper's* (March 1952).

"How to Be an Employee." *Fortune* (May 1952).

"Productivity is an Attitude." *Nation's Business* (April 1952).

"Myth of American Uniformity." *Harper's* (May 1952).

"The Employee Society." *American Journal of Sociology* (January 1953).

"The Liberal Discovers Big Business." *Yale Review* (June 1953).

"The American Genius Is Political." *Perspectives U.S.A.* (1953).

"Today's Young People: More Responsible Than You Were." *Nation's Business* (June 1953).

"Integration of People and Planning." *Harvard Business Review* (November–December 1955).

"America Becomes a Have-Not Nation." *Harper's* (April 1956).

"Organized Religion and the American Creed." *Review of Politics* (July 1956).

"Marketing and Economic Development." *Journal of Marketing* (January 1958).

"Business Objectives and Survival Needs." *Journal of Business* (April 1958).

"Potentials of Management Science." *Harvard Business Review* (January 1959).

"Long-Range Planning." *Management Science* (April 1959).

"Work and Tools." *Technology and Culture* (Winter 1959).

"Politics for a New Generation." *Harper's* (June–August 1960).

"The Art of Being an Effective President." *Harper's* (August 1960).

"The Baffled Young Men of Japan." *Harper's* (January 1961).

"The Technological Revolution: Notes on the Relationship of Technology, Science and Culture." *Technology and Culture* (Fall 1961).

"Economy's Dark Continent." *Fortune* (April 1962).

"Big Business and the National Purpose." *Harvard Business Review* (January 1963).

"Twelve Fables of Research Management." *Harvard Business Review* (January 1963).

"Japan Tries for a Second Miracle." *Harper's* (March 1963).

"Care and Feeding of the Profitable Product." *Fortune* (March 1964).

"If I Were a Company President." *Harper's* (April 1964).

"Automation Is Not the Villain." *New York Times Magazine* (January 10, 1965).

"American Directions: A Forecast." *Harper's* (February 1965).

"Crash Next Year?" *Harper's* (June 1965).

"Is Business Letting Young People Down?" *Harvard Business Review* (November 1965).

"The First Technological Revolution and Its Reasons." *Technology and Culture* (Spring 1966).

"This Romantic Generation." *Harper's* (May 1966).

"Notes on the New Politics." *The Public Interest* (Summer 1966).

"How to Manage Your Time." *Harper's* (December 1966).

"Frederick W. Taylor, The Professional Management Pioneer." *Advanced Management Journal* (October 1967).

"Worker and Work in the Metropolis." *Daedalus* (Fall 1968).

"On The Economic Basis of American Politics." *The Public Interest* (Winter 1968).

"The Sickness of Government." *Nation's Business* (March 1969).

"The Owner and Future Manager." *Management Today* (May 1969).

"Management's New Role." *Harvard Business Review* (November–December 1969).

"The Surprising Seventies." *Harper's* (July and September 1971).

"What We Can Learn From Japanese Management." *Harvard Business Review* (March 1971).

"How Best To Protect The Environment." *Reader's Digest* (March 1972).

"Multinationals and Developing Countries: Myths and Realities." *Foreign Affairs* (October 1974).

"How to Make the Presidency Manageable." *Fortune* (November 1974).

"Six Durable Economic Myths." *Wall Street Journal* (September 6, 1975).

"Managing the Knowledge Worker." *Wall Street Journal* (November 7, 1975).

General Management and the History of Management

Alford, Leon P. *Henry Laurence Gantt.* Easton, Pa.: Hive Publishing, reprint of 1934 edition, 1973.

An able appraisal of one of the great pioneers of scientific management, who has been called the forerunner of modern industrial democracy.

Allen, Louis A. *Management Profession.* New York: McGraw-Hill, 1964.
Sound reference book which discusses the basic principles and techniques of management.

Appley, Lawrence A. *Formula for Success.* New York: American Management Associations, Inc., 1974.
"One of the best business books of 1974" (Library Journal), this volume written by the former chairman of the board of the American Management Association, gives the reader the benefit of his experience in dealing with the problems that confront executives.

Babcock, George D. *The Taylor System in Franklin Management.* Easton, Pa.: Hive Publishing Company, reprint of 1918 edition, 1972.
The first introduction of the Taylor system of management into the American motor vehicle industry.

Beer, Stafford. *Management Science.* New York: Doubleday, 1968.
Lucid description of operations research applied to management.

Bonaparte, Tony H. and Flaherty, John E., eds. *Peter Drucker: Contributions to Business Enterprise.* New York: New York University Press, 1971.
This volume is a collection of essays written by prominent thinkers in management and the social sciences on the topics which Drucker has spent most of his life investigating.

Burger, Chester. *Survival in the Executive Jungle.* New York: Macmillan, 1964.
Contains numerous practical survival tactics for the executive competing in big business. Relevant case examples are included.

Burnham, James. *The Managerial Revolution*. Westport, Ct.: Greenwood Press, reprint of 1960 edition, 1972. *This classic work describes and examines the continuing social revolution of the world. Topics discussed include capitalism and socialism and their part in world politics.*

Cannons, H. G. T. *Bibliography of Industrial Efficiency and Management*. Easton, Pa.: Hive Publishing Company, reprint of 1920 edition, 1973. *An annotated bibliography with a special reference to scientific management and the efficiency movements.*

Church, Alexander H. *The Making of an Executive*. Easton, Pa.: Hive Publishing Company, reprint of 1923 edition, 1973. *The success of an enterprise depends upon the management with the focusing point in the chief executive.*

Dailey, Charles. *Entreprenurial Management*. New York: McGraw-Hill, 1971. *Orientated around the courageous and risk-taking manager. Also includes a discussion of entreprenurial management versus bureaucratic management.*

Davis, Ralph. *Principles of Business Organization and Operation*. Easton, Pa.: Hive Publishing Company, reprint of 1937 edition, 1973. *The first book in the U.S. to differentiate management functions. Completely reset with new introduction and table of contents.*

Dennison, Henry S. *Organization Engineering*. Easton, Pa.: Hive Publishing Company, reprint of 1931 edition, 1973. *An admirable statement about organization based on a lifetime of activity as a business executive and leader devoted to the cause of science and the humanities.*

Emerson, Harrington. *Twelve Principles of Efficiency.* Easton, Pa.: Hive Publishing Company, reprint of 1919 edition, 1974.
The doctrine of efficiency reduced to practice.

Ewing, David W. *The Managerial Mind.* New York: Free Press, 1964.
Deals with intellectual characteristics, tension, nonconformity, manipulation and creative management.

Fayol, Henri. *General and Industrial Management.* London: Sir Isaac Pitman & Sons, Ltd., 1949.
One of the early classics in general management.

Fuller, Don. *Manage or Be Managed.* Boston: Cahners Books, 1963.
Packed with specific techniques for effective management as they relate to human relations, human engineering, job enrichment, and work simplification.

Gantt, Henry L. *Work, Wages, and Profits.* Easton, Pa.: Hive Publishing Co., reprint of 1919 edition, 1974.
A discerning study emphasizing the human element in industry.

General Electric Company. *Professional Management in General Electric,* Vols. 1–4. Easton, Pa.: Hive Publishing, 1975.
The growth of GE has been the result of planning and design. These volumes illustrate the history and organizational flexibility that keeps GE in the role of an industrial giant, exercising managerial disciplines and holding stewardship responsibilities to the share owners, customers, employees, and to the public generally.

Gilbreth, Frank. *Primer of Scientific Management.*

Easton, Pa.: Hive Publishing Co., reprint of 1914 edition, 1973.
A classic work in the field of scientific management, this book covers the Taylor system of scientific management (including time study), applications of scientific management, the effect of scientific management on the worker and relation of scientific management to other lines of activity.

Gilbreth, Frank B., et al. *Scientific Management Course.* Easton, Pa.: Hive Publishing, reprint of 1912 edition, 1974.
A landmark series of lectures given at the YMCA in Worcester, Mass. in 1912, in which the early proponents of the new doctrines of scientific management sought to explain them to the general public. In one of the first attempts at popularizing Taylor's principles, Harrington Emerson, Frank B. Gilbreth, B. M. Franklin and others described the methods and results of the science.

Harvard Business Review on Management. Editors of The Harvard Business Review. New York: Harper & Row, 1976.
Covers all aspects of management. This book includes essays by such important thinkers as Chris Argyris, James Bryant Conant, Peter Drucker and Richard Vancil.

Heyel, Carl, ed. *Encyclopedia of Management.* 2nd ed. New York: Van Nostrand Reinhold, 1973.
This is a ready reference to every specialized area of management. Two hundred contributing authors —leaders in their respective fields—have written over three hundred alphabetically arranged entries ranging in size from concise half-page statements to detailed thirty-page articles.

Heyel, Carl. *John Diebold on Management.* Englewood Cliffs, N.J.; Prentice-Hall, 1972.
Compendium of Diebold's philosophy on management.

Jay, Anthony. *Management and Machiavelli: An Inquiry into the Politics of Corporate Life.* New York: Holt, Rinehart and Winston, 1968.
A highly illuminating interpretation of the psychology and conduct of modern corporations based on the theory that the corporation reflects the same principles of management as the medieval political state.

Koontz, Harold and O'Donnell, Cyril. *Principles of Management.* 5th ed. New York: McGraw-Hill, 1972.
One of the classic textbooks in the field of management. This edition presents a systems approach to management. Also included are thirty-five short case histories.

Loring, Rosalind and Wells, Theodora. *Breakthrough: Women into Management.* New York: Van Nostrand Reinhold, 1972.
A thoughtful pragmatic presentation of all the relevant factors involved in recruiting, employing, training, and advancing more women into higher management positions.

Maynard, H., ed. *Handbook of Business Administration.* New York: McGraw-Hill, 1967.
This contributed volume of over 2,000 pages provides information on all aspects of management.

Mayo, Elton. *The Human Problems of an Industrial Civilization.* Cambridge, Ma.: Harvard University Press, 1946.
Author's initial opinions about the Hawthorne experiment. The first five chapters provide a concise summary of the Hawthorne studies.

Moore, Russell F., ed. *AMA Management Handbook.* New York: American Management Associations, Inc., 1970.
Over one hundred specialists contribute articles

covering the major functions of business. This practical handbook contains 1,200 pages.

Niles, Mary Cushing. *Essence of Management.* New York: Harper & Row, 1958.
Synthesizes the social sciences with the organization theory of scientific management. The book is drawn from twenty-five years of the author's experience as a management consultant, lecturer, and author.

Parkinson, C. Northcote. *Parkinson's Law.* Boston: Houghton Mifflin, 1957.
Introduces the concept "work expands so as to fill the time available for its completion" which is known as Parkinson's Law.

Pollock, Ted. *Managing Creatively*, Vols. I and II. Boston: Cahners Books, 1971.
Volume I, Managing Yourself Creatively, *helps the executive deal with his own idiosyncrasies and improve himself both as a manager and person. Volume II,* Managing Others Creatively, *shows the executive how to evaluate his own performance with subordinates, peers, and superiors.*

Randall, Clarence B. *The Folklore of Management.* Boston: Little, Brown & Co., 1959.
Exposes the myths, half-truths and oversimplifications of management. Chapter titles include the myth of the production wizard, the myth of the rugged individualist, the myth of the overworked executive, the myth of the perfect balance sheet and the myth of the wicked politician.

Robb, Russell. *Lectures on Organization.* Easton, Pa.: Hive Publishing Company, reprint of 1910 edition, 1972.
"Constitutes . . . the single most authoritative . . . exposition from an American to be found in the literature of organization," Harry A. Hopf, management historian.

335

Ross, Joel E. and Murdick, Robert. *Management Update: The Answer to Obsolescence.* New York: American Management Association, 1973.
A survey of twelve crucial areas of management with examples and illustrations. Topics covered include: management information systems, organizational development, social responsibility, strategic planning, and decision making.

Simon, Herbert A. *The New Science of Management Decision.* New York: Harper & Row, 1960.
Fine treatment of problem-solving theory and how it relates to decision making.

Sloan, Alfred P. *My Years with General Motors.* New York: Doubleday, 1964. Former best-seller by the chief executive officer of GM. It tells the story of GM over the twenty-three years that Alfred Sloan was the CEO.

Taylor, F. W. *Scientific Management.* New York: Harper & Row, 1911.
This classic work explains the underlying principles of scientific management. Taylor states the principal object of management should be to maximize its profits while developing excellence so as to maintain its profitability over the long term. This should also apply to employees who should receive maximum wages for achieving a state of high efficiency.

Thompson, Clarence B., ed. *Scientific Management: A Collection of the More Significant Articles Describing the Taylor System of Management.* Easton, Pa.: Hive Publishing Company, reprint of 1914 edition, 1973.
A collection of all major articles before 1914 on the subject.

Uris, Auren. *The Executive Deskbook.* New York: Van Nostrand Reinhold, 1970.
Practical ready reference volume dealing with those day-to-day problems confronted by the executive.

The book contains numerous helpful checklists, charts and other illustrations.

Urwick, Lyndall F., ed. *The Golden Book of Management.* London: Newman Neame, 1956.
A historical record of the life and work of seventy pioneers edited for the International Committee of Scientific Management.

Management by Objectives

Carroll, Stephen J., Jr. and Tosi, Henry L., Jr. *Management by Objectives.* New York: Macmillan, 1973.
Describes several research studies on management by objectives. Appendixes include interview and mail questionnaires, questionnaire study results, forms, etc.

Humble, John W. *How to Manage by Objectives.* New York: American Management Associations, Inc., 1973.
How-to book for making MBO work in every area of an organization. Topics covered include choosing of objectives, establishing realistic profit goals, and improving compensation.

Humble, John. *Management by Objectives in Action.* New York: McGraw-Hill, 1970.
A practical source book of case material which shows how management by objectives works in a business atmosphere.

Mali, Paul. *Management by Objectives.* New York: John Wiley and Sons, 1972.
A systems approach for installing, developing and maintaining management by objectives in a company.

Odiorne, George S. *Management by Objectives.* New York: Pitman Publishing Corp., 1965.
Describes a system of management that defines in-

dividual executive responsibilities in terms of corporate objectives. Must reading for the student or executive interested in management by objectives.

Reddin, W. J. *Effective Management by Objectives.* New York: McGraw-Hill, 1971.
Specifically written as an MBO guide for the manager who wants to set objectives for his own position.

Time Management

Cooper, Joseph D. *How to Get More Done in Less Time.* Rev. ed. New York: Doubleday, 1971.
Contains numerous practical methods for saving valuable hours of time. Illustrated with numerous practical case histories of successful executives in action.

Engstrom, Ted W., and MacKenzie, R. Alex. *Managing Your Time.* Grand Rapids, Mich.: Zondervan Publishing House, 1968.
An excellent practical introduction to time management, this book contains numerous real life examples. Selected reference lists follow each chapter.

Feldman, Edwin B. *How to Use Your Time to Get Things Done.* New York: Frederick Fell Publishers, 1968.
Step-by-step program to enable the executive to double his output.

Larkin, Alan. *How To Get Control of Your Time.* New York: Peter H. Wyden, 1973.
Practical guide to managing your personal and business time. Subjects covered include short-term and long-term goals, establishment of priorities, and organization of a daily schedule.

Loen, R. O. *Manage More by Doing Less.* New York: McGraw-Hill, 1971.

A practical guide for making the manager more efficient. The book distinguishes managing from doing in day-to-day activities.

McCay, James T. *Management of Time.* Englewood Cliffs, N.J.: Prentice-Hall, 1959.
Underscores the intimate relationship between time pressures and rate of personal growth.

MacKenzie, R. Alec. *Time Trap.* New York: American Management Associations, Inc., 1972.
Contains numerous practical tips that managers can use to make themselves more productive.

Webber, Ross A. *Time and Management.* New York: Van Nostrand Reinhold, 1972.
A judicious balance of philosophy and application, this book is full of examples drawn from business, government, and nonprofit organizations; at the end of each chapter is a detailed reference section containing relevant articles and books, many of which are accompanied by commentary.

Social Responsibility

Anshen, M., ed. *Managing the Socially Responsible Corporation.* New York: Macmillan, 1974.
This contributed book explores the financial and political implications inherent in managing a socially responsible corporation.

Backman, Jules, ed. *Social Responsibility and Accountability.* New York: New York University Press, 1975.
Contributed volume analyzing the major social issues confronting business. Noted leaders whose observations appear include: David Linowes, James Hester and Oskar Morgenstern.

Bauer, Raymond and Ackerman, Robert. *Corporate Social Responsiveness.* Reston, Va.: Reston Publishing, 1976.

Discusses the role of the corporation in a dynamic environment. The book identifies and suggests solutions for the critical management problems of corporate social responsiveness. Corporate examples include: Avon products, Eastern Gas and Fuel Associates, and Borden, Inc.

Chamberlain, Neil W. *The Limits of Corporate Responsibility*. New York: Basic Books, Inc., 1973.
Describes and evaluates corporate policies in fields such as consumer protection, environmental control, educational reform, urban renewal and international diplomacy.

Heilbroner, Robert L. and Paul London, eds. *Corporate Social Policy: Selections from Business and Society Review*. Reading, Ma.: Addison-Wesley Publishing, 1975.
Contributed essays dealing with subjects such as forming the corporation, board memberships, morality, environmental protection, multinationals, and the social audit.

Human Resources Network. *The Handbook of Corporate Social Responsibility*. Radnor, Pa.: Chilton Book Co., 1975.
A compendium of what today's corporations are doing in terms of job training, summer jobs for youth, prisoner rehabilitation, the arts, housing, etc. Also, the book discusses corporate social planning and the social audit.

Jacoby, Neil H. *Corporate Power and Social Responsibility*. New York: Macmillan, 1973.
Comprehensive "social assessment" of the American corporation.

Linowes, David F. *The Corporate Conscience*. New York: Hawthorn Books, 1974.
Presents a social audit system that takes into consideration the impact of corporate decisions on society and the environment. In this context, con-

340

sumer protection, employment training, and environmental protection are discussed.

McKie, James W., ed. *The Social and Economic Responsibilities of Business.* Washington, D.C.: Brookings Institution, 1975.
Contributed volume by nine economists, a political scientist, and a legal scholar examining social responsibility in business from several viewpoints.

Seidler, Lee J. *Social Accounting: Theory, Issues and Cases.* New York: John Wiley and Sons, 1974.
Substantial collection of essays which should give the executive background and insights for handling social accountability. Actual case studies of how social accountability can be accomplished and measured are included.

Stone, Christopher D. *Where The Law Ends: The Social Control of Corporate Behavior.* New York: Harper & Row, 1975.
Explains why the legal system cannot get major corporations to respond ethically to issues of public concern, and presents proposals for possibly changing current corporate behavior. Subjects covered include elimination of inside directors and the social audit.

Walton, Clarence. *Corporate Social Responsibility.* Belmont, Ca.: Wadsworth Publishing Co., 1967.
Incisive analysis of many of the difficult issues confronting business executives.

Managerial Performance

Barnard, Chester I. *Functions of the Executive.* Cambridge, Ma.: Harvard University Press, 1968.
Presented here is a comprehensive theory of cooperative behavior in formal and informal organizations. The author demonstrates that the executive, to lead effectively, must make decisions that lend quality

and morality to the coordination of organized activity and to the formation of purpose within an organization.

Blake, Robert R., and Mouton, Jane S. *Managerial Grid*. Houston, Tx.: Gulf Publishing, 1972.
Here is a graphic tool that enables a manager to measure his own effectiveness against his company's and to see the change necessary to increase his impact.

Cleveland, Harlan. *Future Executive: A Guide for Tomorrow's Managers*. New York: Harper & Row, 1972.
Describes the executive working in large complex organizations. The author views the "new" executive as low-keyed with high boiling points, the ability to let others contribute to the decision-making process and a high degree of optimism.

Fiedler, Fred. *Theory of Leadership Effectiveness*. New York: McGraw-Hill, 1967.
Introduces the concepts of "organizational engineering"—fitting the task to the man so people can be better utilized.

Fiore, Michael V., and Strauss, Paul S. *Promotable Now: A Guide to Achieving Personal and Corporate Success*. New York: John Wiley and Sons, 1972.
A clear understanding of what promotability is, how to achieve it, and how to foster it in others.

Flory, Charles, ed. *Managers for Tomorrow*. New York: New American Library Inc., 1967.
Written by the staff of the management consultant firm, Rohrer, Hibler, and Replogle, this book examines the characteristics of the successful executive.

Flory, Charles, ed. *Managing Through Insight*. New York: New American Library Inc., 1968.
Written by the staff of the management consultant

342

firm, Rohrer, Hibler, and Replogle, this book highlights the core values and personality constructs that are required in managers who inspire to insightful managing.

Heyel, Carl. *Appraising Executive Performance*. New York: American Management Association, 1958.
Systematic periodic appraisal of managers by executives. Appraisals are based on judging tangible performance, management skills, behavior characteristics, attitudes, motivation, understanding and health.

———. *Organizing Your Job in Management*. New York: American Management Associations, Inc., 1960.
Concentrates on how an executive can organize his own job. Book includes chapters on time management, delegation, and communication.

Jennings, Eugene. *Executive Success*. New York: Appleton-Century-Crofts, 1967.
Case histories of executives in crises. Many of the case histories represent actual life situations and have been documented as such.

Juran, Joseph M. *Managerial Breakthrough: A New Concept of the Manager's Job*. New York: McGraw-Hill, 1964.
Shows that company survival and growth require managers to continually increase their levels of performance.

Kellogg, Marion S. *What to Do About Performance Appraisal*. rev. ed. New York: American Management Associations, Inc., 1975.
Outlines how to appraise performance in all aspects of management (e.g., coaching, salary administration, estimating future growth, and career counseling). Numerous helpful reference charts are included.

Levinson, Harry. *The Exceptional Executive*. Cambridge, Ma.: Harvard University Press, 1968.
Presents the solid findings of behavioral science on the art of management and defines the role of executive leadership.

McGregor, Douglas. *The Professional Manager*. New York: McGraw-Hill, 1967.
Provides insights to help the manager realize his goals as well as furthering the goals of the organization.

McQuaig, Jack H. *How to Pick Men*. New York: Frederick Fell Publishers, 1963.
Discussion of management appraisal and selection.

Odiorne, George S. *Management and the Activity Trap*. New York: Harper & Row, 1974.
Analysis of managerial mistakes that develop from the manager's inability to cope with change. Also the author describes how to avoid this syndrome and how to climb out if once in.

Randall, Clarence B. *The Executive in Transition*. New York: McGraw-Hill, 1967.
Discusses every aspect of executive behavior as seen from the many years of line experience from the former chairman of the board, Inland Steel Company.

Sampson, Robert C. *Managing the Managers: A Realistic Approach to Applying the Behavioral Sciences*. New York: McGraw-Hill, 1965.
Behavioral sciences used as analytical tools for managerial problem solving.

Schleh, Edward. *Management by Results*. New York: McGraw-Hill Book Co., Inc., 1962.
Makes the premise that the objectives of the company must coexist with those of the employees.

Silber, Mark B., and Sherman, Clayton. *Managerial Per-*

formance and Promotability: The Making of an Executive. New York: American Management Associations, Inc., 1974.
Provides guidelines for the manager who wants to improve his organizational behavior and move up the corporate ladder.

Vance, Charles C. *Manager Today, Executive Tomorrow.* New York: McGraw-Hill, 1974.
Provides practical techniques for developing the art of being well organized, wrestling with corporate problems and extracting ideas and viewpoints from others.

Zaleznik, Abraham. *Human Dilemmas of Leadership.* New York: Harper & Row, 1966.
This book presents a psychological study of leadership. Clinical and theoretical concepts are discussed in terms of psychoanalysis.

Long-Range Planning and Futuristic Management

Ackoff, Russell Lincoln. *A Concept of Corporate Planning.* New York: Wiley-Interscience, Inc., 1970.
An introductory book on planning, concentrating on the nature of planning, design, organization, and control.

Aguilar, Francis John. *Scanning the Business Environment.* New York: Macmillan, 1967.
Theory based on the results of questionnaires which show formal and informal methods to monitor the business environment on both short term and long term basis.

Ayres, Robert U. *Technological Forecasting and Long-Range Planning.* New York: McGraw-Hill, 1969.
Good overview on formal procedures of technological forecasting.

Bright, James R. *Technological Forecasting for Industry*

and Government. Englewood Cliffs, N.J.: Prentice-Hall, 1968.
Systematic study of technological forecasting. Topics discussed include the history of forecasting and applications to actual situations in industry and government.

Bright, James R., et al. *A Guide to Practical Technological Forecasting.* Englewood Cliffs, N.J.: Prentice-Hall, 1973.
Contributed volume including essays by individuals such as Ted Gordon, Clive Simmonds, Wade Blackman, and Joseph Martino.

Christopher, William M. *The Achieving Enterprise.* New York: American Management Associations, Inc., 1974.
Discusses goal setting and goal achievement. Topics included are sales volume, morale, capital budgeting, R & D, planning communication and organizational change.

Ewing, David. *The Human Side of Planning.* New York: Macmillan, 1969.
Focuses on improving planning effectiveness through better team work and collaboration.

Ewing, David, ed. *Long Range Planning for Management.* New York: Harper & Row, 1964.
Best collection of the expert's views on long-range planning. The book includes essays on management by: Peter Drucker, Robert Schaffer, Michael Kami, Simon Ramo, and George Steiner.

Martino, Joseph. *Technological Forecasting for Decision Making.* New York: American Elsevier Publishing Co., Inc., 1972.
Compendium of techniques for technological forecasting. The most comprehensive book on the subject.

Schon, Donald A. *Beyond the Stable State*. New York: Random House, 1971.
Expands his theory of "dynamic conservatism." Illuminated by case histories.

Schon, Donald A. *Technology and Change: The New Heraclitis*. New York: Dell, 1968.
Expands the theory of "dynamic conservatism" by which a company actively resists innovation; and how companies are finally forced to accept changes they profess not to want.

Steiner, George A. *Top Management Planning*. New York: Macmillan, 1969.
Comprehensive state-of-the-art survey of management planning.

Organizational Management and Management Psychology

Allen, Louis A. *Management and Organization*. New York: McGraw-Hill, 1958.
Describes techniques by which companies can improve the quality of their professional management. The book covers such subjects as divisionalization, delegation, centralization, and decentralization.

Argyris, Chris. *Personality and Organization*, New York: Harper & Row, 1957.
This classic work explores the causes of organizational ineffectiveness and suggests ways of overcoming it.

Bennis, Warren. *Changing Organizations*. New York: McGraw-Hill, 1966.
Collection of the author's own essays which describe the causes and consequences of change in organizational behavior.

————. *Organizational Development: Its Nature, Origins and Prospects*. Reading, Ma.: Addison-Wesley Publishing Co., 1969.

347

A primer on organizational development that includes numerous proven examples.

_____. *The Temporary Society.* New York: Harper & Row, 1969.
Foreshadows much of the thinking presented in Alvin Toffler's Future Shock. *The author predicts the demise of bureaucracy and outlines the types of organizations that will ultimately replace it.*

Campbell, J. P., et al. *Managerial Behavior, Performance and Effectiveness.* New York: McGraw-Hill, 1970.
Examines current practices of government and industry for identifying managerial effectiveness.

Dyer, Frederick C., and Dyer, John M. *Bureaucracy vs. Creativity: The Dilemma of Modern Management,* Vol. 2. Coral Gables, Fl.: University of Miami Press, 1969.
Primarily in favor of the creative person, the authors still defend the right of the bureaucrat to his last file cabinet.

Hersey, Paul and Blanchard, Kenneth H. *Management of Organizational Behavior: Utilizing Human Resources.* 2nd ed. Englewood Cliffs, N.J.: Prentice-Hall, 1972.
Stresses motivation, behavior, leadership, and change within organizational settings. A selected bibliography is included.

Huse, Edgar. *Organization Development and Change.* St. Paul, Mn.: West Publishing Co., 1975.
The first fully integrated text that describes methods for organizational development and change, describes how the techniques can be used and also describes research results.

Kahn, R., et al. *Organizational Stress: Studies in Role Conflict and Ambiguity.* New York: John Wiley and Sons, 1964.

Does an excellent job of describing managerial roles and the effects of role ambiguity on the manager.

Kahn, Robert L. and Boulding, Elise. *Power and Conflict in Organization.* New York: Basic Books, 1964.
Contributed volume that examines reasons for conflict and discusses ways to exercise power without causing conflict.

Kepner, C. and Tregoe, B. *The Rational Manager.* New York: McGraw-Hill, 1965.
This text describes fourteen concepts that the manager can use to analyze and solve management problems.

Lawrence, Paul R. and Lorsch, Jay W. *Organization and Environment.* Cambridge, Ma.: Harvard University Press, 1967.
An understanding of the organizational characteristics which allow firms to deal effectively with different kinds and rates of environmental change and especially of technological and market changes.

Leavitt, Harold J. *Managerial Psychology.* 3rd ed. Chicago: University of Chicago Press, 1972.
Examines human problems within the supervisory and management ranks. Topics covered are: individual behavior, one-on-one behavior, behavior in committees and small groups, and the nature of business organization.

Levinson, Harry. *The Great Jackass Fallacy.* Cambridge, Ma.: Harvard University Press, 1973.
In a book that ranges widely from psychology to executive stress, the author writes about present day management theories.

Likert, Rensis. *Human Organization: Its Management and Value.* New York: McGraw-Hill, 1967.
Describes a science-based management system called system four. This system's approach shows how to achieve higher productivity.

Likert, Rensis. *New Patterns of Management*. New York: McGraw-Hill, 1961.
Unique theory of organization that uses such procedures as budgets, goals, and work simplification. Discusses measurements for decision making.

Maslow, A. H. *Motivation and Personality*. New York: Harper & Row, 1954.
A general theory of human motivation based upon synthesis primarily of holistic and dynamics principles.

Roethlisberger, Fritz and Dickson, William. *Management and the Worker*. Cambridge, Ma.: Harvard University Press, 1939.
Complete account of the Hawthorne experiments.

Schein, Edgar. *Organizational Psychology*. 2nd ed. Englewood Cliffs, N.J.: Prentice-Hall, 1972.
Integrated overview of organizational psychology by stressing the types of psychological problems that arise as an organization hires, organizes, trains, manages and develops its people.

Schein, Edgar. *Process Consultation: Its Role in Organization Development*. Reading, Ma.: Addison-Wesley Publishing Co., 1969.
Focused upon the moment-to-moment behavior of the consultant. Relevant case studies are included.

Simon, Herbert A. *Administration Behavior: A Study of Decision-Making Processes in Administrative Organizations*. New York: Free Press, 1957.
Constructs a set of tools—concepts and a vocabulary —suitable for describing an organization and the way an administrative organization works.

Thompson, J. D. *Organization in Action*. New York: McGraw-Hill, 1967.
A theoretical treatment of organizational behavior that emphasizes the problems of uncertainty.

Motivation and Productivity

Ford, Robert N. *Motivation Through the Work Itself.*
New York: American Management Associations,
Inc., 1969.
*Deals with the problems of motivating employees
to higher performance. Topics covered include turnover, grievances, productivity, and employee satisfaction.*

Gellerman, Saul W. *Management by Motivation.* New
York: American Management Associations, Inc.,
1968.
*Deals with concrete problems of organizational
change, recruitment, and training and the improvement of competence.*

Gellerman, Saul W. *Motivation and Productivity.* New
York: American Management Associations, Inc.,
1963.
*This important work discusses the relationship be-
tween individual productivity and the surrounding
environment.*

Herzberg, Frederick. *Work and the Nature of Man.* New
York: T. Y. Crowell, 1966.
This book discusses the general theory of work.

Herzberg, Frederick, et al. *The Motivation to Work.*
2nd ed. New York: John Wiley & Sons, Inc., 1959.
*Reports the finding of a large sample of systemati-
cally collected data regarding individual experiences
of job motivation.*

Hughes, Charles L. *Goal Setting.* New York: American
Management Associations, Inc., 1965.
*Explains how to recognize the needs for self-fulfill-
ment and job satisfaction and how to stimulate
goal-seeking behavior in all employees.*

Maher, John, ed. *New Perspectives in Job Enrichment.* New York: Van Nostrand Reinhold, 1971.
Volume consisting of contributed chapters on job enrichment by noted authorities such as Robert Ford and David Sirota.

Marrow, Alfred J., et al. *Management by Participation.* New York: Harper & Row, 1967.
Findings of a study designed to increase organizational effectiveness of attitudes, behavior values, and leadership.

Marrow, Alfred J. *The Failure of Success.* New York: American Management Associations, Inc., 1972.
This contributed volume contains tested techniques for solving such problems as absenteeism, industrial sabotage, shoddy workmanship, alcohol, and drug abuse.

Maslow, A. H. *Motivation and Personality*, 2nd ed. New York: Harper & Row, 1970.
A general theory of human motivation based upon synthesis primarily of holistic and dynamics principles. Important work which describes the author's concept of the hierarchy needs, including basic biological needs, safety and protection and care needs, needs of affection and love, respect, status, and self-actualization.

McClelland, David Clarence. *The Achieving Society.* New York: D. Van Nostrand Co., Inc., 1961.
This classic work describes the basic concepts in motivation.

McGregor, Douglas. *Human Side of Enterprise.* New York: McGraw-Hill, 1960.
Studies the management of human resources in light of social research findings. Also, the author discusses Theory X and Theory Y.

Myers, M. S. *Every Employee a Manager: More Mean-*

ingful Work Through Job Enrichment. New York: McGraw-Hill, 1970.
Treats job enrichment. Case examples show how the appreciation of this concept can result in accelerated learning time, improved attitudes, reduced costs, and increased productivity.

Executive Stress

Gowler, Dan and Legge, Karen, eds. *Managerial Stress.* New York: John Wiley & Sons, 1975.
Discusses individual responses to stress; the effect of stress on relationships; stress, motivation and learning; leadership style in stressful and non-stressful situations.

Johnson, Harry J. *Executive Life-Styles: A Life Extension Institute Report on Alcohol, Sex and Health.* New York: T. Y. Crowell, 1974.
First book to tell the truth about the sexual behavior of the American executive—an authoritative study based upon information provided by thousands of businessmen who are given an annual health checkup by the Life Extension Institute.

Levinson, Harry. *Executive Stress.* New York: Harper & Row, 1970.
Designed to help the executive examine his own daily experiences. The book discusses the theory behind mental health and work, reasons for stress, stress problems, stress and the family. Specific suggestions on how to cope with stress are included throughout.

McQuare, Walter and Aikman, Ann. *Stress.* New York: Dutton, 1974.
This book explains how career problems, family hostilities and the many tensions of urban living actually alter body chemistry.

Rosenman, Ray and Friedman, Meyer. *Type A Behavior and Your Heart*. New York: Knopf, 1974.
Discusses a type of behavior characterized by time, urgency, competitiveness, aggressiveness and hostility, which the authors assert is the number one cause of heart attack.

Schoonmaker, Alan N. *Anxiety and the Executive*. New York: American Management Associations, Inc., 1969.
Discusses causes and effects of anxiety. A section also covers solutions. Appendices contain material on choosing a counselor and a goal analysis questionnaire.

Multinational Management

Aitken, Thomas. *The Multinational Man: The Role of The Manager Abroad*. New York: John Wiley and Sons, Inc., 1973.
Concentrates on the role and background of the manager in foreign subsidiaries of international companies.

Bagley, Edward R. *Beyond the Conglomerates*. New York: American Management Associations, Inc., 1975.
Predicts by 1990 more than three dozen 'super-corporations' will dominate the entire free world economy. He takes a look at the positive and negative effects of the giants on people, public institutions, and the third world.

Ball, George W., ed. *Global Companies*. Englewood Cliffs, New Jersey: Prentice-Hall, 1975.
Contributed essays by notables such as: George W. Ball, Charles Kindle Berger and Eugene Rustow which examine the controversy amidst the expansion of multinational companies. Topics discussed include, power of multinational companies and establishment of restrictions of multinationals.

Barnet, Richard J., and Muller, Ronald E. *Global Reach*. New York: Simon & Schuster, 1974.
Describes how several hundred corporations dominate the world economy and shows what this means for consumers, workers, and businessmen. The authors advance the premise that this new method of conducting business is undermining the power of governments to control inflation, maintain employment, and collect taxes.

Brooke, Michael Z. and Remmers, Lee H. *The Strategy of Multinational Enterprise*. New York: American Elsevier, 1970.
Based on a six-year research project, this volume studies over eighty manufacturing companies and thirty banks in seven European countries and the United States.

Dunning, John H., ed. *Multinational Enterprise*. New York: Praeger Publishers, 1972.
Analyzes the role of the multinational enterprise in the transfer of materials across national boundaries and its impacts.

Levinson, C. *Capital, Inflation and the Multinationals*. London: George Allen and Unwin, 1971.
A popular controversial volume that is highly critical of MNEs.

Phatak, Arvind V. *Managing Multinational Corporations*. New York: Praeger, 1974.
Discusses the role of the headquarters of a multinational company. Includes bibliographical notes.

Rolfe, Sidney E. *The International Corporation*. Paris: International Chamber of Commerce, 1969.
Extensive survey of the history, problems, costs, legal aspects, etc. of MNEs.

Rolfe, Sidney E. and Damm, Walter, eds. *Multinational Corporation in the World Economy: Direct Invest-*

ment in Perspective. New York: Praeger Publishers, 1970.
Contributed volume published for the Atlantic Institute, the committee for Atlantic Economic Cooperation and The Atlantic Counsel of the United States.

Sethi, S. Prakash and Holton, Richard H., ed. *Management of the Multinationals: Policies, Operations, and Research.* New York: Free Press, 1974.
The nature, organization and functions of large multinational corporations are described by scholars, researchers and business executives.

Stopford, John M. and Wells, Louis T., Jr. *Managing the Multinational Enterprise.* New York: Basic Books, 1972.
Important work based on a study of 187 firms.

Vernon, Raymond. *The Economic and Political Consequences of Multinational Enterprise: An Anthology.* Cambridge, Ma.: Harvard Business School, 1972.
Valuable collection of articles dealing with multinationals.

Vernon, Raymond. *Sovereignty at Bay: The Multinational Spread of U.S. Enterprises.* New York: Basic Books, 1971.
Based on a massive research project conducted at Harvard, the author states that MNEs are most important to the efficiency of international economy. At the same time, he believes there are political problems associated with the development of MNEs.

Miscellaneous References

Cohen, Peter. *The Gospel According to The Harvard Business School.* New York: Doubleday, 1973.

Guishiani, D. *Organization and Management: A Socio-*

logical Analysis of Western Theories, Moscow: Progress Publishers, 1972.

Phillips, Kevin. *Mediacracy.* New York: Doubleday, 1975.

Machlup, Fritz. *Production and Distribution of Knowledge in the United States.* Princeton, N.J.: Princeton University Press, 1962.

Marcuse, Herbert. *Counterrevolution and Revolt.* Boston: Beacon Press, 1972.

Toffler, Alvin. *Future Shock.* New York: Random House, 1970.

Index